Loop H
Olympic Mountains

Timothy D. Paschal

P.O. Box 4123 Sequim, WA 98382

Published By I.B. Group LLC
ISBN: 9798218224912
LCCN: 2023911077

Sixty six statements of caution are contained within the body of "Loop Hikes in the Olympic Mountains". Those statements reflect the risks of hiking in the Olympic Wilderness. The details enumerated within this book: distances, altitudes, compass bearings, etc., were reliably present as of the date of publication. The dynamic elements: trail conditions, re-routing, weather, animal behavior, etc., cannot be guaranteed. When entering the wilderness, you are your first, best and at times only resource. If that reality concerns you, then I suggest you reconsider. The unexpected, the unbelievable and the unplanned can fall upon you at any time. Your judgement alone is responsible for your wellbeing.

Cover and Interior Design: Rae Baitx // www.raebaitx.com

Cover Photograph: William D. Baccus, Physical Scientist, Olympic National Park.

"The photo was taken from the shoulder of Elk Mountain looking towards Grand Valley and Grand Pass. The snow-covered ridge is unnamed and divides Grand Valley from Cameron Creek. The photo was taken in early August of 2011. It was a cool summer and the heaviest snow year in two decades, so conditions are much more like early to mid-July."
-William D. Baccus

Dedicated to the memory of

Daniel T Baker

a friend, a leader,
always an inspiration,
always on our minds

Mt. Olympus, Benjamin Komar, Interpretive Ranger, ONP

“Mental mettle is forged at the hearth of a philosophical furnace.”

Timothy D. Paschal, 1992

Table of contents

Loop Hikes in 5 to 10 Days

Loop Hikes Over 10 Days

Very Long Loop Hikes

Appendix

Author's Notes

Why have I written this Book?

There are a lot of experiences in life, each with its own learning curve. Mine, in some instances, has been perilously steep. Hopefully, the information and insights I've compiled in this book will have a positive effect on how you approach venturing into the Olympic Mountains. Your exposure to the wilderness will test your endurance, resourcefulness, commitment to others and in numerous ways your belief in yourself. What you learn from your experience will be reflected in how you approach future challenges throughout your life.

The wilderness is as good a classroom as it is an experience. You'll be enriched in direct proportion to your degree of attention. Roald Amundsen, the first person to reach the South Pole, once said, "adventure is just bad planning." Matshona Dhliwayo a philosopher and author said, "Mistakes are lessons inside out." Accept the reality of what you've done and who you are, then improve both.

As of this writing, there are limited and costly privately run trail shuttle services in some parts of Olympic National Park and the surrounding National Forest. This book solves that problem via loop hikes that start and finish at a common point. Loop hikes eliminate the need for a ride on the other end of the hike. They have the same advantage as "in-and-out hikes" but they cover more terrain and only repeat a small portion of a trail occasionally and often not at all. I believe Roald Amundsen would endorse loop hikes.

In 1957 my father bought me a Trapper Nelson backpack, invented in Bremerton Washington, the tried and true standard of that time. That pack became the first step in my learning curve. You'll probably never own one, and an online search will tell you why. A Trapper

Nelson pack comprised three basic elements: an absolutely non-anatomically compliant wooden frame (better suited as a table than a companion for your spine), two narrow unpadded shoulder straps guaranteed to carve canyons in your shoulders and a shapeless heavy canvas bag. A bag that no matter how it was loaded, and believe me I tried every imaginable way, was dead set on toppling you over backwards. To counter the backward pull created by this piece of "backpacking technology of the day" the laws of gravity demanded that you compensate by walking bent forward at the waist. So, your first lesson based on my experience is, unless you're starting a wilderness museum, don't buy a Trapper Nelson Pack.

Saddled by my good old Trapper Nelson, I walked into the forest and it gently began to change my outlook on many levels. The transition that began so slowly on that first hike emerged as an emotional and attitudinal force taking root in my youth and building to a constant throughout the rest of my life. From that day in 1958 to the present, I owe who I am and what I've become to the beauty, expanse, challenges and hardships of the Olympic Mountains. Little did I know that a weekend, under the pain and strain of my Trapper Nelson, hiking the North Fork of the Skokomish River, would be the first of innumerable wilderness experiences that would test, refine and mold both my body and my mind.

My backcountry experience developed as a contest between what I thought I knew and how well that knowledge stood up to the reality of what I faced. At any one point in time throughout my developmental experience, I thought I was prepared physically and mentally for the challenges I selected. At different times and in differing degrees I learned that there would always be unexpected challenges that awaited me. The unflinching reality and unforgiving accountability of the wilderness would always be and always was my classroom. Over time I evolved to understanding my capacities, respecting the limits of my skill-set and as a result experiencing more joy and less pain.

The Olympic Mountains are a highly popular destination for people from all corners of the world. It's natural and unique attractions draw millions each year including a significant number of hikers who want to experience the wilderness at the price of a load on their back, sweat on their brow and a trail beneath their feet. The number of wilderness permits for overnight(s) camping routinely exceeds 100,000 permits each year. Considering that one permit can represent up to twelve people, the number of backpackers each year far exceeds the number of permits.

You will, as I did, transition incrementally from seeking a physical or mental test to achieving a clearer and more holistic view of yourself. In doing so, the lesson that you've learned will guide your approach to life's challenges and therein, the fulfillment of the rest of your life recorded as memories and internalized as elements of your character. Your experiences will shape your view and approach to every challenge in any future context forever. I want you to experience and, to the fullest extent, enjoy one of the most exquisite places on Earth. In doing so, I believe your efforts will enhance your character, resilience and levels of joy as you face the inevitable difficulties that lie ahead irrespective of the trail.

1.Tim at the Door, Kathryn E. Paschal ©

Who am I? Why should you listen to me?

I'm Tim Paschal. I grew up in, around and about the Olympic Mountains and therein, Olympic National Park. This area, referred to as the Olympic Peninsula, roughly encompasses the northwest corner of Washington State as well as the continental United States. I was born and raised in Bremerton about sixty miles southeast of the Olympic Mountains. At age eleven I took my first hike. That singular experience left me with a longing to return to the grandeur that is the

Olympic Mountains. I've been captive of those mountains ever since. Being a student of the Olympic Junior College Mountaineering Class, the first in the nation, taught me basic mountain climbing skills and put me in contact with and under the tutelage of some of the notable climbers in the Olympic Mountains: Glenn Kelsey, Chuck Maidan, Doc Barton, Kent Heathershaw, George Martin, Chet Ullin and Dave Sicks. Much later Barbara, my wife, and I enjoyed a number of hikes with Robert Wood and weekends cross-country skiing sometimes in the company of Jack Hughes, Olympic National Park's quintessential ranger.

Several of my winter climbing and backpacking buddies went on to loftier achievements than I. Dan Baker and Dennis Pruitt were part of the first ascent of Mt. William Fairchild in 1963 and Craig Anderson was part of the climbing team for the first American ascent of K2. My last climb, like my first, included Dan and Craig on a "guys and wives" climb of Mt. Baker in 1984. They summited with their wives, but Barbara and I were turned back 600 feet shy of the top of the Roman Wall.

Over the course of my life, I've day-hiked, backpacked, cross-county skied, climbed and snow-shoed these mountains. I spent fifteen years as a volunteer at the Olympic National Park Visitor Center in Port Angeles. I'm committed to helping others gain a better understanding and therein a greater enjoyment and appreciation of the Olympic Mountains.

As a means to that end, I created ***olympicnationalparkvisitor.info*** and now have written ***Loop Hikes in the Olympic Mountains*** for day hikers and backpackers.

Because I've had this close and endearing relationship with this wonderful place throughout my life, I believe that my trove of hard-won and hard-earned experience can save you time, money and heartache. Further, I intend to tease your sense of exploration by pointing out the less obvious and help you better understand your chosen venture. From time to time, I'll underscore my advice with tales from the trails of my experience.

As I did each week at the Visitor Center, I'll do my best to fill your wilderness prescription. However, since I can't speak with you in person, I'll describe a range of experiences that could be characterized with labels from easy to extreme and let you identify the size, shape and fit that suits your interest and developing capacities. Along the way I'll describe some of the challenges and joys awaiting you.

The Olympic Mountains are constantly changing and as such, present a variety of challenges and rewards. Seasons, weather, rain or snowfall, direction, altitude, terrain, temperature, length of day, and the calendar can make any one or two of these factors determine either the joy or pain of your experience. I believe the information and stories you'll find in this book will help tip the scales in your favor, giving you success and joy and leaving less room for distress and gloom. Here I paraphrase Henry Ford, "one of the greatest discoveries a person makes, one of the greatest surprises, is to find you can do what you were afraid you couldn't do". Be as informed, observant and prepared for whatever you've chosen and understand and respect your limitations as you sort your options in the face of each and every challenge. For precisely the aforementioned reasons I've written the first book of its kind, dedicated exclusively, to Loop Hikes in the Olympic Mountains.

Introduction

Pay Close Attention to this Paragraph.

In spite of the Book's narrative nature in which the static details of any of these hikes can be enumerated: distances, altitudes, compass directions etc. The dynamic elements: trail conditions, weather, re-routing of trails, Park restrictions and the behavior of any animal at any time cannot be guaranteed. You are headed into a wilderness where you are your first and best resource. You truly are on your own. If that reality concerns you then I suggest you reconsider. Even when your estimate of your self is, in your mind, a match for a chosen quest, the unexpected, the unbelievable and the unplanned can fall upon you at any time. When it does, you are the only resource for a resolution of the event.

What can you expect?

The Olympic Mountains are a near circular confused jumble of steep ridges and ragged peaks partitioned by nine major rivers and cut by innumerable creeks and streams. The average elevation is between six thousand and sixty-five hundred feet containing around two hundred named peaks. There are a handful of peaks near or above seven thousand feet with Mount Olympus leading the way, double digits short of eight thousand feet. The rivers, creeks and streams descend from glaciers and snowfields melting high in the mountains. The short distances from mountain peaks to sea level defines their descent; they run fast and deep. The only exceptions to this aquatic behavior occur during freeze-up, in the dead of winter and very late in summer stretching into early fall, during the late hiking season. Some, but not all, of the loop hikes in this book include the need to ford rivers.

For those hikes where fording is necessary, I've noted that requirement and cautioned you concerning the seriousness of fording. Hikers have lost their lives attempting fords where they should have turned back. If you are considering a loop that includes fording you should: consult with the Wilderness Information Desk in the Olympic National Park Visitor Center in Port Angeles. I suggest you do a web search for "Stream Crossing Techniques" and read the National Park Service's web-available "Safe River Crossings" and 'Swiftwater Rescue Manual" The Rangers in the Park's Wilderness Information Center can advise you as to the advisability of your plans. In addition, you should consult the USGS website for current water conditions. Also, if you visit online the State of Washington Dept. of Ecology, River and Stream Flow Monitoring page, you can compare years of data and thereby compare it to the weather pattern in any year against the weather pattern in the current year. By doing so you'll have a better sense of what the fording conditions may be. These searches will allow you to choose your hike based on the available data.

These mountains are the land of up and down. Flat ground simply isn't part of the overall equation. While many trails wind their way up river valleys, the initial minimal elevation gain soon gives way to a more demanding gradient. The outcome of the following tale will make my point. Barbara, my wife, and I were on a hiking trip in the Tetons National Park where we earned deep concern from a ranger who worried about our abilities, experience and safety. Our plan was to hike the Granite Canyon Trail to the Teton Crest. The trailhead was nearby and easily accessible. The route would take us a little over nine miles up the canyon gaining about twelve hundred feet of elevation to a patrol cabin. The trail then left the Granite Canyon Trail gaining the last twenty-eight hundred feet in three steep miles between the cabin and the Teton Crest at ten thousand four-hundred feet, and just north of Rendezvous Peak.

The ranger's concern reflected her belief that we didn't understand nor have the strength and stamina required by a twelve mile route that gained about four thousand feet. On our behalf, she was honest enough to share that specific doubt. We replied that we understood the demands of the route and that our proving grounds were the Olympic Mountains, which we hiked on a frequent basis. At that point she commented that she was satisfied with our experience. Hiking in the Olympic Mountains certainly qualified us for both long and steep trails. Her shift from concern to confidence was based on her own experience. Over the previous three years, she had served as a backcountry ranger in Olympic National Park. If we could manage the severe ups and downs of ONP, she knew we most certainly were up to hiking to the Teton Crest. The Olympic Mountains aren't the only place that will put you to the test of heart, legs, and lungs, but it is certainly worthy of its place as proving ground for same.

Tough terrain isn't the only condition you will be up against. Summer really starts in the Olympic Mountains around mid-July and fall can set in as early as mid-August or not start, in a good year, until mid-October. The days from May to August are long and while northwest heat doesn't compare to many places in the country, a long climb up a south and west-facing ridge can be brutal. The availability of water after snow-melt can be diminished, particularly in the high country.

If you've hiked at altitude, you know that the higher you go the more UV exposure you gain; the last thing you need is a sunburn. While most trails start between twelve and eighteen hundred feet of elevation, they often gain several thousand feet within a day's travel. In most places treeline occurs above five thousand feet, leaving higher campsites fairly exposed to the sun and wind.

If the wilderness coast is where you're headed, the cost of the wonderful views is your exposure to the elements. Prevailing westerly winds often bring rain in all seasons. In summer, when the rain relents, the fog takes its place. Coastal fog caused by warm days and on-shore winds can persist into the afternoon leaving everything cold and damp. Strong on-shore winds in the fall and winter can, at times, deliver twenty-foot surf conditions. Combined with night time extreme high-tides, these conditions demand caution and careful decision-making regarding travel and campsite selection. High surf on an extreme high-tide can toss drift logs around like matchsticks, an event you'll not want to be close to.

Spring arrives in the lowlands about the end of March but that same season doesn't arrive in the high country until July. Winter's snowpack lingers in the shade of the forests, on north and east-facing ridges and ground shaded by higher ground to the south and west. Trails that start out perfectly snow-free can disappear into snow a short distance from trailheads, first in patches and then seemingly forever. Trails in the Olympic Mountains are not flagged with markings or reflectors on trees and when buried in snow, any flat spot between two trees can masquerade as the path forward.

There are over six-hundred miles of trails in the Olympic Mountains, many of them intersect with others and some thereby create loops. Almost always, trail intersections are marked with signs indicating some, but not all, destinations and distances in a particular line of travel. You can depend on the information, but you're going to need a good topo map to identify any destination not specified on the sign.

These brief descriptions just scratch the surface of what you'll need to be prepared. More advice is always better and Olympic

National Park's Wilderness Information Center, located within the Park's Visitor Center in Port Angeles, is the best place to acquire it. Rangers in the W.I.C. have, at their disposal, numerous sources of current trail reports and personal experience to advise you regarding your chosen plan. They are very good at identifying the difficulties you'll encounter. Listen closely and, if needed, don't be shy about asking for alternatives. Your safety, level of enjoyment and success will be dependent on the choices you make. Because a book is static regarding information and the wilderness is dynamic, I'll post an annual update on trail conditions. You can access these updates on my website *loophikes.com* any time after January 1st.

Most places I've hiked, but some I haven't.

In my sixty plus years of experience I've hiked in nearly all the different areas within these mountains, but I haven't trodden them all. Of those I haven't personally experienced, I've talked with countless climbers and hikers who have. As I describe hikes and places throughout this book, I'll make it a point to differentiate information based on my experience from that of others. As an example, don't drink the water without filtering, boiling or treating it and don't believe that you can use a kitchen filter to get the job done. Giardia is present everywhere and it's paramount that you boil, treat or filter your water at 0.5 microns or smaller. Start with the assumption that none of the water in the Olympic Mountains is safe to drink. I've never had Giardia; I learned this lesson by listening to Park Rangers. Attending to water and avoiding Giardia ensures intestinal happiness ten days after your hike.

I believe that these mountains and their trails hold more than a lifetime's trove of treasured experiences. In that same regard, I'd be hard-pressed to identify a destination that was utterly distasteful in and of itself. Repeatedly I've been rewarded by the beauty, serenity, majesty, diversity and expanse of this unique, mysterious, and truly captivating place on the planet. So much so that at times a new destination went wanting so that an old acquaintance could be revisited in its stead. You can have a lot, but sometimes you can't have it all. Life's too short and youthful strength too fleeting. I encourage you to do what you can while you can.

Your capacity is the product of the incremental expansion of your experience.

The wilderness will shape you. This truism certainly applies to wilderness skills and your stamina, but more importantly it applies and subtlety affects your psychological side as well. Being prepared goes far beyond ensuring you've brought along enough energy bars. Resources, be they items or skills, are important but stamina both physical and mental, in direct proportion to the task at hand, must be along for the ride if the journey is to be reviewed as a success.

We've all had experiences that required us to "dig deeply" in order to meet the demands we've faced. Successful or not, digging deeply implies a degree of separation between what's at-hand and your ability to access what might be resting on your mental or physical shelves. As your capacity grows, so will your "at-hand" resources. Simultaneously, the separation between your hand and your shelf decreases. The current best of what you've become, mentally and physically, must stand ready to meet the immediate and sometimes imminent challenges that you'll face.

Even as resources migrate from shelves to being available at-hand, new and more refined resources fill the shelf space made available by this form of transfer. Take a moment to re-examine that photo of me headed for my first backpacking trip. I was young, fresh and eager to experience the wilderness. Although 1958 was an entirely different outdoor-gear age from today, I believed at that time I was capable; so certain, as I stood at that door, that I rebuffed my mother's last question, "do you have everything?" I know today that I'll never set out with "everything" but I've learned enough and experienced enough to tip the scales toward success.

In the picture I'm wearing Levi's, stiff and unforgiving logger's boots, a cap without a full brim, a backpack of dubious comfort and design and a sleeping bag open to the elements. What could go wrong?

Very little did, but that was pure luck. It wasn't cold and it didn't rain. If either or both of those conditions had occurred, articles of cotton clothing become sponges and constantly suck heat from the body. Although I had a poncho, I would have been forced to choose between covering my sleeping bag or myself; it wasn't big enough to do both. I was hiking in on Saturday and out on Sunday; why would I need a second set of clothes? My boots were sturdy enough but my legs struggled with their excessive weight by the end of each day. Sheer chance was my benefactor.

The one lesson I did learn, I've already spoken to, the misery of my Trapper Nelson. If you're wondering if I told my mom, I didn't, then or ever. I didn't want to give her a reason to clip my wings. At the same time, I errored when I discounted my mother's telling of her experiences, in her effort to help buffer my own.

For the most part, throughout my experience, I've learned the hard way. Every misfortune, large or small, I viewed as a problem to be solved, a closed door to unlock and an example of being bested by reality. You only know what you think you know. The most useful tool I gained was developmentally and incrementally a better understanding of myself and my capacity. Measuring your optimal ability, both mental and physical, against your informed opinion based on the level of difficulty contained within the challenge before you, is an imperative methodology of estimating your odds for success. Attempting things that are slightly more difficult than what you have recently accomplished is an empirical basis for a decision to move forward, emphasis on slightly. To attempt something because someone else wants you to or by achieving it you would receive praise are the major ingredients of regret. When faced with such a proposition in which your understanding of yourself doesn't match the demand of the venture, avoid the risk; that's a decision which is both imperative and empirical. You will evolve and the venture will always be there when you're ready. Who you are, often unfolds as a great surprise.

A cold dark Friday night greeted us as we piled out of the old truck. The weather wasn't promising. Even in the dark, it gripped our bodies with a malevolence expressed by a biting wind and raking ice crystals. The grade and the conditions of FS Road 2419 had brought the truck to a halt well short of Big Creek. The four of us, undeterred by our immediate circumstance and eager to get started, grabbed our gear and bent to the task of strapping snowshoes to our boots. The dying moan of the truck's departure was expected, stirring little thought beyond knowing it would return Sunday. For us, winter climbing started like this. As usual, we weren't concerned with the conditions and were enticed by the chance to summit Mt. Washington once again. Free of restraint and revisiting a bond of reliance, strength and commitment to each other's safe return, we started up the road. Our only remaining task was to find Big Creek and the Mt. Washington shelter; hoping it wasn't more than two snow-blown miles farther on. At least an hour beyond our greatest desire, seriously tired of shoeing through the dark and tired of the unrelenting windblown snow, we found the shelter. Our first goal achieved, we made camp and got comfortable, if that's possible, in five feet of snow and ice.

An opaque morning broke cold and still with a thick smothering fog. Just another contentious obstacle; we shrugged it off. Our youth, strength and over-advertised experience made us feel certain that we would overcome anything the mountain would throw at us. We were quick with breakfast and spent minutes sorting our packs to essential climbing gear, including the most basic, lunch. Our climbing plan was to move a mile or so above the shelter searching for a draw that curved north then west to the base of the mountain. We moved up the road for about an hour; the silence only broken by the soft fall of snowshoes on fresh snow. In less time than we hoped, it became clear that the shroud of fog was doing its best to defeat our plan for the day. We weren't going to find anything familiar in this obscure terrain. Hard as we tried, it defied definition. Turn back or press on became a very short conversation. We were here to climb a mountain; the alternative held no allure and had even fewer votes. In that undefeatable and undeterred teenage spirit, we carried on with the belief that the fog would clear. Our over-inflated confidence, bolstered a distorted belief that we could surmount whatever lay ahead.

I'll share with you, the reader, an insight that I never shared with my climbing partners. All my life I'd been afraid of heights. I took up mountain climbing for two reasons: one, my friends were interested in it and two, I believed that by climbing mountains, and being exposed over and over again, I could train myself to not fear heights. It didn't work; I'm just as fearful now as I was then. Literally I've broken out in a sweat and my hands are aching as I write about this climb.

Believing that we'd found the draw we were seeking, we left the road and started clawing our way uphill. With the snowpack loose and deep, the slope steep and the brush thick, it was a toss-up whether we were better off with or without snowshoes. Without them every step was thigh-deep but with them every step resulted in an entanglement with the brush. Determination pushed us forward knowing that the conditions would eventually improve. The slope was an avalanche track where the slide alder and vine maple had been bent downhill creating an endless opposition to our upward intentions. We slogged through a wilderness that was unrelenting, didn't care and gave no quarter to those who ventured therein. As hoped, eventually the slope eased and the brush relented. Our progress came to an abrupt and surprising halt. The slope ended at what appeared to be the base of a cliff-face, a few paces ahead. We had no idea as to its height or its difficulty. The face, the fog and the snow under our feet was, at the moment, our entire universe. Was this the initial climbing point? If it is, what's the climbing route on this face? Where does the face top out? Where are we? Given that there were no answers to the worrisome questions that confronted us, we should have leaned into our training and the reasoning it had preached; when you are disoriented, it's best to retreat, learn from the experience and try another day. Disoriented was a given; but after a minimal discussion of the situation, we pushed caution aside blind to the danger that we unknowingly faced. The summit was above us and foolishly we were dead set on going there. It was precisely at that moment when we abandoned a reasoned consideration of what was being risked and blinded by our inexperience, we crossed the threshold of a very dangerous and deadly space. We pulled out rope and assorted climbing gear, tied the snowshoes to the back of our packs and started up the face, free-climbing the lead, from one belay point to the next. I was third of four on the rope. The climb went smoothly until a cold breeze cleared the fog and a much colder one froze my heart. Our climbing route had veered west leaving the ridge, our starting point, far off to our right.

What I faced horrified me; my inner fears drained my reservoir of self-confidence and stopped me in my tracks. We were hundreds of feet above the rock-rubble at the base of the cliff-face that was twice as high. I was captive of what I believed to be a certainty; that rock pile, so far away and yet so near, was going to be my fatal end. I began to sweat, every joint in my body began to ache and my breathing became rapid and shallow. I desperately needed and was obsessed with the thought of a safe place; anywhere, but not here. I panicked, incapable of movement. I don't want to die! I was held captive by that one all-consuming, overwhelming and paralyzing thought. In that instant, the lion that was my reality was consuming the mouse that was my courage, my confidence, myself. I'll make a mistake. I'll miss a placement. I'll fall….

Scared spitless, I was emotionally frozen and had just realized that there were several hundred feet of void between me and anything I could call safe, stable, and horizontal. I wasn't moving and, as part of a rope-team, that meant the team wasn't moving. I couldn't think of moving; I could barely breathe. Cold as I was, I began to sweat and my hands ached from the inside out. Time and space were a mental miasma, an emotional quicksand that slowly devoured me. My legs began to shake and I was fixated on being anywhere but where I was.

The rest of the rope-team asked my reason for the abrupt halt. As a motivation, they reminded me, unnecessarily, that sitting still in the cold was the precursor to being less flexible, less mobile and

2. Mt. Washington, USFS

a danger to all of those literally tied to me. In the end, advice and encouragement became expletive-laden admonishments. We were teenagers, after all, and getting colder by the minute. I could feel my limbs stiffen and knew deep down I couldn't stay where I was. I could climb or I could fall or both. An emotional sun began to peek over an otherwise dismal horizon. I began to extricate myself from an I-Max sized perspective of despair and began to identify my resources for success. The list was short but effective. There was a hand-hold available, not beyond my reach but at the outer limits of my skills. I was on belay; they wouldn't let me fall and if I missed the move, the fall wouldn't be more than ten feet. I've fallen before and though a fall of ten feet wasn't pleasant; it also wasn't fatal. Three of my friends were in danger because I was scared to move and I faced up to a reality; they would do it for me, I needed to do it for them. My rational assessment became my emotional crutch; I made a decision. "Ready to move", I called out. "On belay", was the response. "Climbing", I shouted and with all my will, I focused on one thought; you've made tough moves before and you can make this one today. I shifted my weight, swung up and out to the right, made the move, grasped the handhold and continued onward and upward.

We summited Mt. Washington that day and I went home with one more critical piece of my development. Don't forget who you are and what you've accomplished; always measure the scope of your resources against the challenge at hand.

As you proceed through the rest of this book, you'll find me intertwining tales of my experiences. These tales exemplify my incremental development, or the absence thereof; in either case my degree of development became the focus and determinant element of why I succeeded or suffered.

Assess the elements of incremental growth necessary for you to achieve such an objective, and instead of being reckless, try being deliberately careful. Constructively, select a series of progressively challenging experiences that will, in the end, match what you want with what you've got. It's a much more enjoyable way to grow. This approach is adaptable to most situations and certainly isn't restricted to outdoor pursuits. Both my wife Barbara, a physical therapist, and I, an educational administrator, benefited professionally and personally by its use. It's not so much a technique, as it has become a point of view. A quality that has rescued us from any number of tough situations. It doesn't always lead to accomplishing an immediate goal but if applied it will lead you, more often than not, to a plan for achieving the end you seek.

"Stuff happens", especially when nature is part of the equation.

Prepare, prepare, prepare and in spite of your preparation in the end, while most issues are resolved, your "preparedness-insurance policy" just doesn't or can't cover everything. Sometimes circumstances or needs that you couldn't have foreseen or events that you've never encountered before land smack-dab in your lap. These issues or events occur more frequently to the novice and less so for the experienced wilderness traveler. Be assured, they can befall anyone at any given time. In all cases, unimagined or unexpected "stuff happens". Sometimes it may be subtle and more of a nuisance but at the other end of the spectrum it may be a dangerously critical issue. What follows are a series of backpacking experiences that Barbara, my wife, and I have endured that make the point that the unexpected is sometimes the lure of the hike and at other times the bane of the undertaking.

I met Barbara over thirty-five years ago and among many of her other attractive qualities she liked to hike. So, what better date than a weekend backpack trip to Marmot Pass up the Big Quilcene River, below the south face of Buckhorn Mountain, in the Olympic National Forest. We shared a love of the outdoors. I seized the opportunity to score some points; after all, I was in the interview stage of our relationship, grasping at anything that would cast me in a better light. Winning your mate's heart is the first test of both dedication and ingenuity.

I'd picked this particular hike because it was within the National Forest which allowed Barbara to bring her dog, Qui, along. Never get between a woman and her best friend if your goal is to be her next best companion. Well, stuff happened! It was late May or early June in a spring that had been stunning. Clear skies and warm at sea level, so we packed our gear expecting similar conditions at Marmot Pass. This was the first mistake for me, the experienced one, and for Barbara the novice. Generally speaking, the ambient temperature decreases by three-degrees Fahrenheit for each thousand feet of elevation gain. Marmot Pass is six-thousand feet above Barbara's house near Olympia, the capitol city of Washington State. Although we both knew that spring nights were cooler than the days, at Marmot Pass they would be about eighteen degrees colder than what we had thought they would be. I, we, never gave it a thought because we never had thought about it. You only know what you think you know and if you don't think you're guaranteed not to know. In my case, I knew of this climatological certainty but was operating in the swooning mode of the maybe future husband. That was an absolute distraction from reality and though unacceptable given the risk, thoroughly understandable given the attractive distraction.

Leaving the car at the trailhead, we hiked the first relatively flat mile in the shade of the forest, cool but comfortable enough. The next five miles climbed slowly up the ever increasingly exposed south flank of Buckhorn Mountain. The scree was light colored and reflected more than a reasonable amount of the day's heat upon us. Qui's tongue practically dragged on the trail, my everything had turned into a sweat mop, and Barbara, taken by the flowers and the views, was hot but loving the so-backcountry grandeur, she seemed unbothered.

Six miles and 3,500 feet of elevation later we shed our packs at Camp Mystery, a short mile below Marmot Pass. We set up camp, grabbed a snack and headed up to the Pass. Fifteen minutes later we came across a stock camp with horses hobbled in a meadow; through which ran the only water source in a two-mile radius. Boiling all of our water just shifted from a generalized precaution to an outright necessity; "stuff happens" again!

We moved onward and upward toward the Pass. Just short of our goal we circled around an old rockfall that was home to a colony of Olympic Marmots. They are unique to the Olympic Mountains; isolated from their brethren by extreme periods of glaciation during the Ice age. Our focus shifted radically from horses to marmots, easily described as walking rugs, with enough fur hiding their feet to give them the image of floating across the ground. Luckily, Qui was only slightly interested.

Arriving at the Pass a few minutes later, the view was everything to be expected. Standing on the Pass and facing west, from left to right we had a clear view of the Needles, an uncommon picket spire formation above Royal Basin, Mt. Deception at 7,788 ft., Mt. Claywood at 6,836 ft., doing its best to block the view of the lower two-thirds of Mt. Olympus standing due west at 7,969 ft., the tallest mountain in Olympic National Park. Shifting our view southwest, at about two o'clock was Mt. Anderson at 7,321 ft. in its pyramidal glory, hiding Chimney Peak at 6,917 ft. from view, as it stands guard on the northwest wall overlooking the Enchanted Valley on the Quinault River. Finally, to our far left was a truly spectacular view of Mt. Constance at 7,756 ft., the third highest peak in the Park.

We retreated to Camp Mystery, ate a quick meal and spent the rest of the evening viewing the wild flowers that were out in all their glory. Worn by the long day we crawled into our tent for a good night's sleep, wrong! Having ignored the possibility of a near freezing night, we paid the price. It was a night of endlessly trying to stay warm and very little sleep. Even Qui was cold enough that he snuggled between our sleeping bags grateful for our body heat, we were grudgingly shedding in quantity.

Undeterred by our Marmot Pass adventure and emboldened by what we had learned, we took on Royal Basin next in the middle of

3. Royal Basin, ONP, 2006

summer's heat and the peak of mosquito season. Summers in the mountains are notorious for frightful populations of a variety of flying insects all of which are persistent, insidiously aggravating and dead set on biting, stinging or injecting any and every poor backpacker with substances that cause rashes or itching or both. I thought the heat and the climb up Royal Creek was going to be the hard part.

Royal Lake sits about a two hundred feet below Arrowhead Meadow that qualifies as the shallowest of lakes or the soggiest of marshes, take your choice. Regardless of description, it qualifies as being the mosquito capitol of anywhere you'd like to name. Swarms of the marauders were thick enough to satisfy the director's needs in a horror film's terror scene.

Barbara and I shed our packs, set up the tent and stayed there until early morning. The cool of the night carried into the early morning giving us the chance to make a quick breakfast. We enjoyed the alpine ambiance of Royal Lake, set in its glory at the eastern foot of the Needles and overlooked by Mt. Deception due south.

Both of us knew summer was bug season, but both of us failed to access that lobe of our brain mass; you know that place where we store everything that gets lost forever absent an ugly experience that causes a resurgence of insight and in this case seasonal adjustment. Fall, yeah, I remember fall when most of the bad bugs have disappeared from Royal Lake as well as hundreds of other wilderness areas; yeah, I remember, now! What was I expecting in the middle of summer? I not only lost points with my future permanent hiking partner, but she was also well on her way to assuming the role of chief cautionary consultant. Well done, Timmy!

There are a number of places in the Olympic Mountains that I haven't traveled and one in particular by choice. The Skyline Trail, in the southwest quadrant of the Park, begins a half-mile short of the North Fork Camp Ground on the North Fork Road northeast of Lake Quinault. The thirty miles of mostly rough trail follows the Skyline Ridge to the northeast, gaining and loosing elevations between North Fork, at 500 ft., Kimta Peak, at 5,399 ft. and skirting well below Mt. Seattle's summit at 6,246 ft. before the trail joins the North Fork Quinault at 3,520 ft., just below Low Divide about seventeen miles up-river from the North Fork Campground.

Although the views throughout the length of the Skyline Trail are reputed to be breathtaking, water is a big challenge in this undertaking. The level of availability of water between a wet year and a dry year can and does vary severely. As I've pointed out before, taking anything for granted and not planning for contingent actions is a recipe for at least regret and at most a critical threat to your wellbeing.

Knowing what the current and forecasted weather will be is insufficient on the Skyline. How does the past winter, spring, and early summer compare to previous years? Visit the State of Washington Dept. of Ecology, River and Stream Flow Monitoring. There you can compare years of data and compare it to the weather pattern in any year against the weather pattern in the current year. What has the previous winter and spring brought to this area? If the answer is, it's been a dry, cold winter and spring with a diminished snowpack containing a low water content. Then the only guaranteed water sources are at the trailhead, at Three Lakes 6.9 miles in, at Lake Beauty 14 miles in, and Low Divide 8 miles farther on. This hike is difficult, exposed, at higher altitudes, and the last half of it is rated as "way-trail" that has not been maintained year after year. Ample skills with Topographic maps and a Compass are a requisite for this hike.

I've not hiked this trail but have listened closely to those who have. Few are eager to repeat the adventure, but those who return time and again do so for the beauty, solitude and the extreme privilege of visiting probably one of the most unspoiled wilderness areas in the Park. This is the enchantment and allure that the Skyline affords. They all admit that regardless of their desire to hike the Skyline, they do so with extreme caution and preparation. After all, miles of infrequently traveled terrain leaves you exceptionally dependent on the diligence of your research, preparation and a willingness to accept, regardless of your efforts, that ""stuff happens"".

Your enjoyment is usually directly proportional to your preparation, but understanding and accepting that the unforeseen can and often does materialize, helps to fortify your will, stamina, and creative problem solving. If it's sufficient, you'll carry that enjoyment home as well as being capable of providing a great story, for all that will listen. My recommendation: find someone who's hiked the Skyline, pick their brain and pack yours to overflowing with all the research you can find. Bear cannisters are required and there is no longer a bridge across Big Creek. Resolve to make choices based on your capability. Avoiding a misjudgment is far better than rescuing yourself from your misguided choices. Always make capability-based choices.

When it's time to make a decision, avoid undo hesitation. It only makes the inevitable look worse. Barbara and I were taking my two children on a day hike up the Duckabush River in the southeast quadrant of the Olympic National Forest. We were headed up the Duckabush Trail to Five-Mile Camp, which by the way, is 6.8 miles from the trailhead; go figure? At about three miles into the hike the trail which, up to this point had been an easy walk, turned abruptly into a steep climb over Big Hump an elevation gain of 1,500 ft. with fifty-two switchbacks. Grumbling set in at about ten switchbacks and grew increasingly more serious the higher we climbed. The promise of a great lunch and wonderful fishing did little to quiet the "I don't want to do this anymore" chorus. We finally topped-out and regained our spirit of adventure as we cruised through the last three miles. Five-Mile is a good destination. We immediately set up for lunch. Settling down on the edge of the river near a deep hole, fishing was our only thought along with all the high hopes that every fisherman holds in his heart. The kids' spirits soon lagged and we called it quits after catching but one small trout. The four of us shared the four bites of trout that our efforts had provided. We downed the rest of lunch, cleaned up, repacked our things and headed for the car.

Everything went along swimmingly until part way down the Big Hump we found ourselves on a new trail. This was disturbing since there is no branching of the Duckabush Trail until mile sixteen and we were inside mile four. We backtracked to find the old trail but no matter how hard we looked; we couldn't find it. A trail crew had filled the old trail with brush to discourage its use and connected the old with the new, in the time we had been at Five-Mile Camp. "Stuff happens"!

We guessed that the new trail would reconnect with the old trail at some point farther on. The good news was it did, the inconceivable news was that the new trail's only bridge, just yards short of reconnecting with the old trail wasn't finished. With no one nearby our only option was to cross twenty feet of incomplete bridge over a steep rock-laden ravine about thirty feet deep. As the "experienced one" in the lead, my credibility was at that moment lower than the bottom of that ravine. Honey, or Daddy was missing in action. The family's eyes said it all, "what now fool"? "Stuff happens", but uniquely this time,

I was being held responsible for this particularly right-in-front-of-us stuff, that was seriously happening.

Don't take it personally, I told myself. They need someone to be responsible for this decidedly surprising misadventure and they've picked me because I'm tallest. Fine, I told myself if that makes you feel better; but what are you going to do about this very real sad state of affairs? My decision was not received well; build the rest of the bridge. The kids fell into hysterical laughter and Barbara knew I'd lost my mind. After a lot of convincing, off-the-cuff made-up engineering talk and noting that the one true fact, was that there was no alternative. I moved forward with the plan, such as it was.

The trail crew had laid down and secured the stringers, the underlying supports for the deck of the bridge. A ready supply of deck planks were piled nearby. My plan was to carry and place, one by one, the planks on the stringers until the deck of the bridge was in place, albeit unsecured; we'd have to walk very gently. Wouldn't you know it, the very first time the family puts me in charge and in complete control, I came up short on deck planks. The trifecta of Stuff is happening to me; what part of that is fair or deserved or anywhere in the karma rule book? Improvise! So, I rearrange the planks with a gap of a few inches between each. Actually, I did it several times widening the gap to the limit of my audience's acceptance and still came up short. I needed to cross the final five feet with two planks wherein my razor-sharp mathematical mind split five feet into thirds and worked up the courage to balance on one while I placed the next. Mission accomplished! I had hidden my fear while solving that pesky-plank-puzzle, or so I thought. "No-Way", was the universal reaction from the onlookers. A serious discourse ensued and, in the end, it was agreed that I'd carry the kids across, Barbara would cross on her own and I would forever be the one that got us lost and nearly killed on the Big Hump. Don't take it personally, I told myself. They need someone to be responsible for this decidedly surprising misadventure and they've picked me because I'm tallest.

For the record, none of us have been back since. My solution that day never has outshone the cloud of that unexpected and unimaginable problem. The point here is, the unimaginable happens and in this instance in a compounded manner. Never leave home thinking everything will work out, sometimes it doesn't. Expect that possibility and prepare the best you can.

Fishing for bees can be painfully disappointing.

Nearly sixty years ago, three of my hiking friends and I left the Lower Lena Lake trailhead on the Hamma Hamma Road just before dark. Our plan was to camp overnight three miles up-trail at Lower Lena Lake, break camp early on Saturday morning and move on another four plus miles to Upper Lena Lake, just inside the southeastern border of Olympic National Park. We planned on a little fishing at Upper Lena and exploring Scout Lake, situated a few miles to the west.

It was late in July, warm and sunny with broken clouds overhead; what could go wrong? Though it was a little late in the morning for fishing we threw down our gear and gave it a good try to no avail. We set up camp and set out on the way-trail in the direction of Scout Lake. After about two hours traveling through the magnificence that the high country provides in abundance, the clouds, which had been broken that morning, had now consolidated into a deck that obscured the summits of Mt. Bretherton to our south and The Brothers to the northeast. The temperature was falling and the wind was freshening from the southwest. From our experience we were just one thunder clap short of a summer storm, not uncommon but also not expected. Time to return to camp. Scout Lake would always be there, if and when we returned to this delightful area of the Park.

4. Upper Lena Lake, ONP, L. Kirk, 2006

No sooner had we arrived back at Upper Lena Lake, a wind driven rain arrived, along with the distant roll of thunder. Time to leave. Open ground is not where we wanted to be if thunder's partner, lightning, was about to join this climatic dance. We threw everything back in our packs as though we were in a race; the fact was we were. Down-trail we went. My tent partner and I led the way and the other two followed a short distance behind, but close enough to hear them arguing over some issue related to fishing. As time passed their voices fell out of range and little was thought of it.

About an hour later we were stopped on the trail taking a water break, both intake and outflow. As we were climbing back into our packs, the missing twosome arrived in a rage with each other. Something in excess of brotherly bonding but just short of a bar fight. The initial argument that we had heard earlier was over not breaking down a fishing pole but rather letting it fly in the sky like a CB antenna on an eighteen-wheeler. The impetus of this fight to the finish, which had intruded upon our otherwise solitude, was the bee's nest that the fishing pole had raked out of an overhanging tree. From bad to worse, the nest fell square on the pack of the angrier of the two. The "friend" with the pole thought the event hilarious, definitely a social faux pas, if not an outright rage igniter. In time, all the laughing or swearing calmed down and we hauled our entertainment or sorrows, as the case may be, on toward Lower Lena Lake.

Just when you think it's bad, something worse refocuses your lens on the maladies of life in general. The thunder had increased and now the skies opened up. Even a hard rain didn't quite cover this event. We reached Lower Lena Lake and immediately broke out our shelter halves. No longer in service today, shelter halves were, at some time past, the army's idea of a two-man tent with each occupant responsible for carrying half the tent. The tent was buttoned together and supported by two segmented tent poles. Being neither compact nor light, it met both our needs and our "army-surplus" budget. Great, but you had to have both halves to have a whiff of backcountry architectural success. My partner had overlooked his shelter-half when leaving Upper Lena. Unfortunately, the button holes refused to stretch the four miles between these two lakes.

Okay, lets add insult to injury! My "tent partner" makes a quick deal with the "all sting and no honey duo" to shoehorn himself in with them, leaving me to enjoy the unlimited space of a drenched forest for the night. "Stuff happens", sometimes cloying as ostracism in the rain. Find a solution or drown. Mine was a downed hollowed-out log about four feet in diameter, forty feet long and lying at an "acceptable version of horizontal". It would do, and I wasn't about to go shopping extensively for a better shelter solution in a downpour?

I shoved my pack in the hollow and when nothing bigger than a spider crawled out, I proclaimed the space vacant and available for immediate occupancy. Wrapping myself in my ground cloth, I settled in for a dry but adventurous night. I awoke in the morning to my friends' screaming my name into the wilderness, hoping that forgiveness for their heartless transgression of the previous evening would lead me to call back and assuage their self-induced assault on their collective conscience.

The storm had passed, all was forgiven and we celebrated with a breakfast of oatmeal and hot Tang, a tasty invention of the new U.S. Space Agency, NASA. Some stuff is truly one-off and as such it can't be anticipated, but the solution can't be erased. Therefor it is forever in your arsenal, at the ready for a possible imitation-application, varied only by the circumstance of a future episode of "stuff happens".

Your enjoyment in the wilderness is proportional to your preparation. Across time you are solely responsible for creating and expanding your level of preparation. Because most of your experience-based know-how is developed in a progression of incremental advancements, give each outing your best shot at success. Understanding your limitations, and what you're up against, your acuity at finding positive solutions and your drive to succeed should always be inventoried against the challenges of the proposed quest.

The Ten Essentials are easily identified and should be with you at all times.

A quick online search will identify the Ten Essentials and offer places to acquire them. In addition, if you are considering a loop that includes fording, you should: consult with the Wilderness Information Desk in the Olympic National Park Visitor Center in Port Angeles. I suggest you do a web search for "Stream Crossing Techniques" and read the National Park Service's web-available "Safe River Crossings" and 'Swiftwater Rescue Manual" The Rangers in the Park's Wilderness Information Center can advise you as to the advisability of your plans. In addition, you should consult the USGS website for current water conditions. Also, if you visit online the State of Washington Dept. of Ecology, River and Stream Flow Monitoring page, you can compare years of data and thereby compare it to the weather pattern in any year against the weather pattern in the current year. By doing so you'll have a better sense of what the fording conditions may be. These searches will allow you to choose your hike based on the available data.

That said, the Ten Essentials are only as useful as your understanding of how to use them. A jack in the trunk of your car is useless if you can't associate its use with fixing the flat that has you stranded. More to the point, the prospect of someone happening by who knows what a jack is and how it is to be used may be common on a roadway, but you are likely to be the only help you have, facing a wilderness problem in the wilderness.

One of the Ten Essentials is a current topographic map of the surrounding area of your expected route of travel. Custom Correct Maps in Port Angeles, WA provides a series of maps that cover the entirety of the Olympic Mountains. These maps are available at the

Park's Main Visitor center in Port Angeles and at Brown's Outdoor Store, 112 W. Front Street in Port Angeles as well as several other outlets. Owning the map and being able to use it are two entirely different things. That map might as well be a sandwich wrapper if your ability to use it is restricted to following the line that represents the trail, from where you parked to your destination.

Brown's Outdoor is a good place to buy supplies; they have everything you might need. If you are considering a multi-day hike you might find it easier to contact Brown's (360) 457-4150 and arrange to pick up your supplies when you come through Port Angeles. It could be easier than paying excess baggage fees. Worse yet, stove fuel is banned on all flights.

To be more precise, never hike without a quality topographic map, one with 1:62,500 or better scale. Such a map if used knowingly, gives the route, the gradient of the trail, the possible sources of water in the vicinity and the related routes and trails in reasonable association with your position.

5. Wildfire, John McColgan, BLM

One example where this type of information could be critical is a forest fire, where the worst kind of "stuff happens". Assume your return route, the one and only trail out of where you are, is blocked by a lightning strike fire that is slowly working its way up-trail. What's available from your current position? A topographical map is as close as you can get to your eye in the sky, allowing you to find available trails in the general area. If you've practiced reading them when you're not facing a crisis, you'll develop a sufficient map-reading skill base to assist you in any situation. If you know how to interpret the contours, they can point the way to an off-trail traversable route over the nearby terrain. Obviously, you have a number of choices in hopefully several different directions.

Your experience should remind you to check the direction of the wind; fortunately, in this case, it's the direction of smoke drift from the fire, if it's visible. The next check box is fires usually follow the wind and climb up ridges' both of which could eliminate some of the available routes identified by the contours. Pick the best option still available to you. Your first goal is to avoid the fire's advance and secondarily increase your exit options to a trail and optimally a road. Alternatively, and assuming no reasonable escape from your present position, the map will identify water bodies, streams, rivers and lakes; all of which may become your option of last resort.

Carrying a map does you little good if you can't accurately read, interpret and orient to the information in your hands. My final words on this subject, "It's all about you and always on you every time you risk the isolation of the backcountry; your preparation too often becomes your salvation, so be prepared".

Short Day Hike Loop Hikes

Ending is so much better when you finish where you began. Loop hikes that can be done in a day exist in every quadrant of the Olympic Mountains. In the eastern quadrants they begin and end at various trailheads in the Olympic National Forest. They come in a variety of lengths and difficulty; so, match your ability to the challenge described, and choose wisely. Some like: The Hall of Mosses, the Spruce Nature Trail, both near the Hoh Visitor Center, the Living Forest Trail at the Park Visitor Center in Port Angeles and the Quinault Rain Forest Nature Trail Loop are very short, 1.5 miles or less, but interesting and easily traversed.

Some are at altitude and best attempted between mid-July and mid-September; a week or two earlier in a warm and dry year and a couple of weeks later in a wet and cold year. The following hikes can be done in a day. The question is, whose day? If you are experienced, fit and accustomed to long days on the trail any of these loop hikes are for you. If you have reservations about the difficulty or length of the hike, listen to your own best counsel, your intuitive self. Start with a hike that suits your skill and endurance levels, and one that is the best measure of your comfort and confidence zone. The following loop hikes vary significantly in their length, difficulty, trail gradient, and the highlights along the way.

Marymere Falls Loop

NW Quadrant, Custom Correct Map, "Lake Crescent-Happy Lake Ridge", (1.8 mi., difficulty 0.74, easy, beautiful trees, a waterfall, trailhead restrooms and Lake Crescent Lodge)

The trail starts on the front steps of the Storm King Ranger Station, just off of U.S. 101 on Barnes Point, along the south shore of Lake Crescent. Most of the first-mile of the trail is flat and winds leisurely through the old growth virgin forest to a bridge spanning Barnes Creek on your right. Crossing the bridge, the remaining quarter-mile rises up to the base of the 90 ft. falls. You'll spend about thirty minutes hiking from your car to Marymere Falls. Reverse your course of travel and you'll return to your car in the same amount of time. As an alternative return trip, turn left shortly after having re-crossed the bridge and follow Barnes Creek down-stream. Take the next right turn and head toward Lake Crescent. A few paces from the lake you'll find on your right a grove of old growth Western red cedar trees (Thuja plicata), near the lake's shore. Take a right at the intersection, circling the grove to your right. Your car is just ahead. This alternative adds about 10 minutes to the return portion of the hike. At the intersection if you turn left instead of right, you'll be a few paces from the Lake Crescent Lodge, a great place to visit. Marymere Falls is an easy hike, less than two miles in length and suitable for anyone who hikes and can handle stairs.

6. Quinault Rain Forest, USFS

7. Merymere Falls, ONP

Staircase Loop

SE Quadrant, Custom Correct Map, "Mount Skokomish-Lake Cushman", (2.6 mi., difficulty 0.7**, easy, huge trees, rapids, pools and red sandstone)**

To get to the Staircase Ranger Station follow U.S. 101 to Hoodsport and turn to the west on Lake Cushman Road. Follow the road past Lake Cushman to its intersection with FS Road 24, the Staircase Road, and turn left. Shortly after the turn you'll see the road change from pavement to gravel as it skirts along the northern shore of Lake Cushman. You'll know you've arrived in Olympic National Park when the road changes back to pavement. The Staircase Ranger Station is a mile farther on, but first you'll come to the fee station. The loop starts at the ranger station and heads up-stream on the east side of the river. You'll return to the ranger station via the vehicle bridge at the end of this 2.6-mile loop. The trail follows what, in my youth, was the road between the ranger station and Big Log Camp. For about a mile, the trail skirts well above the river offering great views of the deep pools and rapids along the way. The trail then turns directly toward the river and the suspension bridge where you'll cross to the opposite side.

Stop on the bridge. The views are up close and beautiful. Notice the gravel island in the middle of the river under the bridge. Numerous wooden and even steel bridges were constructed in pairs that took hikers from one bank to the island and then to the opposite shore. In succession, every one of them was destroyed by the river during winter storms. The suspension bridge was the ultimate solution to constantly replacing bridges.

As you cross the river, you'll find a lush and vibrant near-Rain Forest. While the Skokomish River Valley doesn't technically qualify as rain forest it is the nearest thing to one. You'll see huge Douglas fir, western hemlock and Western red cedars as you hike the 1.4 miles from the bridge to the ranger station.

The trail follows the river closely, for the most part, allowing you the opportunity to enjoy the rushing rapids and the serene pools. You viewed these from above on your hike up the river. Now you can get up close and personal.

On your way down-stream you'll come to a sign that identifies 'The Red Reef". This is an outcropping of red sandstone. The red sandstone you're looking at was first laid down as mix of sandy sediment and clay, on the seafloor between 66 million and 2.6 million years ago. The tertiary period began about the time of the mass extinction of the dinosaurs. The red coloring comes from iron

8. Staircase Rapids, ONP, Docier, 2008

oxide within the mix. The western, southern and a bit of the southeastern areas within the Olympic Mountains all primarily consist of compacted sedimentary deposits that were uplifted as rock. The uplift was a function of the Juan de Fuca Plate subducting under the Continental Plate over millions of years. The ground beneath your feet, at this moment, is continually being uplifted, ever so slowly, at a rate of about a quarter of an inch a year. The rate of uplift in the Clearwater River Valley, situated between the Hoh and the Queets rivers near the southwest coast of Olympic National Park, is the greatest rate of orogenic uplift in the world.

The Olympic Mountains are astounding. The variety of ecosystems, plants, animals, rocks and human history make this place a gem. Olympic National Park's designation as a World Heritage Site is well deserved. Thank you for visiting; I hope you enjoyed your time here.

Krause Bottom – Geyser Valley Loop

NW Quadrant, Custom Correct map, "Hurricane Ridge", (6.5 mi., difficulty 43.1**, moderate, exceptional river hike, and the chance for an organic treat at Michael's Cabin)**

(A Special Note: the trailhead is at the end of the Whiskey Bend Road a spur off the Olympic Hot Springs Road. As of this writing, 2022, the Olympic Hot Springs Road remains washed out. The road is barricaded at Madison Falls just off of U.S. 101 up the Elwha River entrance to the Park. Hiking from Madison Falls is permitted; however, be advised that the Whiskey Bend trailhead described as the start/end point for this loop is 9 miles distant from Madison Falls. The description that follows for the Krause Bottom Loop assumes the road has been repaired and your start point will be at Whiskey Bend. Contact the Olympic National Park Wilderness Information Center at 1-360-565-3100 for current information.)

Starting at Whiskey Bend, the trail parallels the Elwha River, well above the river on its eastern flank, through stands of big Douglas fir trees (They were initially mistaken as true firs by Scottish botanist David Douglas around 1700. In fact, Douglas firs, "Pseudotsuga" and hemlocks, "Tsugas" are members of the pine family, "Pinus"; regardless, the name stuck). Within the first hundred yards of the trail, look to your left, focusing closely on the uphill side of the biggest trees for a hand's width notch in the ancient bark, about six feet off the ground. These notches are called "blazes" and were cut into these trees in the winter of 1889-1890 by the famous Press Expedition. It was sponsored by the Seattle Press newspaper as a means of increasing readership in the "age of adventure". The blazes were cut into the bark to mark the trail of the expedition so that the expedition members could find the trail as they shuttled supplies from one camp to the next in three to six feet of snow. Deep snow explains why they were cut well off the ground.

At just short of a mile a sign announcing an overlook points off the trail to the right. Less than a hundred yards later you'll find yourself standing on a rock outcropping looking down and across the Elwha at Elk Meadow on the opposite bank. This meadow is frequented by Black Bear and Roosevelt Elk; however, I've never had the pleasure of such a sighting, in all my stalwart attempts. The trail continues on, to your left, appearing to complete a loop and return you to the Elwha trail a short distance above. My advice, retrace your steps and regain the trail the same way you left it. The route to your left, in search of the main trail, is incredibly and unnecessarily steep just before you reach the top. Save your energy for the views ahead.

Back on the main trail and about a quarter-mile ahead you'll come to a trail sign pointing to the right and down-slope to Rica canyon. This half-mile trail dropping down to the river is doable. But take your time; it's steep. The trail ends at the river's edge; turn right. A few hundred yards will deliver you at Goblin Gates, a dual monolithic obstruction to one of the biggest rivers in the Park. Trust me, the river's response to this geologic insult is rife with water-laden fury. Watch your step; this is no place for a swim!

Anywhere along this loop you'll see xylophagous fungus often referred to as Conk fungus. Trees that have conks will eventually lose their structural integrity and fall to the forest floor, decay and add to the nutrient base for trees and plants that will follow.

Retrace your steps and then continue up-stream along the bank of the river. Two important items before you go too far. First, you'll soon encounter a broad shady grassed area just off the trail to your left, a wonderful spot to have lunch. Secondly, you'll find, about a third of a mile farther on, a spur trail to your left. If you take it, you'll climb slowly up to the main Elwha River Trail and turning left you'll return to the trailhead. This exit can cut your hike almost in half, a little over three miles total, and return you to Whiskey Bend. If you decline the offer, your next destination is Humes Ranch about a half-mile distant.

Along the way, the broad expanse of Geyser Valley, which by the way doesn't have geysers, demonstrates the sheer power of the river.

Will Humes (l), Orlin Burdick, Grant Humes (r), Humes Ranch, 1905. Photo by Frank Pearson (Gerry Humes collection).

9. Humes Ranch, University of Washington Digital Collection, 1905

This waterborne energy is measured by the immense piles of rounded rock, sized anywhere from boulders to gravel, to sand. As the river traverses the valley, it meanders back and forth, forever shifting its course from one side of this expanse to the other, endlessly carrying its rock burden down-stream and eventually depositing it in the Strait of Juan de Fuca. Arriving at Humes Ranch you're treated to a detailed replica of Mr. Humes cabin sitting above a nearby riverside flat that in its day was a combination garden and orchard. Settle in under the branches of the old growth cedar tree dead ahead and, rain or shine, enjoy a restful view of the river.

On the trail again, head back to Humes cabin and turn right. Climb uphill for a short half-mile where you will turn left heading for the main Elwha Trail. The trail takes you back to the Whiskey Bend Trailhead and along the way passes Michael's Cabin. If it's fall, stop at the cabin and pick an apple from Michael's orchard. You'll have to stretch to reach one since the bottom five feet have been cleared by the Black Tail Deer and Black Bears, permanent residents throughout the Olympic Mountains.

Ozette Triangle Loop

NW Quadrant, Custom Correct map, "Ozette Beach Loop", (9.5 mi., difficulty 4.12, easy, scenic ocean beaches, be careful of the tides)

The trailhead for this hike is a few hundred feet west of the Ozette Campground at the extreme west end of the Hoko-Ozette Road, south of state route 112 and west of the town of Clallam Bay. The southern and northern legs of this triangular loop are over low marshy ground. As such, the trail consists of a continuous string of cedar puncheon, rough split planks, which do a marvelous job of keeping you up out of the mushy ground, especially in the wet season. The puncheon, if wet, tends to be slippery; watch your step and use hiking traction devices if you have them. If you forgot to bring them, they are available at Brown's Outdoor store on Front Street in Port Angeles. Ian or Eric can provide you with current trail information as well as meet any of your equipment needs.

I'll describe this hike south to north but it can be just as enjoyable and at no disadvantage done north to south as well. Heading southwest from the trailhead it's about a three-mile walk through a relatively young forest made up primarily of Spruce, a conifer that's accustomed to wet ground. This leg and its northern counterpart have risen a few feet above sea level recently. "Recently" in this case is measured on a geologic time scale; within the Holocene epoch, the past 11,700 years. Your reward, about three miles out, is your arrival at Sand Point and your introduction to a small piece of the last remaining fifty-six miles of wilderness coastline in the lower 48 United States. The coastal section of Olympic National Park was added by an act of Congress in 1953. This was one of Harry Truman's last acts as President, fifteen years after the creation of the rest of the Park in 1938. Aside from the beautiful beach and the sea stacks, those photo-perfect rocky projections off-shore, the air straight off the Pacific Ocean is about as clean and fresh as you'll find anywhere. Complementing the continuous roar and unending white curling surf, the water is either yachting blue if it's sunny, or battleship grey on any day not of the same description.

The next leg of your journey is a three mile walk north on the Pacific beach. Water at Sand Point is the one reliable water source on this loop. All water in the Park must be treated to avoid Giardia.

It is important that you're informed of, and cautious about, ocean tides. On your Custom Correct map, "Ozette Beach Loop", you'll see two orange dots along your route north. The first is a short half-mile from Sand Point and the second is about a mile north of the first dot. These dots range up and down the Park's coast line and each has been assigned a particular numeric value. The southern one is 5.5 ft. and the northern one is 5 ft. These are indicators of how high the tide may rise before it rises to a point that the entire beach is awash, leaving a hiker no beach to walk on. The alternatives, to no beach to walk on, are bad and worse. The bad, find a high dry drift log and wait, sometimes hours, for the tide to recede. The worse, attempting to traverse the mile between these two dots by walking on the drift logs. I highly recommend you Do Not try to walk the logs. It's a slip, fall and break a limb risk that is compounded by being in a remote wilderness, miles from help. One last point, the drift logs look big and stable. "Big" yes but "stable", unfortunately, not always. Time your hike so that you pass between these two dots before the incoming tide reaches five feet or more; always travel the beach with, and refer to, a tide chart. If you don't have a tide chart, it's time to reverse course and save the rest of this hike for another day. In planning for this hike, time your arrival at the beach such that you traverse the beach when the tide is below five feet during the roughly two hours of transit.

Situated just south of the northern dot, the Wedding Rocks are a feature that, based on your level of curiosity, could add an additional hour to your transit time. I recommend you add that hour to your itinerary. It's well worth the planning and absent such a plan you will be tempted to either risk missing your tide window, jogging the beach leg and missing its' beauty or being forced to pass on the unique opportunity the Wedding Rocks provide. Prepare well for this hike and remember, "Time and Tide Wait for No One", credited to St. Marher, 1225 and revised by Geoffrey Chaucer, in the 15th century.

At the end of this three mile beach leg, you'll arrive at Cape Alava with Ozette Island to your west patiently awaiting the millennia that must pass before it joins the rest of the beach or it succumbs to erosion. To the northwest and miles distant are the Bodelteh Islands, part of the Flattery Rocks, so named by British Captain George Vancouver during his 1792 exploration of the northwest coast. Collectively called Sea Stacks, these rocks, reefs and micro-islands are sprinkled along the coast from Shi Shi Beach to the north and to Ruby Beach to the south.

As you gaze off-shore you are looking over a piece of the most protected marine sanctuary in North America. The protectors consist of a number of U.S. governmental agencies and Environment Canada working in partnership with you to protect and preserve this valued

10. Ozette, Sand Point Trail, ONP, 2004

piece of Planet Earth. Please leave only your footprints and pack out your trash and that of others that you happen upon.

Leaving the beach, head southeast three and a half miles, over the cedar puncheon, returning to the trailhead near the Ozette Campground. You've now experienced a piece of the Pacific Coast marine environment that is one of three critical elements that led to the designation of Olympic National Park as a United Nations World Heritage Site in 1981. Through times past, you've now shared the experience of the early explorers, Heceta, Pérez, Cook and Vancouver. They saw what you've seen today.

Mt. Muller Loop

NE Quadrant, Custom Correct map "Lake Crescent-Happy Lake Ridge", (16 mi., difficulty 14.92, south facing ridge, views, small meadows, stock and bikes)

The Mt. Muller Trailhead is at the end of Forest Service Road 2918 on your right about 5 miles after you leave Lake Crescent headed for Forks on US 101. What you'll see first is the Clallam County PUD electric substation at the intersection of FS 2918 and US 101. The road forks just before the trailhead with a stock camp off to your left and the trailhead straight ahead.

At the trailhead you have a choice. It's a loop, but you might not have the same hiking experience depending on the rotation that you'll need to choose. Briefly, done clockwise, the trail to your left, you'll climb steeply, traverse the ridge west to east and descend gradually returning to the trailhead via the trail on your right. I recommend this choice.

The first 3 miles is the most difficult section of the loop. You'll gain 2,200 ft. as the trail ascends the ridge roughly following Littleton Creek, at a distance on your left. At 3 miles you'll come to an

11. Muller Ridge, USFS, 2006

intersection with a trail that comes from the west and continues to the east. Turn right and follow the trail to the east. Having reached the ridge, the trail generally traverses its crest. It leads you through a mix of forest and small meadows gaining 500 feet over the next 5.5 miles. At the end of this section, you'll arrive at the summit of Mt. Muller at 3,748 ft. The summit clearing allows you views of Lake Crescent to the east. Swinging around to the west: Mt. Angeles, Griff Peak, Unicorn Peak, Aurora Peak, Boulder Peak and Sourdough Mountain all within Olympic National Park and Sore Thumb directly south in the Olympic National Forest.

The trail continues east along the ridge and in the next 2.4 miles loses about 1,000 feet of elevation. As the trail begins to descend more sharply it abruptly changes directions, at first decidedly west then south as it loses more elevation and then west as the gradient lessens. You'll arrive at a clearing, now within earshot of US 101, where you will briefly join the Olympic Discovery Trail, itself leading west. After a few hundred yards the ODT breaks off to your left leaving you 2 miles short of your trailhead just beyond Littleton Creek. Aside from a lot of exercise this 16-mile loop loses most of its appeal on anything less than a sunny day.

Loop Hikes in Two or Three Days

Some hikers, eager and fit, may see the following hikes as doable in a day by traveling light and hard. I wouldn't argue that they can be done that way; I just don't recommend it. Doing these hikes in a day relies almost entirely on endurance and leaves little room for error, miscalculation or just stuff that can happen. Move more slowly, carry necessary resources and enjoy the view along the way. If you seek an endurance challenge join an organized long-distance running club; this experience is intended as a hike in the Park not a sprint.

Barbara and I hiked from the Dosewallips Campground to Dose Meadows, 14 miles in one day, carrying heavily loaded packs. A day later we hiked the same 14 miles on our way out. 14 mile days with heavy packs wasn't enjoyable; in all our years on the trail since, we never repeated such an undertaking. Take the time to experience the wonderment of the wilderness.

Sol Duc Resort Loop

NW Quadrant, Custom Correct map "Seven Lakes Basin", (14 mi. difficulty 17.15**, counterclockwise, moderate, views, a waterfall and a high-country lake)**

Summary: Sol Duc Hot Springs Resort Trailhead, Mink Lake, Deer Lake, Sol Duc Falls, Sol Duc Hot Springs Resort Trailhead

By starting from the Sol Duc Hot Springs Resort and taking the trail due south to Mink Lake, I've started you on this loop counterclockwise to put the elevation gain at the front end of the hike. The highest point today will be 4,130 ft. where the Mink Lake trail intersects the Bogechiel River Trail on the Little Divide. Three and a half miles later and about 600 feet lower, the end of day-one will be Deer Lake 7.6 miles distant from the Sol Duc Resort.

The trail, rising to the south, immediately starts to gain elevation as it climbs between two buttresses on the north face of the Little Divide. During the Ice Age all the valleys in the Park were choked with ice. These alpine glaciers slowly carved their way down-slope shaping the terrain into steep-walled valleys. Even as they moved, the glacier itself supported the valley walls with its mass of ice. When the Ice Age began to loosen its mile-deep grip on parts of the Olympic Peninsula, the alpine valleys were the first to melt out. Initially, they formed meltwater lakes trapped behind the dam of thick continental ice near the shoreline of the saltwater bodies that nearly surround the Olympic Peninsula. The icy water eventually drained from the valleys leaving unsupported steep valley sidewalls; too steep to support their own weight given the poor makeup of the soil. Soon the ridgetops began to slide down the valley walls but as they fell, they spread out near the bottom of the slope. Two of these slides, side by side, created a support for the walls, called a buttresses, and at the same time the top of the slides put dips in the ridgeline giving the ridgetop a silhouette of a serrated shape. As you travel around the Park, you'll notice that nearly every valley and every ridge share these same characteristics.

Back on the trail you'll climb 1,400 ft. to Mink Lake, midpoint of day-one. Mink Lake is 2.5 miles beyond the trailhead and home to an old shelter in Bogachiel Park. The area is flat and, in some places, marshy; it's a bench holding two small lakes. This is a good place to rest a bit. Unfortunately, you're still captive between the buttresses and not high enough to catch any views out of the Sol Duc with the exception of Aurora Ridge rising some 4,000 ft. to the north and separating the Sol Duc area from Lake Crescent hiding due north.

12. Sol Duc Falls, NPS

This view, if you can call it a view, dominates the horizon to the north of your location at Mink Lake.

Time to saddle up and push on. The last 1.8 miles will top out on the Little Divide at 4,130 ft. where it intersects the Bogachiel River Trail. The best news is that you've gained all of the elevation on this loop; what lies ahead today and tomorrow is downhill. Better yet, what's left today is to turn east and enjoy the last 3.5 miles to Deer Lake; "a walk in the Park". Yes, a terribly cheesy phrase, but I just couldn't pass it up. The ridge slowly loses elevation, but the first two miles provide superior views of Boulder Peak and Mount Appleton to the northeast and a peek-a-boo view of West Peak of Mt. Olympus, the highest point in the Park at 7,969 ft., looming over the White Glacier. It's the source of Mount Tom Creek that feeds into the Hoh River far below.

About a mile before arriving at the lake you'll rise up and over the lip of the bowl that holds Deer Lake to the east. You'll then start a 500 ft. descent first heading southeast then switching to the north and intersecting the High Divide trail a short distance south and up-slope from the lake. At the junction turn left to the north through meadow land; you'll find the lake nearby. Deer Lake at 3,520 ft. is nestled in the uppermost range of the contiguous forest, just at treeline, and as such provides both wind-shelter and shade for your stay. Don't plan to gather around a campfire. You may have seen the sign at 3,500 ft. just above Mink Lake on your climb that warned, "No Fires above this point, Camp Stoves Only". This is an environmental protection provision and is fiercely enforced by the Park's backcountry rangers and local hikers as well. I suppose as a substitute, you could sit around a roaring camp stove and tell outrageously exaggerated stories of past events. On second thought, retire to the tent and get some well-deserved rest.

If you have the time and energy, either the afternoon you arrive or before you depart on day-two, I suggest a quick and easy walk up the High Divide Trail, a little over a mile, to open meadows of huckleberries which come ripe in the end of August. If it's the end of August to very early September, you're in for a marvelous experience. The Park has its share of Black Bears and as fall arrives in the high country, they go into "hyperphagia", a state of hormonally forced eating in preparation for winter. You and the Bears will be sharing the same meadows. While I know of no Bear attacks within my lifetime in the park, you still are well advised to give these 250 to 350 pounds of less than cuddly, four-by, fuzzy paw walkers their space; the Park requires you to stay at least 50 yards from bears. Take along something to sit upon or sacrifice your oldest hiking pants because you'll need to sit in the meadow on the blueberries. Worry about the stains if you want, but don't worry about squishing the berries, trust me, the bears will clean-up after you.

You'll notice that the Bears are head down in the feast and are paying no attention to you, or so it seems. No matter where you choose to sit, inevitably a Bear will steer in that direction. At the point at which the Bear believes you have encroached territorially, never mind that the Bear is the only entity that is on the move, the Bear will stop, raise its head and stare at you. This is your clue to slowly get up and move away, out of the Bear's current line of travel. When the head drops down again, you're out of their annoyance zone. Just to be sure, redouble the distance; if nothing else you won't have to move as often. Needless to say, the photo ops are astounding and the organic refreshments are literally at your fingertips. Enjoy!

Back to reality. Time to break camp and get on with day-two. As you leave the lake, you'll cross its outlet, the head of Canyon Creek on its parallel journey with you to the Sol Duc River 2.9 miles down-trail. Before you get too excited, the trail from Deer Lake down to Sol Duc Falls is what I refer to as "rocks and roots". The trail descends about 1,500 ft., at the low end of strenuous, through heavy stands of subalpine conifers before it transitions, at about 2,500 feet, to mainly Douglas fir, Western hemlock and an understory of rhododendrons which bloom in late spring and early summer at most of the lower elevations. Along the way it is punctuated with the knee creaking task of stepping down off of moderately variable-sized rocks and roots; take your time. As you approach Sol Duc Falls, you'll hear it as a faint low beating sound and the nearer you draw, it rises to cacophonous proportions.

At the falls, which never run short of water thanks to the massive watershed from which the Sol Duc River draws, you'll cross a bridge centered on this, one-of-a-kind, experience. After you've gotten your waterfall-fix, but before you move on, stop and look above the falls and then down-stream. What does the stream either side of the falls area look like? Broad and shallow with ripples fits the description both up and down stream. Now look near the bridge; it runs through a deep narrow slot with sheered walls that are squared off at the bed of the chute. The chute was created by the river's erosion of a wide sandstone intrusion between two slate layers that over time were uplifted and rotated ninety degrees to stand on their edges. The sandstone being much softer than the slate has been warn-down forming the river chute under the bridge. This is one of many similar erosive events, but the one that is easiest to visit.

With less than three miles left, retrace your steps from the bridge a couple hundred feet toward Deer Lake and take the intersecting Lover's Lane Trail on your right. The gradient is nearly flat and unlike the incessantly trodden rock and gravel surface of the trail on the opposite bank of the river, the soft duff of this trail is pleasant and quiet. Here the forest is thick, almost to overgrown, and littered with dead-fall coated in moss. With an annual rainfall of about 90 to 95 inches, the Sol Duc Valley comes up about 40 inches short of the rainfall of the Hoh Rain Forest. Qualified or not, the short three miles of forest environment through which you're hiking is similar to, but no substitute for, the Rain Forest in the Hoh Valley, on the west flank of the Park.

A long hour later you've arrived at Sol Duc Hot Springs Resort. For a small fee, if you brought your swim attire, you can soak away your accumulated backpacker's aches and pains in the Hot Springs; a wonderful way to end this two-day loop. By the way, stop in the souvenir shop next to the lobby and take something home to remind you of the wonderful memories of this beautiful and diverse area of Olympic National Park.

Deer Park Loop

NE Quadrant, Custom Correct map, "Gray Wolf-Dosewallips", (17 mi., difficulty 12.31, lots of elevation gain and loss, views and differing types of forests)

Summary: Slab Camp Trailhead, Deer Park Campground, Three Forks, Side Camp, Camp Tony, Slab Camp Trailhead

The trailhead for this loop is at the end of Forest Service Road 2875. A short distance past the Dungeness Bridge on U.S. 101, a mile west of Sequim, turn left onto Taylor Cutoff Road; there's a gas station on the southeast corner of the intersection. Taylor Cutoff runs due south flat and level, then rises up and swings to the right becoming Lost Mountain Road. The road now climbs, tops-out and swings left into a more open and flat area dotted with houses and small farms. The road runs nearly straight for about half a mile before it begins a definite turn to the right. At that point, look left to see FS Road 2875. The attending sign, if it hasn't been stolen, will announce Slab Camp Road. Turn left onto FS 2875, or Slab Camp Road, if you must, and follow it to its end about 5 miles away. Take care to avoid the mistake of turning onto FS 2870 on the left just over a mile from the beginning of FS 2875 at the intersection with Lost Mountain Road.

The Deer Ridge Trail is commonly hiked by the locals and way-finding ought not to be a concern. The trail begins in a heavy and healthy forest at about 1,400 ft. and gains 4,000 ft. of elevation in the 4.5 miles to Deer Park. There are two springs at the Deer Park Campground, but to be safe, consider it a dry camp so you'll not only have to carry water for the first day, but the second as well.

The trail climbs Deer Ridge and the higher you climb the more spectacular the views; the reward for your hard work. On the climb you've crossed into Olympic National Park which requires a backpacking wilderness permit for one or more overnight stays within the Park. You can get the permit in person at the Park's Visitor Center in Port Angeles or easier yet, take care of it online. Contact the Wilderness Information Center at 1-360-565-3100, for more information.

After setting up camp at Deer Park, treat yourself to the view from the top of Blue Mountain just a few hundred feet above the campground. It's a truly 360° view of the interior of the Park and the surrounding lowlands along the Strait of Juan de Fuca. Northeast, across the entrance to Admiralty Inlet, the Cascade Range rises with the majesty of Mount Baker with its 10,778 feet of permanent snow and ice. It's no surprise since it holds the rights to claiming the world record of the greatest snowfall accumulation in most years, across the

13. Lowland Forest, USFS

ages. Skiing on Mount Baker routinely carries on into June. Looking southeast you'll spy Mt. Constance at 7,756 ft. and more southerly just to its right Mt. Deception at 7,788 ft. To the southwest at 7,321 ft. is Mt. Anderson in the far distance. You'll also see left to right, Sentinel Peak at 6,592 ft., Mt. Claywood at 6,836ft., Mt. Cameron at 7190 ft., and McCartney Peak at 6,784 ft. There are about two hundred named peaks in the Park and you're looking at most of them including Mt. Olympus at 7,969 ft. just west of McCartney.

If it's a clear night, the next treat is an astronomical extravaganza brought to you by the total absence of any competing background light; you'll now know why the Milky Way was given its name. Don't forget the satellites; those look-a-like stars but traveling across the night's sky faster than the rotation of the earth. Time to hit the bag, tomorrow will bring its own rewards and challenges.

Snowshoe Hares, (Lepus americanus), in the Olympic Mountains do not turn white in the winter as do their brethren in the Cascade Mountains. One theory states that the hares are accommodating to a warming climate where a brown background has become more prevalent than a white background. A different theory believes that the acquisition of the "agouti gene", through cross breading, keeps Snowshoe Hares from turning white in the winter

Day-two requires a trip down Blue Mountain involving about the same amount of elevation change as day-one, only in reverse. The remainder of day-two on this loop includes: 4.3 miles from Deer Park down to Three Forks on the Gray Wolf River, then down-river just short of 5 miles to Camp Tony and finally a 3 mile climb back to the trailhead a distance of about 12 miles total on the day. It could be done in one day, but two is better in my opinion. I tend to go on hikes

14. Snowshoe Hare, ONP

just to be out there; I'm reluctant to focus on the getting home part. My best recommendation, make it a three-day experience. So, day-two could be one of three alternatives. The first is do the 4.3 miles to Three Forks or Gray Wolf Camp and leave the remaining shy eight miles for day-three. The second alternative is pass up Three Forks and move on to Slide Camp, an additional 2.6 miles down the Gray Wolf, leaving just over 5 miles for day-three. Finally, the third alternative is to hike all the way to Camp Tony leaving a mere 3 miles left for day-three. Choices, choices, choices, what's a hiker to do?

Maybe some more information will prompt a preference. I've got both kinds of news. I'll start with the bad, really not so bad but a little less than good. Other than the fact that you're in a river valley, often out of sight of the Gray Wolf, which is making its presence known primarily in audio. There aren't any views to speak of and it's cold. The forest in the Gray Wolf Valley is robust and dense and the trail follows the river which runs in a steep walled-in terrain below Blue Mountain to the north with the Gray Wolf Ridge rising to between 6,000 and 7,000 ft. to the south. What little sun visits this stretch of the river shows up late and gives up early, exacerbating the chill of the near constant down-stream breeze.

Got it? So, what's the good news? The distances between Three Forks, Slide Camp, Camp Tony and the trailhead are all between 2.5 and 3 miles. Between Three Forks and Camp Tony the trail gently contours the south flank of the river losing about 500 feet of elevation in the distance between these two points. Even the climb from Camp Tony to the trailhead is an easy 1,000 vertical feet spread over 3 miles. The better good news? Beyond Three Forks the tough part is over. Whether you choose to go all "Packasorus Rex" and bust all the way out on day-two, or take three days to experience the experience, you'll at least remember this hike for its contrasts.

Lake Angeles-Heather Park Loop

NE Quadrant, Custom Correct Map, "Hurricane Ridge", (13 mi., difficulty 12.79, strenuous, high country views, late summer and fall only)

The trailhead for this hike can be found by driving five miles up the Hurricane Ridge Road from the Park's Visitor Center just above Port Angeles via Race Street. When you reach the Entrance Station do not go through the Station, instead turn right. The road winds around about a quarter of a mile past some seasonal Park staff housing and ends in an upsloping rectangular parking lot. The Lake Angeles trailhead is halfway up the far side of the parking lot marked with a large kiosk.

From the trailhead to the lake is a distance of three and a half miles. The tread is exceptionally good, easy on the feet and usually well maintained due to its year-round use by the locals. The gradient of the trail averages about 350 ft. of elevation gain each mile, the boundary between moderate and strenuous. The entire length of the climb to the lake is through a healthy and vibrant conifer forest which provides cooling shade in the heat of summer and retains winter's snow pack well into spring in most years.

As you draw near the lake, you'll notice the increasing exposure of bedrock outcroppings and the accumulation of boulders. This is evidence of the work of the Angeles Glacier before it melted into the cirque it was carving in the north wall of Klahhane Ridge. You'll approach the lake via a short spur trail to your left, the only spur on the ascent to the lake. Taking the spur, you'll cross over the remnants of the last moraine and find the north end of the lake. Take the time to visit the lake from this vantage point. As you look south across the lake, you'll notice two features. First, the small forested island that appears to be drifting in the middle of the lake. Secondly, look across the lake at the sheer rock headwall at the lake's southern end, a testament to the power of glaciers and their ability to scour away solid rock by their irresistible weight and the force of glacial ice on the move.

Retreat to the main trail and turn uphill to begin your 765 ft. climb to the crest of Klahanie Ridge at 5040 ft. The trail ascends steeply following above the west edge of this mostly shoreless lake. You'll arrive at a sloping bench above the headwall at the south end of the lake with the ridge rising before you. Cresting Klahanie Ridge you're welcomed to a common element in the Park, basalt. The two outer ridge bands of the Park are the remnants of a number of islands and sea mounts made up of marine extruded volcanic basalt, squeezed out of mother earth one undersea liquid burp at a time. They grew over time to form islands, not that different from their sisters in the Hawaiian chain. The rock is friable, at best, due to the severity of rapid underwater cooling. These islands drifted northeast on the Juan de Fuca Plate until they refused to subduct and were dismantled as the Juan de Fuca Plate slid under the North American Plate. The line of travel then pushed this immense mass of plate debris into a corner of what was then the Pacific Northwest, creating two huge broken ridge wrinkles on the landscape. Those wrinkles today comprise the north, east and partial south faces of the Park.

The top of Klahanie Ridge, like its brethren around the exterior of the Park, is a jumble of broken rock, in this case pushed in places into a knife-edged crest. You'll mount just such a crest near the middle of Klahanie Ridge's northeastern extremity. The first quarter-mile is no wider than two boots side by side, steep on both faces and severely broken into short steep rises and falls. Just when you've had enough high-altitude gymnastics, the trail settles down taking you to Victor Pass three miles southwest of Lake Angeles.

Take a break, you've earned it. Looking away to the south, nearly two hundred peaks are in clear view on a good day. This view conjures the wanderlust of both the most novice or hardened of hikers. A vast wilderness calls; will you answer?

Looking over the north side of Victor Pass you can see the Strait of Juan de Fuca and on the distant Canadian shore the exquisite city of Victoria, British Columbia. If it were not for: Abraham Lincoln, a near Pig War between the British and those upstart Americans and a European-styled arbitrated decision by Kaiser Wilhelm I, Victoria and the southern portion of Vancouver Island would be part of Washington State. The result however left Vancouver Island to the British and the

15. Lake Angeles, ONP, 2009

San Juan Islands as part of Washington Territory. Ah, nothing like a good fight and an independent referee to settle the smoldering rage over an arbitrary "Strait" line, the 49th Parallel, when reason demanded a bend and a curve.

Time to get moving. You can see the trail as it leaves Victor Pass and curves down and across the bowl to the north. Then it swings west and climbs via several switchbacks to a low point between Mt. Angeles proper and "second top" after which it drops down the west face and traverses north below "second top". This stretch of narrow trail runs at a fairly constant elevation across a steep scree slope and passes by Thumb Rock, an old volcanic dyke composed of harder and more weather resistant rock. It stands alone as both a sentinel and a vestige of the past. The trail comes to an abrupt end a few hundred yards short and a hundred yards below Heather Park. Turn right and scramble up a steep rock chute. Breaking over the top you'll find yourself in the aptly named fields of heather of Heather Park. A little over two miles north of Victor Pass and a rock scramble later, you can easily walk to the top of "first top" in the middle of Heather Park and enjoy a wonderful view of the Strait's south shore as it runs west towards Neah Bay.

It's downhill from here. Four miles of trail that quickly descends north into the forest on its way back to the trailhead. If you're tired, you should be. Over the 12.5 miles in this loop, you've gained and then lost about 4,000 ft. of elevation, not counting all the smaller ups and down along the way.

Happy Lake Ridge Loop

NW Quadrant, Custom Correct Map, "Lake Crescent Happy Lake Ridge" (17.8 mi., difficulty 15.45, two lakes and high ridge views)

Summary: Olympic Hot Springs trailhead, Boulder Lake, Happy Lake, Olympic Hot Springs trailhead

Special Notes:

1) The Happy Lake loop is within the Elwha drainage. Normally, the end of the Olympic Hot Springs Road is the trailhead for this loop. However, at this writing, 2022, the Olympic Hot Springs Road remains washed out. The Road is gated at Madison Falls just off of U.S. 101 up the Elwha River entrance to the Park. Hiking from Madison Falls is permitted, however, be advised that the trailhead described as the start/end point for this loop is 8 miles distant from Madison Falls. The description that follows for the Happy Lake Loop assumes the road has been repaired and your start point will be at the road's pre-washout terminus, the normal trailhead.

2) Boulder Creek Campground and the Olympic Hot Springs area has a year round burn ban, stoves only. Contact the Olympic National Park Wilderness Information Center at 1-360-565-3100 for current information.

The trailhead is a barrier at the end of the Olympic Hot Springs Road which, in its day, extended about two miles farther on and ended at the Olympic Hot Springs Resort. The Lodge burned to the ground in the 1920's and was rebuilt and survived the economic ups and downs over the decades until a snow storm in the 1960's destroyed several of its buildings. The Park removed it in 1972.

As you hike southwest from the trailhead, the road has been overgrown but patches of asphalt remain. The trail contours below the crest of Happy Lake Ridge, some 3,480 ft. above you on your right. At about 2.5 miles the trail forks. The downward fork runs down to Boulder Creek, crosses a bridge and reverses its direction leading you to what remains of Olympic Hot Springs.

These springs are undeveloped and consist of several shallow pools encircled by rocks. The hot water seeps from the sidehill above the pools and flows continuously through them, flushing them with clean water frequently. If it has rained recently, either over a prolonged

16. Boulder Lake, ONP

period or as a downpour, the cold rain water mixes with the hot water and makes for tepid conditions for a day or so until the hot springs once again gain control and raise the temperature in the pools.

The up-slope trail at the fork is your hiking trail. From the fork to Boulder Lake, you'll be skirting below Crystal Ridge on your right. At the top of the first rise, you'll pass through the Boulder Creek Campsite. Continue on about a mile to the next fork. To the right is Boulder Lake, your destination for the day. Before you start up to the Lake, drop your packs, secure your food, grab your camera and hike about a half mile up the left fork. Just down-stream of where the trail crosses Boulder Creek you'll find a spur trail on your left that takes you quickly to a double waterfall. A peaceful and camera-perfect place not usually noted on most maps.

Back to your packs, saddle up and start the 2.7-mile and 1,960 ft. climb up the north fork of Boulder Creek to Boulder Lake, its source. This is not the easiest part of the loop. The trail has a number of short steep segments and is rife with rocks. On a more pleasant note, it is bordered by Alaska Cedar lending a fresh fragrance to the air.

Arriving at the north shore of the lake, the area is open for the most part. Looking across the boulder-strewn lake you'll see Boulder Peak at 5,600 ft., a mile distant to the southwest. You can scramble to the top of Boulder Peak; the way is steep so be careful; "stuff happens". The 360° views are outstanding on a fair day. Leaving the lake to the southeast, a way-trail leads to Three Horse Lake a little more than a mile distant. The way-trail contours above the north fork of Boulder Creek, paralleling the creek at a half mile distant to the west.

Up early the next morning and beginning the climb to Happy Lake, a strenuous 5 miles to the northeast. The elevation gain of 960 ft. and the rough and rocky condition of the trail as it steeply climbs most of the first mile to the crest of Happy Lake Ridge will be offset by the ever increasing views that open up. That said, take your time with the first mile of this trail. The Happy Lake junction is at the four mile mark as you traverse the Ridge. Happy Lake is half a mile north of that trail junction, in a setting of subalpine trees and small meadows. This is your destination for today.

Happy Lake is the one of the sources of Barnes Creek which flows into Lake Crescent some 4,700 ft. below and to the northwest. The views at the junction are worthy of your attention. A curve in Klahanie Ridge to the southeast hides a view of Hurricane Ridge at its western terminus. Due south is Mt. Olympus at 7,969ft. over twenty miles distant which overshadows Mt. Appleton fifteen miles closer but only 6,000 ft. in height.

Due north of the ridge you have a clear view of the Strait of Juan de Fuca and the Elwha Spit, growing by the day as the Elwha River lays down its silt and debris burden as it enters the Strait. The spit is the direct result of the Park removing two dams built on the Elwha in the early 20th century. The near 100 years of silt build-up behind both those dams has continued to move down-stream since the dam removal began in 2011. As the river meets the Strait its velocity slows which diminishes its capacity to carry the weight of its burden. The end result is that the river continuously deposits material, building a sweeping spit in a northeasterly direction, just off its entrance point on the Strait of Juan de Fuca.

The third day's trek splits the remaining 4.5 miles between more ridge-walking and a steep descent to the Olympic Hot Springs Road. If the day is hot, you'll appreciate the drop in elevation and a return to the cooler shade of the forest. Meeting the road turn uphill and 1.5 miles farther on you'll return to the trailhead at the road's end. You started this loop hike three days ago and have covered nearly 18 miles in the effort. I hope taking the time to enjoy the views and surprises along the way was worth your effort on this trail.

17. High Divide Trail, ONP

High Divide Loop

NW Quadrant, Custom Correct map, "Seven Lakes Basin", (18.4 mi., difficulty 19.99, good camps with water, some of the best views in the Park, waterfall, entirely within a restricted reservation area)

Summary: Sol Duc Trailhead, Sol Duc Falls, 7-Mile Camp, Heart Lake, High Divide, Deer Lake, Sol Duc Trailhead

I'll deal with the restricted reservation designation first. Unlike most places in the Park, the number of people allowed to overnight in the area is limited and all camping must take place in designated camp sites. These restrictions derive from a need to protect this extremely popular camping area. This area's high-country beauty and desirability are at the same time its worst enemy and its greatest threat. Reservations may be made at *recreation.gov* up to 6 months in advance. There is less reservation demand November to March then it increases through spring, peaks from June to August and decreases in the fall. Contact the ONP Wilderness Information Center at 1-360-565-3100 to get more specific help regarding when to request your permit and any other restrictions that may apply at the time that you plan to experience this loop.

The trailhead is at the end of the Sol Duc Hot Springs Road, 25 minutes and just short of 15 miles off U.S. 101. The first short mile takes you, and nearly all the 3.5 million Olympic National Park visitors each year, to Sol Duc Falls. This first mile is a very busy place except early in the morning. You can get an early start by camping the night before in the Sol Duc Campground. It's a good idea to reserve a site through *recreation.gov*. Your reservation has to be at least four days in advance of your arrival.

So, let's try this again. Up early on day-one, pack up and move the car up to the trailhead parking area, about a mile up the road at 1,880 ft. of elevation. Hike the short mile and enjoy and uncrowded view of Sol Duc Falls. As you approach the Falls, you'll hear them before you see them. The trail splits right and left at a shelter just before the falls. Drop your packs at the shelter and follow the trail to the right down to the Bridge that fronts the Falls. It's photo time! Before you leave to retrieve your gear take a minute and inspect the chute that runs under the bridge; an uplifted sandwich with hard slate on each side and soft sandstone filling between the slate. For eons the river has been grinding away at the rock and, as you would guess, the softest rocks erode much faster than the hard ones.

Back at the shelter and strapped-up, head uphill on the Sol Duc River Trail. In short order, the trail levels out and stays so for about 2.5 miles. At that point you'll traverse a curve to the right that has you walking in a rock gutter, narrow and about a foot deep through its 20-yard length. Coming out the far end, the trail abruptly starts uphill and persists. You'll have gained 1,000 ft. over the first 4 miles by the time you reach the Appleton Pass junction on your left. Another short mile will have you arriving at 7-Mile Camp at 3,350 ft. This is a good place to take a break and replenish your water.

Heading on another 2.2 miles you'll cross the now smaller Sol Duc River and climb beyond treeline through alpine meadows to reach Heart Lake at about 4,700 ft. Your destination lies 8.6 miles from the trailhead. If you didn't snag a campsite at Heart Lake your campsite is most probably in Sol Duc Park a mile short of the lake.

Set up camp and hike up to the crest of the High Divide at the eastern base of Bogachiel Peak. The view of Mt. Olympus, about six miles distant is "in your lap" quality. If you can't get a good photo here throw your camera away, sit down and cry for a while.

You're standing where Barbara, my wife, and I stood years ago on one of many backpacking trips to the High Divide. It was an overcast day and as we stood discussing the future of the weather and enjoying the view when a clatter on our right startled us. A herd of mountain goats "Oreamnos americanus", ran down from Bogachiel Peak. Billys, nannys and several kids, about twenty in all.

Up until this event, we'd only encountered goats one at a time, never in these numbers and never with kids. We were both unsettled primarily by the presence of the unpredictable kids. The goats, being naturally curious, encircled us standing off about thirty feet and slowly walked, almost in line, as they circled us. If trouble erupted, we anticipated it would start with the kids and once started be finished by the adults charging us. The image of tangling with 350 pounds of agitated muscle and horns inspired abject fear in us both.

One hormone driven "eager beaver" kid was already horns down and pawing the ground on the verge of charging us. This didn't bode well for our future. What to do? With hearts racing and taking perhaps our last breaths, Barbara and I stood back to back rotating to our left matching their rate of circumnavigation. We agreed to keep eye contact with the kids, me to the left and Barbara to the right. I'd been told that while adult goats can be triggered to aggression by being stared at, kids on the other hand find it off-putting and keep their distance faced with a stare from a creature bigger than themselves. Were they right? I hoped so; our lives depended on this thin second-hand advice. My wisdom bin had just scraped bottom. Our, attempting-to-be-calm, internal "don't panic" voice was getting hoarse and fading in the stress of this predicament.

Try as we might to restrain it, our unbridled outward response, consisting of all action and no brain, was about to burst forth. At that point I thought it was do or die, but wait, hold on, yes, yes, yes, the goats are giving up! Evidently, we weren't interesting enough; should we be insulted? The whole herd started to mill about like we didn't exist. I snapped several keeper-photos, one in particular of a nanny and her kid. Mom looking disheveled, in mid-process of shedding the thick heavy and dirty coat of last winter, while her kid was sporting a new coat of flawless, pristine white. Soon thereafter they turned up-hill and bolted away.

Wow, I thought steep trails and narrow ledges caused you to sweat, strained your heart and made you yearn for home. Add a herd of mountain goats to the list of emotional spasms and wilderness stress. I was soaking, breathless and, because we'd survived, ecstatic. Yet another episode of "you never saw it coming, survived the terror of the moment and now can't wait to tell someone about it." Obviously, I'm still telling the story and my thanks to you for being my newest audience.

The High Divide is the photo point for all the magnificent pictures you've seen of Mt. Olympus. Perhaps, the Skyline Trail at Kimta Peak and Dodger Point are the only other places that would challenge the High Divide for its scenery. If you've the energy for it, climb up Bogachiel Peak. At 5,474 ft., it rises a scant few hundred feet above the High Divide Trail. If you elect to take this opportunity, you'll cash in on a reward that cost you little extra effort.

Day-two and dawn beaks, it's time for a high-country breakfast absent a table but with a world class view. Well-fed it's time to break camp, clean up the area, your trash, any trash, yours or not, and hike up to the divide. This will be a short but glorious day in the high country. Deer Lake lies about 6.5 miles to the northwest along the divide. If you've decided to skip a scramble up Bogachiel Peak, you ought to consider a quick drop-in at Seven Lakes Basin.

You'll arrive at the Seven Lakes Basin spur a mile northwest of Bogechiel Peak. If this side trip calls, drop your packs on the divide and hike down into the basin. You'll be entering one of the most sought-after backpacking destinations in the Park. If you tried to get a campsite reservation and were turned away, you're about to find out why.

In my energy-abundant youth some of my hiking buddies and I did this loop in reverse in two days, spending a cold late spring night at Lunch Lake. Snow in the Basin was spotty, the lakes had thawed but the Divide 700 feet above us was calf deep in snow. We "could'a-should'a" retreated up the trail that brought us down into the basin, but oh no, we had "a better plan". We headed off-trail east across the basin intending to climb up and over the southeast corner of the basin on to the divide, a half-mile west of the Sol Duc Trail junction. We were certain that this would save us miles and time on our way back to the trailhead. The ignorance of youth!

Crossing the basin was a snap, but as soon as we started up the basin's southeastern wall the snow became deeper and just short of the top, waist deep. Being cold and wet were the least of our worries. At its crest the snow had built a cornice that was more daunting than straight up; it actually overhung our position. Should we retreat in the defeat of wilderness ignorance or continue the obvious foolishness and danger of moving forward with this lamebrained plan?

Of course, youthfulness can't conger danger or defeat; we moved forward. It took several hours to achieve the goal of cutting a slot in the cornice and extracting ourselves onto the crest. So much for saving time and energy.

Our dignity reclaimed, we moved along the High Divide Trail focused on regaining the trailhead, some 8 miles down-trail. I was beat but not admitting it to my friends. Falling farther behind, they stopped all too frequently, only to allow me to catch up with their blistering pace. To add insult to injury on the struggling tail of this beast of a misadventure, my pack strap broke. I'd lost the first strap to those dastardly mice at Lunch Lake. They obviously had taken advantage of a poor hiker like me, by working the dark hours of the graveyard shift. They chewed clear through the first strap in a quest for the sweat-salt carefully deposited in that strap over my many years. Now, truly beat and tired, they deliver a time delayed "Coup de Strap". How low can it go? For the second time I improvised with hemp line, a strong but highly uncomfortable solution to my problem. Understand that I was still using my original, absolute-no-comfort model, Trapper Nelson. The Middle Ages had overlooked this form of torture, probably categorizing it as too-severe and inhumane.

I was literally in tears. All I wanted was to be back home. After a good and lonely cry, it dawned on me that crying wasn't the same as hiking, or an effective means of diminishing the problem and accelerating the achievement of my desired goal. The wilderness neither loves nor hates you; it just holds you absolutely responsible for your choices and the quality of your response to what it serves up.

Back up from the basin you're back on the trail with one more mile of High Divide views before the trail swings north-northwest on its last 2.5 miles to Deer Lake. It depends on the time of year. If it's not the end of August into the early weeks of September you'll be traversing high country meadows some of which are abloom with Avalanche Lilies in late June through the first of July and flaming fall color late September into October. But there is a magical window at the end of August into early September; the aforementioned meadows are ripe with huckleberries. All you can eat and a liter a day to take home is the Park's rule. You'll have competition, however, from the Black Bears grazing the berries, getting ready for winter. The bears are normally skittish around hikers and I know of no adverse human-bear incident or encounter in the Park. In these meadows however, they seem unphased by your human and alien presence. Eating is their goal and nature's table is set. As the bears graze head down they may stop, raise their head and stare at you. This is bear sign language for, "I'm headed your way and would you please step off". Do so. You don't want to challenge 250 to 350 pounds of a bear's hard wired reflexes: you can't win, trust me. You don't have to go far and 50 yards is a safe and a Park required distance in this situation. Did you bring your camera?

A mile or so down-trail you'll come to Deer Lake, your stop-over for day-two. If it's hot or windy, you'll love this campsite. Deer Lake sits in a bowl just inside the boundary of the contiguous forest providing cool shade and wind protection from the high meadowland you've just traversed.

Day-three breaks and the final 3.8 miles is only half of what day-one required. The first 3 miles follow Canyon Creek from its headwaters at Deer Lake to its end, near Sol Duc Falls, where it empties into the Sol Duc River. This sometimes-steep grade is rife with what I call "rocks and roots" creating ample opportunity for stepping down; in some instances, a step of mid-calf in height. The virgin forest is robust and just a few inches of rain short of qualifying as a Temperate Rain Forest.

Subalpine conifers give way at about 2,500 ft. to the predominance of Western hemlocks and Douglas firs; misnamed since they really belong to the pine family. You can tell the difference in two obvious ways. The bark on the Douglas firs is thick, rough and bears the deep growth scars of constant splitting and healing to accommodate the annual added girth of the trunk. The bark on Western hemlock has a scalier appearance, not so different from what a fish looks like. The scales provide the same girth expansion relief that the splitting does on firs. The second identifier is at the absolute top, called the "lead" of the tree. The lead on firs stand straight up where hemlock leads droop over in Dr. Seuss fashion.

Arriving at Sol Duc Falls, you'll rejoin the Sol Duc River Trail for the last eight tenths of a mile back to the trailhead. It's been a short day, leaving you plenty of time for a soak in the hot spring's pools at the resort. A great ending to a most wonderous trip in the Daniel J. Evans Wilderness. As a final note, plan well and request campsites early. In every year, you're hard up against stiff competition for this truly prized area of the Park.

18. Boulder Shelter, ONP

Boulder Shelter Loop

SW Quadrant, Custom Correct map, "Buckhorn Wilderness" (21 mi., difficulty 13.0, moderate, dry, long last day, high country views, Marmots)

Summary: Upper Dungeness Trailhead, Camp Handy, Boulder Shelter, Marmot Pass, Tubal Cane Mine, Silver Creek, FS Road 2870, Upper Dungeness Trailhead

This hike begins at the one and only sharp switchback in Forest Service Road 2870 marking the Upper Dungeness Trailhead. From U.S.101 about five miles east of Sequim or about a mile and a half west of Sequim Bay State Park turn south onto Palo Alto Road. Farther on, Palo Alto becomes Forest Service Road 28 as asphalt gives way to gravel. FS 28 intersects with FS 2880, joining from your right. Follow FS 2880 by turning right. Farther on, FS 2880 intersects with FS 2870 which also comes from your right. Proceed straight ahead at the intersection of FS 2880 and FS 2870. You are now on FS 2870 and will remain so all the way to the trailhead. FS 2870 contours to the west and high above the Dungeness River, by an ever so twisting route around the buttresses of Maynard and Tyler Peaks in the Olympic National Forest's Buckhorn Wilderness. Once on FS 2870 and after about 5 miles of this so "twisty-turny" road, you'll descend a long 2 mile grade, slowly turning to your right. At the bottom of that grade, you'll notice vehicles parked on the left side of the road just before the road itself switchbacks in a sharp rounding left turn. Park the car. You've arrived at the Upper Dungeness Trailhead; your dusty, or muddy, driving day is over.

Leaving the trailhead and hiking southwest through mature timber on fairly level ground, you'll arrive at a fork in the trail. The right fork leads to Royal Lake, but you'll take the left fork headed toward Camp Handy. The grade is still easy as you proceed to Camp Handy following the west then the east bank of the Dungeness River. Just beyond Camp Handy the trail begins a 2.6-mile and 1750 ft. climb to Boulder Shelter, the destination for your first day.

Or is it? There are always options and calculated decisions to be made involved is these types of situations. Your point of origin, the trailhead for this loop is 14 miles farther on from Boulder Shelter. Although, much of it is a descending grade to Silver Creek north of your present location and then a 4 mile trudge down FS 2870 back to your vehicle. No matter how you cut it, 14 miles makes a long hard day. Your other option is to hike to Marmot Pass 1.5 miles due north of Boulder Shelter and then turn right and descend a mile to Camp Mystery to set up camp. However, tomorrow from Camp Mystery you'll still have the better part of 14 miles before you reach the trailhead.

Oh Great! Either option requires a long day come sunrise. There are however some other considerations. First, you're already at Boulder Shelter and you can lay down those heavy packs. Part of that weight is water lugged up the trail. There is a small creek just south of the shelter but it could be dry depending on when you arrive. Because that Boulder Shelter in the dry season should be considered a dry camp with no water source within 2.5 miles; the same 2.5 miles between where you are and Camp Mystery. If you stay at the shelter, you'll most likely need to at least drop your packs at Marmot Pass and take a quick side trip to the stream at Camp Mystery to fill up on water for the rest of the 14 miles required by day-two.

In the scenic department, Boulder Shelter and Marmot Pass are exceedingly similar with Mt. Constance to the southeast and both Mts. Mystery and Deception to the west. Except at Marmot Pass you'll get a partial view of Mt. Olympus peeking around the north shoulder of Mt. Deception. From Boulder Shelter, just south of Marmot Pass, even a partial view of Mt. Olympus isn't available. Both vantage points are at or just above treeline, covered in thin soils and struggling grasses for the most part. A major difference are the Marmots. There's a reason it's called Marmot Pass. A colony of the cute ground hugging mammals reside in an old rock slide just below the pass. Water, views and cute wildlife, how much better can it get?

One last incentive to push on. Mice inhabit every shelter in the Park; Boulder Shelter is no exception. On our many hikes, Barbara and I have suffered with the damage that mice can do in the backcountry, even avoiding shelters. We've had both our tent and our packs eaten through, in the dead of night, by these sneaky silent intruders. They severed both my pack straps on one occasion and decimated our food stores halfway through a 10 day outing; thank God for berries in the late summer. Regardless of your choice, I'll resume the hike's features starting at Marmot Pass on day-two. Contouring at about 6,000 ft. the trail swings around the west side of Buckhorn Mountain at 6,988 ft., off to your right, and then starts its descent following Copper Creek, a tributary of the Dungeness River. Traversing the eastern edge of the rain shadow, created by Mt. Olympus and the Bailey Range to the west, the trail passes through the driest portion of the Olympic National Forest. This micro-climate is the driest area on the western Pacific coast north of San Diego, California.

The trail descends a dry and rock-strewn ridge-face running down to Buckhorn Lake, a half mile off to your right. Buckhorn Lake is the headwater of Copper Creek, running north through the narrow valley below. Trees that were struggling at altitude start to become more abundant. They are smaller and obviously showing the effects of a lack of decent soils and insufficient water. About 3 miles down-trail from Marmot Pass, the trail steepens as it abandons the near ridgetop and heads directly down to Copper Creek.

Reaching and crossing the creek, the trail enters into the area of the Tubal Cain Mine, a struggling enterprise that closed operations due to a slump in copper and manganese prices and the brutal winter of 1912-1913. At this point the trail is in close proximity of the southern shaft of the mine, visible at the summit of the tailings pile. Entering the mine shaft is Not Recommended! Your mining curiosity might be better served by examining the cast-off mining equipment spread around the tailings pile.

The trail heads north and skirts above Copper Creek to the east through the next 4 miles. It then descends and, a half mile short of Silver Creek, the trail turns sharply due east. Reaching Silver Creek, it changes direction abruptly to the north and rises a short distance to FS 2870. Turn left and the Upper Dungeness Trailhead, from which you started this hike, awaits your arrival 4 miles distant. You've just completed two days of hiking across one of the drier trails in the Olympic National Forest; congratulations.

North Fork Quinault River – Three Lakes Loop

SW Quadrant, Custom Correct map, "Quinault-Colonel Bob", (21 mi., difficulty 10.11, the river, the lakes and elevations from Rain Forest to Subalpine and back)

Summary: North Fork Quinault Trailhead, Elip Creek Camp, Tshletshy Ridge, Three Lakes, North Fork Quinault Trailhead

After a long drive to the South Shore Road on Lake Quinault, just minutes off of U.S. 101, stop in at the Lake Quinault Lodge for coffee and a chance to experience the grandeur of the lodge's Great Room. You'll have wonderful views of the lake, exquisite interior woodwork, something that just isn't done anymore, and over-stuffed furniture that will put you to sleep; don't spill the coffee!

After your respite from the dreaded yellow-striped asphalt of U.S. 101, drive beyond the lodge on the South Shore Road about 14 miles to where it crosses over the Quinault to join the North Shore Road. After the crossing, bear right to the terminus of the road at the North Fork Campground, the trailhead for this 21-mile loop. I'll describe it in a counterclockwise rotation.

From the trailhead you'll follow an easy grade paralleling the North Fork Quinault River which runs down from Low Divide, 16 miles to the northeast, to its end point at Lake Quinault. The lake and its shores are controlled under an 1856 treaty with the Quinault Indian Nation. As such, the National Park Service controls the lake's north shore and the U.S. Forest controls the lake's south shore, while the lake itself belongs to the Quinault Tribe. These three neighbors get along amicably, much to the public's benefit.

About 3 miles up-trail you'll find Wolf Bar Camp. Wolf Bar camp was the initial stop on my first Boy Scout "50-miler" hike, a cross-Park trek, seven days from North Fork Campground to Whiskey Bend on the Elwha. By the way, it's really only 43 miles, but who counts when you're twelve?

At Wolf Bar, the trail swings to the north. Just short of 4 miles up-trail and a 400 ft. climb you'll reach the end of day-one, at the Elip Creek campsite. You'll have completed the easy part of this loop. You'll find out how easy day-one was tomorrow morning. Elip Creek Campsite is just north of the creek, slightly above and west of the Quinault River. The campsite has no bear wire and the privy is across the creek from the campsite. With Mt. Lawson at 5,201ft. due east, don't expect to wake up with the sun in your eyes.

19. Three Prune Creek, ONP

As you leave Elip Creek campsite, you'll climb the steep spine of a ridge rising to the west of the river. You won't be needing the sun to keep you warm. The relentless switchbacks that climb 2,400 ft. in the first 3 miles of this trail will provide all the heat you'll need. This ridge is flanked on its north side by the Three Prune Creek drainage and on the south by Elip Creek, not that you can see either one far below.

As the trail reaches the top of the rise it contours, first northwest, then west and then due south, around a prominence on your left. The northwest side of the prominence is home to Kurtz Lake. The lake is out of sight and about 160 ft. above the last bend in the trail to the southwest, as the trail finishes bending around the prominence. The trail continues heading southwest and a short mile later it intersects the Three Lakes Trail at 3,760 ft.

Turning left and heading south, the trail climbs quickly over a 4,000 ft. pass and traverses below Tshletshy Ridge, now on your right. The trail runs over open ground for three quarters of a mile. Back in the forest, another short half mile brings you to a stream bed, probably dry, and the half way point between Elip Creek Trail junction and Three Lakes. Another 1.5 miles down-trail you'll arrive at Three Lakes, your goal achieved and the end of a tough 7.5 mile day-two.

Through the summer this alpine bench, the Three Lakes area, is flush with wildflowers and its share of mosquitoes. A short half mile

20. The Brothers, ONP

side trip to the west will take you to the crest of Tshletshy Ridge and you'll be rewarded for your effort with a peek down into the head of Paradise Valley 700 ft. below. This is just about the only view point. The landscape in all other directions rises well above the lakes' elevation at about 3,200 ft. On the trail again, the morning of day-three starts with an easy wander through meadows dotted with subalpine conifers. About a mile down-trail from Three Lakes the trail begins to round two buttresses running to the northeast. As it passes through a stand of Alaska cedar, (Callitropsis nootkatensis db.2010), take a careful look for the granddaddy of Alaska cedars in the Park. It has stood in this grove amongst its brethren for 2,000 years and at 37.6 feet in circumference and with a 27 ft. spread, it is larger than any other of its kind in the U.S

I was 14 and on an outing with the Olympic College Mountaineering Class, the oldest and most enduring college mountaineering program in the country. Too young to be officially part of the class, my friends and I took the class several years in a row by contributing to the equipment fund and keeping the arrangement below the radar; the college version of "don't ask, don't tell". It was 1961 and we were off to climb The Brothers, led by George Martin, Glenn Kelsey and Chuck Maiden. After establishing base camp at trails end in The Valley of Silent Men, a few of my friends and I accompanied Gene Kelsey and Chuck Maiden up the lower part of The Brothers southeast buttress in search of a big Alaska cedar that Chuck had seen on a previous climb. We found it after an hour of climbing through thick brush.

Chuck took numerous measurements and fixed the tree's location with compass and map; old-school location finding was all there was in the early 1960s. Chuck submitted his find to the government for possible inclusion as a record specimen of (Cupressus nootkatensis db.1864), Alaska yellow cedar. As it turned out, the tree near Three Lakes won that honor and holds it to this day, as it should.

The trail from Three Lakes continues to descend through heavily forested ground then begins a series of switchbacks, at about the 1.5 mile mark, which end where the trail crosses the outfall creek from Three Lakes. A mile later the trail, climbing the opposite valley wall, rounds a buttress 300 ft. above where the outfall creek from Three Lakes joins Big Creek on its way to the North Fork Quinault far below. You're just shy of the day's half way point, at 3.5 miles. The trail climbs 400 ft. up the valley wall and then slowly loses 1,000 ft. in the next 2 miles, where it passes the marshes just north of Irely Lake. It rejoins the North Fork Road, a mile farther on. Gaining the road, turn left and finish the loop with a short mile up the road to the trail-head. You've completed 21 miles, including the middle miles where you bore the brunt of two trail sections that first gained and then lost 3,500 ft. of elevation. Put this loop into your book of conquests as a hike well done; you've earned it.

Five to Ten Day Loop Hikes

Grand Ridge – Cameron Creek Loop

NE Quadrant, Custom Correct map, "Gray Wolf-Dosewallips", (28 mi., difficulty 18.09, high country, subalpine lakes, a pass, a dry camp)

Summary: Obstruction Point Trailhead, Grand Ridge, Deer Park, Three Forks, Lower Cameron, Grand Pass, Grand Lake, Obstruction Point Trailhead.

True to the up and down nature of the Olympic Mountains, this loop contains ups and downs spread over two drainages in the Park, Grand Creek and Cameron Creek. The trailhead is easy to find. Leave U.S. 101, (Front Street in Port Angeles) turning left onto Race Street and continuing up Race through 4 stoplights then straight through the one 4-way stop sign, to the Olympic National Park Visitor Center. The V.C. will be on your right, just after the 4-way stop.

Stop at the V.C. and get your backcountry permit at the Wilderness Information Center inside the V.C., if you don't already have one. You'll register at the desk and indicate how many are in your party (no more than 12), your start point/date and end/point date. In this case both, are Obstruction Point. You'll be asked for camping locations by the day and self-identification and emergency information. I recommend an emergency contact number as well. Leaving the V.C., drive 17 miles up to the Hurricane Ridge parking lot. The Obstruction Point Road is on your left just as you get to the parking lot. There's a speed limit sign on your right, opposite the sign, is the Obstruction Point Road. The road quickly dips out of sight from the parking lot. The 7.8 mile road to Obstruction Point is gravel; take your time and drive it slowly. Driving it fast results in either dental repairs or kidney bruising. It's just as hard on the road itself and won't be doing any favors to those who will use it in the future. Slow is a gift to all concerned.

Obstruction Point is a popular trailhead for hikers and backpackers alike. Parking space can become a problem. I suggest you get there very early. If you are staying over in Port Angeles the night before the trip begins, I'd get my permit the day you first arrive in Port Angeles. Early the following morning I'd drive, about an hour, straight up to Obstruction Point, avoiding a long wait in the permit-line at the W.I.C. desk and most likely beat the crowd in the rush for a parking space. There are two trails that leave the parking area. One heads south, it's not the one you want. Your trail leads to Deer Park and heads east across Grand Ridge. This area of the Park lies in a rain shadow and is

21. View South from Grand Pass, ONP, Pablo McLoud

extremely dry by comparison to the rest of the Olympic Mountains. The face of the southern slope on the ridge contains a lot of fine loose scree. If the wind is blowing, it's like a dust storm out there. My suggestion, wait out the wind, it usually eases up late in the day. It's 7.6 miles between Obstruction Point and the Deer Park Campground. There is no water at Obstruction Point, on Grand Ridge and at times, late in the summer, Deer Park. Carry enough water for today and half of tomorrow. This trail is as high, dry and near the sky as any maintained trail in the Olympic Mountains.

With the exception of the last 2 miles on Grand Ridge you'll enjoy views north and south as the trail alternates from the top of the ridge to just below it on the south slope. Southwest, about 3 to 4 miles distant, you'll see a series of unnamed peaks along a ridgeline, running to the southwest at elevations of 6,000 to 6,500 ft. On the other side of that ridgeline is Cameron Creek, which you'll meet in a couple of days, roughly 3,000 ft. below the ridgeline you're looking at.

Farther out, 7 to 10 miles due south and a thousand feet higher, you can see the north end of the south hook of the Gray Wolf Ridge. Given your sightline, you'll see Mt. Walkinshaw at 7,378 ft. blocking your view of Mt. Clark, Martin Peak and Mt. Deception, all over 7,000 feet high. This line of seven thousand-foot peaks marks the inner east range of the Olympic Mountains. Running from north to south it is the greatest concentration of high peaks in the Olympic Mountain complex. We see them as mountains but in truth, they were marine extruded basaltic islands drifting east on the Pacific Plate. When the seafloor of the Pacific Plate subducted under the Continental Plate at the western edge of North America, these seamounts were tipped, broken and squeezed into the eastern and northern inner and outer ranges of the Olympic Mountains forming a roughly wrinkled horseshoe shape on the maps you're using today. To the north you can see Mt. Angeles and Klahanie Ridge, marking the north range of the Olympic Mountains. About a mile short of Maiden Peak, the halfway point, you'll pass Roaring Winds Camp. Barbara, my wife, and I nearly got blown off the Ridge in our attempt to spend a night camped at Roaring Winds; I wouldn't recommend it to the faint of heart.

Arriving at Maiden Peak, at 6,434 ft. and about 200 ft. above the trail on the north, I recommend the short scramble to its summit; the views in all directions are spectacular. To the southeast you'll see Gray Wolf Ridge about seven miles off. The ridge runs to the south and its southern end, twice the distance away, is named The Needles. Its name fits its shape, a distinctly rugged sawtooth shaped ridge containing eleven 7,000 plus ft. peaks.

The Obstruction Point to Deer Park Trail slowly descends through its last 2.5 easterly miles and then abruptly rises to the Deer Park Road near the ranger station. Turn to your right and travel a short half mile up the road to the Deer Park Campground. After you've set up camp and rested a bit, walk the short mile to the summit of Blue Mountain at 6,007 ft. the third highest point on this loop.

If it's a moonless clear night sky, you have a real treat in store. There is absolutely no background light within many miles. I believe you will be as enthralled as I was my first time and every time thereafter. I got the chance to see our universe lit up as a spectacular display of cosmic bodies, satellites, meteors, and the Milky Way. It's hard to imagine just how much you can see on a clear night illuminated by the cosmos

Morning breaks and it's time to eat, pack up and get back on the trail. Today is a short hike but it's all steeply down-trail. Like 3,000 feet down-trail over 4.1 miles. "Oh, your poor toes, your hose bearing holes, the pain of it all adds to your woes, but like it or not down you goes." As "down-you-goes" you'll rapidly transition from an alpine to subalpine to the upper reaches of the lowland forest. This transition is caused by the changes in exposure, temperature, soil quality and moisture. As the elevation of the Olympic Mountain environment declines there is generally a decline in the first two elements and a distinct increase in the last two. As with all generalities there are exceptions to the pattern.

Within the boundaries of the Park nearly all of the forest is virgin. The exceptions are roads, improvements in trails and Park structures, a good deal of which were built by the Civilian Conservation Corps, the CCC, in the 1930's.

In due time you'll arrive at the Three Forks Shelter, an example of the CCC's work. I don't like shelters. Let me be more specific. I wouldn't spend the night in one, if I had a choice. Why my disdain for shelters? Mice! They are in most places in the mountains and everywhere at lower elevations. Over the years, I've had them infest my food supplies, eat through my pack straps, chewed holes in my tents, and generally abused my gear as I've slept.

If you don't like Three Forks, your alternative is Gray Wolf Camp a quarter mile down-stream and on the opposite bank. The bad news is it's out of your way today and again tomorrow morning. If you elect this alternative move down-stream a short half mile, cross Grand Creek, then the Gray Wolf River, and Gray Wolf Camp will be a few paces ahead. In the morning, reverse your route, cross the Gray Wolf then Grand Creek and follow Cameron Creek up-stream. You now know how Three Forks got its name. Look up from Three Forks and you'll see the noses of steep ridges in every direction. It's not a stunning view but it is the reason that Three Forks is a cold camping experience. Of course, cold is relative. In the hottest days of August, you might say it's cool, maybe even comfortable, but that's only on the hottest days. During the rest of the calendar, it's cold.

After you've packed up your campsite, look around for any trash, yours or others', pick it up and carry it out. If previous one-night occupants have been as responsible, this campsite and others will remain as close to pristine as you hoped it would be for your stay. Taking care of the wilderness is every hiker's responsibility; thank you for doing your part. Today's hike travels up Cameron Creek 4.9 miles to Lower Cameron Camp, a very small site. You probably read the sign at Deer Park, "No Open Fires, Stoves Only". That rule applies in the Park at and above 3,500 feet of elevation. The purpose is environmental. All vegetation above 3,500 feet is in a constant survival struggle. Soils are thin and relatively poor. Even though subalpine and alpine plants have adapted, they are still fragile. Dead wood is scarce, but scarce as it is, the nutrients it adds to the soil as it slowly rots is critical. These environments cannot afford you burning their precious fertilizer. Please do your part and only use stoves above 3,500 feet. Three Forks was the only backcountry camp on this entire loop where campfires are permitted.

Lower Cameron Camp lies at about 3,600 feet. The trail up from Three Forks has slowly climbed up and into a widening valley as it gains about 1,500 feet, an easy day. If you've taken my advice, you'll find a small campsite but not near Cameron Creek. Before we discovered the damage that we were doing three or four decades ago, camping "on" the river was looked on as part of the "outdoor experience". That type of attitude and practice caused both erosion and spoiling of river banks, but it also was the source of denuding riverside vegetation and contributed to increased waste, in all forms, despoiling the waters. Take a good look at the ridge opposite the Creek to your north and west. Tomorrow will start with you climbing to its crest. Get some rest, you'll need it, come morning!

Morning? Did someone mention morning? Its arrived, you're packed up, cleaned up and are back on the trail. Moving up-trail 2.1

miles you'll arrive at the junction of the Grand Pass Trail on your right. At the junction you'll find a few small camp sites. As you stand at the junction, Grand Pass towers 2,350 feet above you. That elevation gain has to be achieved in 1.8 miles. As you start up, take your time. Rest and water, in frequent doses, are your friends. If you are thinking that the grade is steep and tortuous in its lower portions, you may think the last half mile to the top is some form of divine punishment. When you finally crest the ridge, you'll go from upslope to downslope from south to north in a single stride. If ever there was a knife-edged ridge, Grand Pass most certainly is it. Congratulations you've just completed the toughest part of this loop.

Once over Grand Pass you are now entering a restricted reservation area, one of several in the Park. These areas have been established to control their use, protect popular areas and reduce the need for closures. The benefit for everyone is that continued use can be sustained. On the Park map, they are designated by red dots at the perimeter and red tents within the designated area. The fact that you're hiking this loop is proof that you've been introduced to and mastered the restricted reservation area protocol. Contact the Wilderness Information Center, W.I.C., at Olympic National Park at 1-360-565-3100. The rangers at the W.I.C. will advise you on how to proceed in securing the reservations you desire. Reservations can be made online at <recreation.gov.>

You're headed to Grand Lake at the low end of this subalpine valley. By comparison to the south side of Grand Pass, you'll feel a good portion of relief. As you navigate the last 2.4 miles, you'll first pass by Gladys Lake, the smallest of the three lakes in the valley. Moose Lake is next and a bit larger than Gladys. A short half mile later a spur trail on your right takes you a few hundred yards to Grand Lake, your stopover for the night. You'll notice designated campsites, which, while they give you a view of the Lake, are somewhat removed from it on purpose. A trail leads northeast from the lake following Grand Creek. This trail is a way-trail, sometimes used as an alternative route back to Obstruction Point. It follows the creek for about a mile and a half, crossing it twice. The farther you go the harder it is to sort the trail from a myriad of game trails particularly in its higher segments.

The crossing of Grand Creek is messy at best, a jumble of small logs or large brush that doesn't afford the best footing. There are many tales of wet feet as a product of hiking a trail in the driest portion of the park. Given the degree of way-finding and the fact that the creek crossings are difficult, at best it's an option, but I don't recommend it for the reasons stated. This is particularly true considering the main trail between Grand Lake and Obstruction Point is well maintained and ascends the same elevation without a "where's the trail" element.

Your trailhead destination tomorrow is at the head of the Valley about 1,500 feet above the Lake.

Unless you're hiking in the late summer or early fall you've noticed the mosquitoes at the Lake. While you may feel bad about leaving the Lake behind, my guess is that you're not missing those thousands of miniature marauders. Feelings aside, you've got 1,500 feet to climb in the first 2 miles and another 1.5 miles beyond that before you rest.

If you are hiking in the afternoon on a hot day, Badger Valley has the effect of a reflector oven. I recommend climbing out of the Valley before the heat sets in. You'll reach the crest of the Valley a mile and a half from Obstruction Point. Just shortly after you reach the crest you'll pass over a few small beds of "pencil slate". Usually slate, a metamorphized sedimentary rock form, is found in a shape that is about the size of your hand and about as thick as a finger. It is a dark grey in color, relatively smooth on its broad faces and irregular around the edges. In this case, the formation created lateral parallel faults across the face and when these weak points failed, they produce pieces of shale that are just about as wide as they are thick and just a few inches in length. Called pencil-slate, they resemble those little pencils that come with some board games.

The terrain welcomes you with an easy rolling trail from the crest to the trailhead and the end of this 28 mile loop. You've now experienced the driest part of the Olympic Mountains, navigated the reservation system, have straddled Grand Pass, hiked the highest driest maintained trail in the Park and gained and lost the 6,000-foot mark three different times. You can be proud of meeting the challenges of the past few days, logged some added experience and hopefully are looking forward to your next backpacking goal.

Cameron Creek – Gray Wolf River

NE Quadrant, Custom Correct map, "Gray Wolf-Dosewallips", (45mi., difficulty 26.81, 3 passes, alpine glory, mountain views and 2 side trips)

Summary: Slab Camp Trailhead, Three Forks, Lower Cameron Camp, Upper Cameron Camp, Cameron Pass, Lost Pass, Dose Meadows, Thousand Acre Meadow, Gray Wolf Pass, Falls Camp, Cedar Lake, Slide Camp, Slab Camp Trailhead.

This loop starts at the end of Forest Service Road 2875. Beginning just past the Dungeness Bridge, a mile west of Sequim, turn left onto Taylor Cutoff Road; there's a service station on the southeast corner of the intersection. Taylor Cutoff runs due south, flat and level, then swinging upward and hard to the right becomes Lost Mountain Road. The road climbs and as it tops out it swings left into a more open and flat area dotted with houses and small farms. The road runs nearly straight for about half a mile before it begins a definite turn to the right. At that point, look left to see FS Road 2875. The attending sign, if it hasn't been stolen, will announce Slab Camp Road. Turn left onto FS 2875, or Slab Camp Road if you must, and follow it to its end about 5 miles away. Take care to avoid the mistake of turning onto FS 2870 on the left just over a mile from the beginning of FS 2875 on Lost Mountain Road.

As FS Road 2875 ends, you've arrived at the trailhead; there are two trails. The one to your right leads to Deer Park, but the one you want is on your left. The trail follows Slab Camp Creek 3.1 miles down-trail to Camp Tony on the Gray Wolf River losing about 1,000 ft. of elevation. You'll become quite familiar with the Gray Wolf by the time you return to Camp Tony on your last hiking day.

The trail now heads up-stream 5.9 miles to Three Forks Shelter or the alternative, Gray Wolf Camp, the end of your first day. The Gray Wolf starts out in the bottom of a heavily forested steep-walled valley. If it's hot, you'll enjoy the cooling effect, but if it's cool and gloomy, not so much. Given the density of the forest canopy and the limited time during the day that the sun shines into this canyon, the temperature persists in the cool range throughout the summer and downright cold in spring and fall. 2.3 miles up-river you'll happen on Slide Camp with Slide Creek running nearby. This is a good spot to take a brief rest before finishing today's hike. The trail humps and bumps along gaining about 1,000 feet by the time you reach Three Forks.

Three Forks is aptly named; it's the point at which the Gray Wolf from the south, Cameron Creek from the southwest and Grand Creek from the northwest come together. The steep spine of forested ridges

22. Lost Pass, ONP

matches the Cardinal Points (N.E.S.W.) of the compass with Three Forks centered among them. This is not unique in the Park, but not at all common either. Your best vantage point for this topographic oddity is on the south shore of the Gray Wolf at Camp Gray Wolf, opposite the shelter site.

Camp Gray Wolf, is in about the same location as the aforementioned view point, on the east bank of the Gray Wolf River. Tomorrow you'll be headed up-stream on Cameron Creek. In order to do that, you'll need to follow the Gray Wolf down-stream a couple hundred yards where you'll cross the river and proceed west past the Three Forks Shelter and on up Cameron Creek. Regardless of your camping choice, beware of the mice. These night time invaders are present throughout the Olympic Mountains. I believe that they are worse at shelters.

Years ago, on one of our early hikes together, Barbara, my wife, and I pulled into a campsite after a long day's hike to find the bear-wire down. We had counted on hanging our food bag on the wire and the two trees tall enough in this alpine area had no lower branches that began to match my ability to pitch a line over them. So, as we crawled into the tent that night, I put the food bag under my head as a makeshift pillow. Surely the mice wouldn't be so bold as to try a pillage raid next to my keen ear. We awoke to an obvious failure of my backcountry skills. The mice, while I was enjoying the bliss of sleep, chewed through the side of the tent and the food bag. They sampled about half of our food sacks, within the bag, and left their calling cards before moving on to their next "sacking of a sack". Needless to say, we survived the rest of the hike on half stores and a crash course in "creative gourmet" based on a wild berry base. Interesting as it was, it wasn't enough that we ever repeated those made-up on-the-spot recipes.

The sun is up, but not so much in your current location. Today will be an easy day with a slight rise in the trail gradient and 5 miles up-trail to Lower Cameron Camp. You'll find the creek running freely between two 6,000-foot ridges to the north and to the south. To the north is an unnamed ridge dividing the Lillian Valley from Grand Valley, an alternate route back to the FS Road 2875 trailhead. To the south is another unnamed ridge dividing the Cameron Creek and the Gray Wolf River drainages; a place you'll become familiar with a few days from now.

This is an opportune moment to make the point that you are only as safe as your ability to pinpoint your location and identify your path to safety. It's an acquired skill but not difficult to acquire. Whenever you stop for a break, set up camp, or any other reason, take the time to study your map and compare it to what you see from your vantage point. The presence of distinguishing features, such as peaks, waterfalls, or the confluence of a stream, can be keys to your current location. Once you know your location, study which alternatives present themselves, providing you a safe exit from your current location. In the Olympic Mountains, the ridge standing before you often, but not always, holds that alternative you're looking for in the next valley. Never travel off-trail without a clear understanding of the topo map and a clearer ability to understand what it's telling you. You're a hiker, not a goat, and therein is the severe difference in capability.

The terrain has changed somewhat by the time you've risen 1,000 feet above Three Forks. At 3,500 feet you're required to use only stoves; open fires are "verboten". You're entering the subalpine zone. You'll begin to see, if you haven't already, Silver Fir. It's a subalpine species but it also grows at lower elevations. It's not hard to spot; it has, wait for it, silver bark. Subalpine trees in general, though just as old as their bigger brethren that you experienced around Camp Tony or Slide Camp, have a smaller stature. Severe weather, exposure and poorer soils add up to a difficult growing environment and a tougher life cycle, all the way around. As such, the number of dead trees begins to make itself known. The rate of death isn't the true difference. The difference is that there is seriously less groundcover and forest density to conceal the fallen trees. As you ascend Cameron Creek to

Cameron Pass the difference between the lower forest and the alpine environment is astonishing.

A new day and you can get up with the sun. I suggest early is better. The day's hike is relatively short, 4.6 miles to Upper Cameron Camp. There is a built-in reason. The upper Cameron Basin is an alpine hiker's wilderness dream. The basin is picturesque with a meadow accented by a slowly winding Cameron Creek, situated below a scree-filled bowl crowned with Cameron Pass at 6,350 ft. hovering 1,300 feet above you to the southwest. Sundown is hours away, so take the time enjoying this very special place, you're earning memories that will last a lifetime.

Please try your best to stay on the trail as you explore. You'll notice a number of "social trails" that have left scars on this pristine meadow. These scars can take decades to heal and if you use them, the decades of healing have to start all over. If we, as hikers, don't accept the inconvenience of taking due care of these fragile places, they will continue to decline to the point of being ordinary. Look around, I've guided you here to observe and experience the majesty of this place and trust that you'll stop short of doing any greater damage to its beauty; "take nothing but memories, and leave no trace." A message from Leave No Trace Center for Outdoor Ethics: LNT.org

The morning arrives and you bid farewell to Cameron Basin. Today will be one of the toughest days of the loop, crossing Cameron Pass. Often Cameron Pass, particularly the north side, is the last pass in the Park to melt out. At worst, with snow and ice remaining, you'll need an ice axe and training in self arrest techniques. At best you'll need good eyesight. It will be hard, beautiful and long; saddle up. Follow the trail until it seems to end in the lower reaches of the scree-bowl that you face. Your task, and you must accept it, is to identify the cairn nearest to you up-slope. A cairn is a pile of rocks of differing height placed at the edge of the trail to mark the path through rough terrain. It won't take you long to find the deficiencies in this way of travel. First, there is very little color contrast amongst the "rock tossed salad" quality of this scree slope. Second, not all cairns are created equal. Some are waist high and easy to spot but most are much smaller, some no taller than your ankle. What! Why, it's not like there's a shortage of building material? Finally, some cairns may just be missing in action, knocked down by some errant hiker or a wayward hoofed mammal.

As you proceed slowly from cairn to cairn, stopping at the first and searching for the next, your scree-bowl time may be wearing but at least it isn't a sweat breaking sprint to the top. Speaking of the top, you're in for a surprise. Unlike some passes in these mountains, where one side is as steep as the other, the back side of Cameron Pass looks more like a knoll than a pass. The ground rolls away gently in all directions, covered sparsely by struggling bushes and clumps of sedges and other high-altitude plants. The exposure at 6,000 feet is extreme. Wind, snow, sun and drought are common and consistent seasonal events. Anything growing up here is tough as nails and has had to adapt seriously to this harsh environment. The conifer bushes you see are really the same trees that you walked through several thousand feet below. At this altitude, given the wind exposure, height is not an advantage as it is in the denser forests at lower elevations, where there is a constant fight for sunlight. Up here tall results in broken or blown out, due to high winds and heavy snow. As such, the tree lowers its aspirations and accepts life in the form of a bush.

The trail breaks southeast and traverses through a series of meadows and copes of slope sheltered alpine conifers. In the alpine summer between mid-July and early August these meadows are raging with wildflower colors. You are in the inner sanctum of the Park. Few hikers are willing to expend either the time or energy required to stand where you stand on this day. The deeper into the Park you travel, the land is less disturbed by mankind. As such, you are experiencing a view of the land altered only by time. If you encounter wildlife, absent mice, you may notice that they are less tense about you being in their space. Barbara and I encountered a huge bull Roosevelt Elk the last time we ventured up here and in one of the meadows a bit farther on a boar Black Bear. Their reaction to us was very similar. They didn't move away, they just raised their heads from grazing and looked at us with an expression of, "who are you and why are you up here?" We moved on and they went back to grazing. The wildlife carries on unbothered by the very few hikers they encounter.

From Cameron Pass to Lost Pass is about 2 miles. Take a break and get off your feet for a bit, you've got a challenge just ahead. From Lost Pass at 6,515 ft., you have a wonderful view of Mt. Cameron behind you to the north and the 7,000 footers, Mts. Mystery, Deception, Clark and Walkinshaw, south to north, in the distance to the east.

Time for the descent, one of the steep ones. This is a drop of over 1,000 ft. in a short mile down to the Dosewallips River (The Dose). To add insult to injury, the trail frequently demands you step down off rocks in the trail that are knee high. Take your time and step carefully; you're a long way from help. The slope is partially south facing and can be blistering hot on a summer day. Almost done. Having intersected the Dosewallips River Trail turn right, southwest. A short distance later you'll arrive at Dose Meadows and an end to one of your toughest days so far.

Would you consider a rest day at this point? If so, I have a suggestion and, yes, it involves a day hike. Hayden Pass at 5,487 ft. is about 2 miles up-trail from Dose Meadows. The pass sits on the southern end of a small ridge anchored by Mt. Claywood at 6,836 ft to the northwest and Mt. Fromme at 6,705 ft. about a half mile to the southeast of Mt. Claywood. This is a piece of a number of ridges and their peaks that form the east flank of the Elwha Valley between the Strait of Juan de Fuca and Low Divide.

A short distance above Dose Meadows the trail crosses the Dose and climbs steeply, gaining about 500 feet, whereupon it veers decidedly right and the grade lessens. The trail continues to climb several hundred yards sweeping to the left around the nose of a small ridgeline. Look for a faint way-trail leading off-trail to your left. This is your entrance to Thousand Acre Meadow, one of the biggest alpine meadows in the Park. If you liked Cameron Basin, you'll certainly enjoy the granddaddy meadow of them all. After exploring the meadow, return to the trail and continue the short distance remaining up to Hayden Pass. Sentinel Peak at 6,592 ft. hovers over you to the southeast, Sentinel's Sister at 6,301 ft. to the south and Mt. Seattle at 6,246 ft. to the southwest. You've now experienced two of three passes on this loop and tomorrow you'll be put to the test by Gray Wolf Pass about 4 miles distant to the northeast.

The intersection of the Gray Wolf Trail is 3.5 miles down-trail from Dose Meadows. Today will begin and end gently, be tough in the middle and the longest day on this loop. The Gray Wolf Trail intersects the Dose Trail at 3,600 feet and climbs to 6,150 ft. over the ensuing 3.5 miles. The first 1,400 feet and 2 miles are achieved via one very long switchback and a shorter cousin. From the 5,000-foot mark to the pass at 6,150 feet the trail consists of a number of shorter switchbacks, relentless climbing and an ever-increasing rock-strewn trail. The views from the pass are similar to those at Lost Pass for the most part. I'll leave it at that. You need to take a break, eat and drink to refuel your lungs and legs; today's not at all over. You've got 4.1 miles ahead of you and albeit down-trail there's at least one section not to look forward to.

From the Pass the trail heads due north dropping steeply down the first 400 feet of elevation before the grade eases. A little after a long mile spent crossing the last open alpine terrain, you start the descent back below treeline. The next half mile twists wildly through about a dozen short switchbacks; steep, short and choppy. You can cheer crossing the footbridge a mile further on and at about 4,000 feet of elevation. The last mile to Falls Camp is a piece of cake considering what you've been through today. Throw down, make camp, eat and relax.

Another rest day perhaps? Yes, I have a side trip, if you're up for it, or you could just lay around for the day; you choose. If you're up for another sightseeing venture, look no further than the way-trail leaving from the camp and following Cedar Creek as it rises 1,300 feet and 2.1 miles later to Cedar Lake. Cedar Lake is the result of the Cedar Glacier melting into its own cirque. This stark but picturesque setting consists of a pristine high-country lake surrounded by glacier-carved headwalls on three sides. It's a primal scene dominated by rock and water two of the earth's elementals. A glacier working as a forming tool and rock, the material to be worked. It's also a great place for echoes, try it out.

Packed up and on the trail again, you'll move down-trail gently for the 5.4 miles it takes to reach Gray Wolf Camp, opposite Three Forks Shelter. Turning northwest you'll follow the Gray Wolf another 2.6 miles to Slide Camp, your last overnight on the loop.

Your last day involves 2.3 miles down to Camp Tony and then the final climb of 1,000 feet and 3.1 miles to the trailhead at FS road 2875. This has been an eventful and tough hike at times. You've covered over 45 miles with another 10 thrown in on rest days. Gaining and losing elevation you've hiked through some of the deep and isolated backcountry in the Park. Sweeping vistas, grinding trails and peaceful solitude were your reward for the price you paid. Sore and tired, absolutely. Ready to go home, certainly. Thinking of what you'll do next? I hope so. That's what ignites the sense of adventure and anticipation in anyone who has laced their boots, bent to the weight of a pack and headed up-trail in anticipation of the challenges that await

Dodger Point-Elwha Loop

NW Quadrant, Custom Correct maps, "Elwha Valley", and "Hurricane Ridge", (42 mi., difficulty 29.38, a hard climb, stellar views, a dry camp, a difficult way-trail, a ford, a lush river valley, best done late summer to early fall)

Summary: Elwha Trailhead (Madison Falls/Whiskey Bend), Goblin Gates, Humes Ranch, Dodger Point, Elwha Ford, Remann's Cabin, Elwha Ranger Station, Elwha Trailhead.

"Not for the young, the old or faint of heart" screamed the long-remembered stop-sign that stood for years at the start of the Lake Constance trail; 4,000 feet of elevation gain in 2 miles. Evidently the Park didn't have a second sign to announce the difficulty of attaining Dodger Point, a dry camp, followed by a way-trail descent and finally a ford of the Elwha. This loop involves serious challenges and if you're not certain that you're up to the demand, you should reconsider right now. You've been advised!

But I'm well ahead of where I need to start. Backing up, you'll find the Whiskey Bend Trailhead at the end of the Whiskey Bend Road. At first, you'll follow the Olympic Hot Springs Road to just beyond the Elwha Ranger Station, where the Whiskey Bend Road, a gravel road, bears off to your left. As of this writing, 2022, the Olympic Hot Springs Road has been washed out several times in as many years; its replacement is under consideration by the Park. The trailhead is at the barrier on the Olympic Hot Springs Road, currently at Madison Falls, 1.75 miles off of U.S. 101. If the road hasn't been repaired or replaced at the time you are considering this loop, your first day will begin with about an 8 mile hike up two roads to Whiskey Bend, where the Whiskey Bend Trailhead is located.

As you start up the Whiskey Bend Road it climbs a short distance and passes a parking area on your right. You may want to take a rest and take advantage of the overlook. This was the location of the Glines Canyon Dam built in 1926 to provide electric power to the mills in Port Angeles. Across the canyon you can see the spillways that regulated the flow of the Elwha and the Glines Canyon Hydroelectric Power Plant, a National Historic Site. It produced electricity continuously until 2014, when it was shut down as the dam removal began. The dam, along with a smaller one down-stream on the Elwha, eliminated the passage of salmon up-river to their spawning grounds for the better part of one hundred years and decimated the Elwha Chinook Salmon, some of the largest salmon on record. The U.S. Department of the Interior bought the dams and in 2016 completed the largest dam removal project ever

23. Mt. Scott from Dodger Point, ONP

undertaken in the country's history. The river is quickly recovering, as are the salmon runs.

On the Road again, you're about 3 miles from Whiskey Bend. On the off chance that the road has been repaired or replaced you've driven to the Whiskey Bend Trailhead. Either way, your first day's camp is at Humes Ranch 3.5 miles ahead.

Leaving Whiskey Bend, and 1.2 miles up-trail you'll come to a spur on your right directing you to Rica Canyon-Goblin Gates; take it. You'll drop a steep and short distance to the bank of the Elwha. If you're interested, turn right and about 100 yards down-stream you'll come to Goblin Gates. At this point the Elwha, which has been free to meander up-stream in Geyser Valley, is severely restricted by two mammoth chunks of basalt, the Goblin Gates. The power and rage of the river is on full display as the Elwha roils and bucks, fighting its way through this natural obstacle; don't fall in.

Rica Canyon, beginning at Goblin Gates, is the last mile and a half of the 11 mile Grand Canyon of the Elwha, a Class IV and V run that begins at Canyon Camp farther up the Elwha Trail. Called by some the "run of no return": extremely narrow, strewn with boulders, drops, holes, steep rock walls and severely restricted scouting and portaging; this is one dangerous run. Once you put in, there are few places where you can get out. The Grand Canyon of the Elwha is no place for less than expert kayakers. It's the toughest 11 miles of kayaking in the area; a true breathtaking experience.

Heading up-stream you'll pass a spur on your left after about 1 mile. Ignore it and proceed a short-mile farther on to a second trail intersection at Humes Ranch. The building is on your left but you'll move straight ahead and down to a small clearing. This is your campsite for tonight. Will and Grant Humes were early settlers on the Elwha and your campsite is in the area of their garden, in the day. It won't take you long to appreciate their choice. Unlike Goblin Gates, the river is calmly passing by, the ground is near level and an old-growth western red cedar is conveniently nearby, offering shade from the sun or an umbrella when it rains. Enjoy your rest, tomorrow will be a long hard day. Since you're doing this loop in the latter half of the hiking season you may end up in a dry camp at Dodger Point. Given the difficulty, I suggest you spend an additional day, which means two dry days; prepare accordingly. If it makes you feel any better, tomorrow won't be the hardest day on this loop. More about that later.

Light dawns, today emerges and the trail awaits. You're packed up and ready to move onward and upward. The trail leads out of the clearing up-stream and to your left, climbing to the junction with the Long Ridge Trail about a half mile ahead. At the junction turn right, navigate a short but messy piece of trail leading to the Long Ridge Bridge. Standing on the bridge, the views up and down stream are a contrast in geology. Down-stream is a gravel quarry's dream. River burden, from boulders to sand, fill Geyser Valley wall to wall and as far as you can see. Obviously, the work of a powerful river. Look up-stream and you not only see a completely different landscape but a look back in time as well. This end of Convolution Canyon is an example of the overly steep canyon walls, common throughout the Olympic Mountains and left by the alpine glaciers at the close of the ice age, 10,000 years ago. At first, the ice supported the walls, then the ice melted into lakes. The lakes were held in place and unable to drain by the unyielding mass of the continental ice sheets in the lower elevations. As the continental ice melted, the lakes drained leaving canyon walls too steep to support the glacial debris of which they were composed. Over the past several thousand years the walls have slipped into the canyon, at times completely blocking the Elwha for short periods of time. Eventually, the river moves the slide material out of the canyon and deposits it down-stream into Geyser Valley and beyond.

So much for hydrology and glaciology, it's time to face your first of several challenges on this loop. Your destination today is Dodger Point, 11 miles and 4,500 feet higher as you ascend Long Ridge. Averaging over 400 ft. per mile, this is a daunting but doable climb. If it makes you feel better, the steepest part is the first 3 miles, a gain of 2,500 feet, as the trail switchbacks, swinging east to west to east again, up and across the northern nose of Long Ridge several times. The last 8 miles follow the constant but lesser grade of the ridge. The trail, for the most part, sticks to the western slope of the ridge crest. You should be carrying enough water for your stay at Dodger Point, but you may be lucky enough to come across a few small tarns along the trail in its last 5 miles, if summer hasn't consumed them. If you do replenish your water supply in the backcountry, regardless of where you are, you should treat, filter (at or below 0.5 microns) or boil the water. Giardia is prevalent; take the time to protect yourself. At 6 miles the forest begins to thin and distinctly so above 5,000 feet. About a mile and a half short of Dodger Point you'll pass a high point on your left and about 500 feet above you. The next high point just ahead is Dodger Point at 5,760 ft. Take a look around, Robert Wood in his "Olympic Mountain Trail Guide" described the view from Dodger Point as "...one of the superlative viewpoints in the Olympics, and the 360 degree panorama is outstanding". It's for this reason that I suggest a rest day, if the weather is cooperating. Make use of this opportunity to view and identify many of the major peaks that surround this splendiferous perch.

To the southwest lies Ludden Peak at 5,854 ft. and directly behind is Mt. Ferry at 6,195 ft. A route just to the northwest side of the line defined by these two peaks has at times served as an exit route from the classic off-trail traverse of the Bailey Range. A piece of that route can be seen heading southwest from the small tarn a mile distant below Dodger Point. That small tarn signals a hard left turn and the beginning of the way-trail you'll follow on your descent to the Elwha.

It's hard but true, the sun is up and it's time to depart Dodger Point. Starting down-trail to the southwest you'll find the tarn a mile distant. At the tarn the trail swings hard left and the day's challenge begins. The descending route is identified as a way-trail. It is seldom used due to the combined difficulties of way-finding and at its end, far below, the fording of the Elwha. Early on in the history of this area blazes in trees and colored flags helped mark the way. Very few of the blazes remain. The reason being revealed by the amount of dead-fall in the forest and flags have been banned for decades; I doubt you'll see any. That leaves cairns as the only assistance which may be available to you.

If you are not comfortable with your ability to meet this challenge, you should not attempt this portion of the loop and retrace your steps back down the Long Ridge Trail. On the other hand, if you intend to move forward, you'll need to: spend a good deal of time studying the detail of a quality topo map, know how to read a compass and set your altimeter at the Dodger Point Lookout at 5,753 ft. You'll come to a point down-trail where being able to orient your physical position relative to compass bearings and altitude will mean the difference between success and failure.

Let me be, just in your face, blunt! If you're good at reading maps, knowing how to use a compass, can track your elevation and have a keen eye for the surrounding topography, you'll manage this route with some difficulty. Anything less in your skill set will result in you throwing in the towel, semi-lost somewhere southeast of and below Dodger Point. You'll have only one remaining clue still working for you; Dodger Point is uphill to the northwest! Return there and hike out the way you came in.

If you're moving forward from the tarn, the trail initially heads east for a short distance and then swings southeast and skirts the low end of a scree field just below Dodger Point. You'll lose about 800 feet by the end of first mile, marked by crossing over the bottom quarter of a narrow treeless overgrown avalanche chute 1,400 ft. below the Dodger Point Lookout.

The descent is steep. It swings first to the east, then back to the west and then drops straight down toward the Goldie River losing about 400 feet of elevation. At that point it abruptly turns east losing elevation more gradually and contours east around the nose of Long Ridge for the last time. The trail then begins to swing north as it crosses the Semple Plateau. It loses less than 500 feet in the last mile and delivers you at the west bank of the Elwha in the vicinity of Remann's Cabin on the opposite bank at 1,451 feet of elevation.

You should consult with the Wilderness Information Desk in the Olympic National Park Visitor Center in Port Angeles. I suggest you do a web search for "Stream Crossing Techniques" and read the National

Park Service's web-available "Safe River Crossings" and 'Swiftwater Rescue Manual" The Rangers in the Park's Wilderness Information Center can advise you as to the advisability of your plans. In addition, you should consult the USGS website for current water conditions. Also, if you visit online the State of Washington Dept. of Ecology, River and Stream Flow Monitoring page, you can compare years of data and thereby compare it to the weather pattern in any year against the weather pattern in the current year. By doing so you'll have a better sense of what the fording conditions may be. These searches will allow you to choose your hike based on the available data.

Looking up and down-stream, a short distance from Remann's Cabin, you'll find gravel bars and fordable places in the late summer and early fall when flow rates on the Elwha are at their lowest. Prior to undertaking this loop, you should review fording on the Resource Page, in the Appendix of this book. Fording is serious business. Hikers have lost their lives. Take your time and choose wisely.

Having forded the Elwha and given what you've experienced so far on this loop, you'll be glad to know all the tough parts are now behind you. Elwha Ranger Station is 1.5 miles down-trail and is waiting for you to set up camp. If the ranger is present don't miss the chance to report your descent from Dodger Point. Recent information is hard to come by, particularly about seldom used way-trails. What you have to report will be useful to those who follow. As you hike down-river from Remman's Cabin be advised that the bear wire at Canyon Camp is down.

The trail ahead of you is in good shape and will seem like a piece of cake compared to Long Ridge. You've got some choices depending on whether your trailhead is Whiskey Bend or Madison Falls. If it's Whiskey Bend, then tomorrow will be the final day on the trail. A distance of 11.3 miles. If it's Madison Falls, then its two more days before you're done. If this is the case then I suggest you do the hike to Whiskey Bend, camp over and finish the last 8 miles to Madison Falls the day after.

You've completed one of the toughest loop hikes in the Park. One that demands stamina, backcountry skills and a will to press on throughout those segments that are more ordeal than pleasure. Since Whiskey Bend, the 42 miles you've been treated to are some of the most stunning view points in the Park. Your skill set has been most certainly tested and honed. You are among the few that have taken up this challenge, in any given year. You should be proud of your accomplishment, joining the ranks of the hardy souls who have trodden this beautiful but difficult Olympic Mountain loop.

Skyline-North Fork Quinault Loop

SW Quadrant, Custom Correct map, "Quinault-Colonel Bob", (47 mi., difficulty 52.86, rugged terrain, dry camps during and after late summer, alpine views, lakes and Rain Forest)

Summary: Irely Lake Trailhead, Three Lakes, Three Prune, Kimta Peak, Lake Beauty, Low Divide, Sixteen Mile, Elip Creek Camp, North Fork Quinault Trailhead, 0.7 miles down-road to Irely Lake Trailhead.

Bear canisters are required on this loop. The Irely Lake Trailhead is located 0.7 miles before the end of the North Shore Road. The North Shore Road intersects U.S. 101 at the northwest end of Lake Quinault. Follow the North Shore Road 14 miles to an intersection. Turn left onto the North Shore Road. The Irely Lake Trailhead is 2.3 miles from the intersection just 0.7 miles before the end of the North Shore Road. If you end up at the North Fork Quinault Trailhead, you'll need to proceed back down the North Fork Road 0.7 miles to the Irely Lake Trailhead on your right with parking on your left.

The first 1.1 miles takes you by Irely Lake on your left. Don't be fooled by the trail gradient to Irely Lake; beyond the lake you're just steps away from a steep, and at times, rough trail ahead. From Irely Lake it's 5.8 miles to today's destination, Three Lakes 2,580 feet above Irely Lake.

The trail climbs steadily at a moderate grade about 2.5 miles to a crossing of Three Lakes Creek, a half mile above its confluence with Big Creek flowing from the west. There is no bridge at the Big Creek crossing; proceed carefully and take your time. The trail switchbacks steeply up the eastern nose of Three Lakes Ridge before it contours to the west for about a half mile. Then more switchbacks and a final gentle mile plus to Three Lakes, nestled in a small subalpine basin.

Enjoy the abundance of water early on. In the next three days finding water can be a challenge and nearly impossible late in the summer. No matter where you find water in the Park, it needs to be treated by filter, boiling or chemicals. Giardia is present throughout the Olympic Mountains. It's a "protozoa-bear" that you don't want to mess with. Dance with it and you'll regret not heeding this warning for the next couple of weeks. If you choose to filter, my preference, you must filter at or below 0.5 microns, the size of most harmful water-borne spores.

Although at 3,180 ft., Three Lakes has a special "Stoves Only" restriction, uniformly enforced at 3,500 feet and above throughout Olympic National Park and the Olympic National Forest. You'll see the sign alongside the trail early tomorrow. This restriction exists to protect the alpine environment where trees grow slowly and the soil needs every fallen rotting branch to feed the struggling flora upon which the fauna depend. It's a tight fragile circle in the high country. Please do

24. Kimta Peak from Promise Creek, ONP

your part to protect it. Others that preceded you did it for you; pass the blessings of their thoughtfulness forward.

The warmth of the morning's sun, if there is any, comes a little late to Three Lakes thanks to the ridgeline due east that hovers 1,300 feet above you. Water bottles full, gear packed, a quick trash patrol, yours or not, around camp and you're ready for the trail. Today's segment is short, or not, depending on the choice you make. Choice one, Three Prune Camp, 500 feet higher and 4.5 miles farther on, at or above treeline for the most part. It's a pleasant hike through the nice end of what will become a rugged and memorable trail. Or choice number two, push past Three Prune an additional 5.2 miles to Kimta Peak at 5,399 ft.; as high, dry and beautiful as it gets on the Skyline Trail. Remember everything within 11 miles up-trail of Three Lakes, on the Skyline, is water-poor at best and often dry. Think about your decision as you move forward.

About a mile and a half beyond Three Lakes you'll pass Reflection Lake on your right just about 150 ft. below and east of the trail. The lake sits precariously in a small meadow perched at the edge of a 2,300-foot drop into Three Lake Creek below. This will be your first chance to find water. When you find water, make use of it. If your water bottles are full, drink, refill and haul as much water as you can. Another mile and a half brings you to the junction with the Elip Creek Trail that never gets within a country-mile of Elip Creek until it intersects the North Fork Quinault Trail 4.5 miles east and 2,700 feet below. Your last reasonable chance for water is Kurtz Lake, about a half mile down the

Elip Creek Trail and about 150 ft. above you on the right. From where the Elip Creek Trail intersects the Skyline Trail, it is 12.6 difficult miles to Lake Beauty, the next reliable water source.

Three Prune is 1.5 miles beyond the Elip Creek Trail and most of that trail alternates between copes of trees and open areas, some rock-strewn and others in meadow. If your decision is to end this day at Three Prune or even if you've decided to move on to Kimta Peak, either way you've got another dry camp ahead of you. On the ridgeline just to the north you will find a pass about 300 feet above your current location. Scramble over the pass and drop another 500 feet down its north slope and you'll find Three Prune Lakes. Three Prune Lakes are a possible but not a reliable water source. You ought to be able to assess your chances for water at the top of the ridge. Do this tomorrow morning if you plan on camping at Three Prune or drink your fill and go over the pass, fill up then gear up and finish the rest of your day. An aside, you should never hike without a Custom Correct quality map in your possession; that applies, in the extreme, to off-trail travel. The Skyline Trail between Three Prune Lakes and Lake Beauty might as well be off-trail.

Three Prune is pretty much the end of an easy-to-follow trail on this loop hike. Trail finding between Three Prune and Seattle Creek is usually tough and at times daunting. Your map and compass skills are definitely going to be put to the test. I suggest you carry an altimeter and set it each day against the elevation contour references indicated on your Custom Correct map.

Whether it's this afternoon or tomorrow morning, off you go to the unparalleled vista and isolation of Kimta Peak 5.2 miles ahead. The first mile beyond Three Prune brings you to the crest of the Skyline Ridge, above Stalding Creek. The next 4 plus miles sticks firmly to this walkway in the sky and continually flirts with about 5,000 feet of elevation as it runs north. To the west is the Queets Valley, one of the least visited or hiked areas in the Park. Yes, far down the valley, you are looking at the Pacific Ocean. Your view left and right encompasses the vastness of one of only six temperate rain forests on the planet and it's right in the palm of your hand. Look northwest. On a clear day just over Rugged Ridge, above the Bogachiel River outside of Forks, you can catch a glimpse of the Strait of Juan de Fuca. It was once thought to be the beginning of the mythical Northwest Passage, a much sought-after trade route between Europe and the Far East. Wait until you get to Kimta Peak. There's a view to beat all views and it's just a few tough miles ahead.

Finding a camp site in the vicinity of Kimta Peak is difficult, but hard ground may be found a mile south of Kimta as the trail crosses a barren shelf or on what's left of the ridgetop just short of where the trail turns east below the Peak. Kimta Peak may be one of the most scenic spots in the Park, even if its accommodation is difficult.

As you near Kimta Peak the trail becomes almost a way-trail. It's easy to get confused by all the wandering animal trails. Old tree blazes and cairns now mark the way forward, past Kimta Peak toward Lake Beauty 5.6 miles ahead. Just below Kimta Peak the trail turns strongly to the east. The view, that I referred to, is your reward for the short scramble up the 150 foot difference between the trail and the peak. From the peak you have the south side of Mt. Olympus staring directly back at you. You're looking into the upper Queets Basin, an area rarely visited and home to the Valhallas, a small group of peaks southwest of Mt. Olympus, named for the Norse gods. Turn east and look down the upper Elwha Valley and to the south the Quinault Valley. Somewhere down there on the Quinault, 4,800 feet below, is your trailhead.

Your starting elevation is 5,260 ft. where the trail turns from north to east, just below Kimta Peak. In the first half mile east, you'll drop to 4,800 ft. then drop abruptly down another 160 ft. and then contour to the southeast a short quarter mile at that elevation. Drop to 4,400 ft. and contour east at that level for a half mile. Leaving 4,400 ft. drop down 50 ft. and contour southeast around one buttress, into and back out of a creek drainage, regaining 4,400 ft. as you round to the east side of the second buttress. Changing direction to the south, travel a short 200 yards and gaining about 75 ft. you'll arrive at a ridge crest climbing steeply to the northeast. Follow the ridge crest to an elevation of 5060 ft. Looking upward to the north you'll see a rock promontory. Ascend at first to the north then slightly to the northeast, as you near the crest, until you attain 5,300 ft. You're standing on Promise Creek Divide. Below you about a hundred feet and due east is a small cirque. Contour the north wall until you are due northwest of the low point in the cirque, a dry tarn in the summer. Start a slow descent northeast from 5,300 ft. to 4,800 ft. over the next half mile and then contour at or slightly above that level for another quarter mile to the northeast. You've arrived at the crest of, or just beyond, a buttress running down to the southeast. Heading east, follow the northeast face of the buttress as you descend to 4,400 ft. over the next quarter-mile, to the crest of a second buttress to the north. Look upward to the north and you'll see a gap in the ridge line above, a short half mile distant. That gap is Hee Haw Pass. Once through the pass head northeast a half mile, skirting below a peak on your right, to the junction of the Lake Beauty spur trail at 5060 ft. Turn left and you'll find Lake Beauty a short half mile away; your destination for today at 4,681 ft. Congratulations, you've just completed one of the toughest sections of one of the toughest hikes in the Olympic Mountains.

Lake Beauty at 4,681 ft. would be a great place for a rest day. Sitting in a mix of alpine trees and meadows, with the campsite on the west side of the lake, it's a place of peace, quiet and rest. If you decide to lay over tomorrow, scramble to the top of the prominence above the intersection with the Skyline and treat yourself to another world-class view of the Olympic Mountains. East of Mt. Olympus is the famous Bailey Range, draining west into the Hoh, southwest into the Queets and southeast into the Elwha. Farther east are all the 7,000 ft.-plus peaks of the Olympic Mountains' Eastern Front with Mts. Anderson, Constance and Deception leading the way.

On whatever day you leave Lake Beauty, you won't have to worry about water any more on the remainder of this loop. From Lake Beauty you'll travel down the northeast slope of the same ridge that brought you up to the Lake. After losing about 1,200 feet and 3.2 miles distant, you'll cross Seattle Creek. From Seattle Creek you'll climb about 700 feet and contour around the nose of Mt. Seattle's southwest ridge. Once around, you'll have a steep descent on the southeast face of the ridge. Then 5.1 miles from the Lake Beauty junction with the Skyline Trail your day ends on Low Divide. Low Divide is a lovely place for another rest day. The Martin's Park Primitive Trail begins at the southwest end of Lake Margaret providing the chance for a 5 mile round trip to Martin's Lakes at the Base of Mt. Christie just southwest of the divide.

There are two hiking days left on this loop. Starting in the subalpine meadows and lakes of Low Divide you'll descend the North Fork Quinault to Elip Creek 9.2 miles down-trail. There is no bear wire at Elip Creek and the privy is across the river from the campsite. Along the way you'll pass by Sixteen Mile Camp and cross from the east bank of the river to its west side for the duration of the loop.

Sixteen Mile became a special place for me at a young age. I was thirteen and on my first Boy Scout 50-Miler from the North Fork Quinault Trailhead, over Low Divide and finishing at Whiskey Bend on the Elwha. Our first night's camp was at Wolf Bar, the last camp you'll pass on your final day. We broke camp the next morning and were headed for Sixteen Mile, 10 miles up-trail. We were young, strong and, as you'll see, foolish. We were moving right along just past Trapper Shelter with a mere 3.4 miles to go when one of the "younger Scouts", I'd been in the Boy Scouts one year longer than he, remembered that he'd left his rod and reel at Wolf Bar. One of my future longtime hiking and climbing partners and I jumped at the opportunity. "If we go get it, it's ours, right?" So much for the Scout Law, "be helpful". The younger scout agreed and we reported to the Scoutmaster that we were going back for the prize. We threw our packs into the brush along the trail and started at a sprint down to Wolf Bar. When we finally got down to Wolf Bar, there it was sitting on a rock in plain sight. We snatched it up, turned on our heels and started back up the trail. Weariness set in about half way back to our packs. How foolish we'd been started to creep into our perspective of this high-energy-low-reward venture that we'd chosen for ourselves. We had a brief scare at the point where we threw our packs in the brush," yea, where exactly was that point?" After a few false starts we finally found our trusty Trapper Nelsons, saddled up and headed for Sixteen Mile. We'd missed dinner but they held some back for us. "If you want it warm, you'll have to build your own fire" the Senior Scout proclaimed. Staring at the plate of cold whatever it was, the thought of doing anything after our 21 mile day on the trail was too much. We ate it cold and crawled into our bags.

Elip Creek Camp is 5 miles below Sixteen Mile. Truthfully, the camp isn't much. Jammed between opposing ridges on all sides the camp is deep in the Quinault Valley and buried in the Rain Forest's thick canopy, cold and dark describes it well.

Up and at it on your last day! Leaving Elip Creek behind, there's 6.5 miles left to go on a hopefully bright morning. Down-stream the trail hits 600 feet of elevation and swings west at Wolf Bar. 600 feet! You were nearly ten times that high just a few days back. You're 2.5 miles from the end of a very tough 47 mile Olympic Mountains' Loop. Hats are off to you and any hiker who has completed the Skyline Loop. Did anyone leave a celebration package in the car?

Grand Ridge – Gray Wolf River Loop

NE Quadrant, Custom Correct map, "Gray Wolf-Dosewallips", (52 mi., difficulty 45.43, high country views, a dry camp, subalpine lakes, alpine meadows, 4 passes, night skies)

Summary: Slab Camp Trailhead, Deer Park Campground, Grand Ridge, Obstruction Point, Grand Lake, Grand Pass, Cameron Basin, Cameron Pass, Lost Pass, Bear Camp, Gray Wolf Pass, Falls Camp, Slide Camp, Slab Camp Trailhead

The trailhead for this loop is at a very sharp left turn in Forest Service Road 2875. To get to FS Road 2875 turn off of U.S. 101 onto Taylor Cutoff Road, just west of the Dungeness River Bridge, west of Sequim. After heading flat, straight and due south for 2 miles, the road turns uphill to the right. At that turn the road becomes the Lost Mountain Road. Follow it uphill to where it crests the hill and crosses through a flatter area with small farms. After the farms the road swings to the right. In the middle of that turn a gravel road appears on your left. Turn on to it. A mile farther on FS Road 2870 veers off to the right; don't take FS 2870. About 3 miles after the FS270 junction, FS 2875 will deliver you to the Slab Camp Trailhead, just before it swings sharply to the left and becomes FS 2878; not that you should care.

Your goal for today is to ascend Deer Ridge to the Deer Park Campground. Yes, I know you could have driven to the campground, but that defeats the purpose of hiking, after all! Deer Park is 2,700 feet above you and 4.8 miles away. The first short mile and a half slowly gains about 300 feet as it contours a steep slope heading south. At this point the trail turns westerly attaining Half-Way Rock, just about the boundary of Olympic National Park at 4,658 ft. Good news, you've gained most of the elevation and Deer Park Campground is about a mile and a half ahead of you. The campground has had a year-round spring, but given climate change that may change as well. If not, you won't find water until you arrive tomorrow at Grand Lake 11.4 dry miles away.

If it's a clear night, you are in for a treat. Consider climbing a short mile to the summit of Blue Mountain. The daytime views are a 360° panorama of the Olympic Mountains and the surrounding national forest; but at night it's a front row seat on the universe. With absolutely no background light, stars, planets, constellations and the Milky Way are right in your lap. Gazing doesn't get better than this.

The night's done, the sun's up and it's time to pack-up and hit the trail, day-two. You are already in the driest area of the Park, the

25. Black Bear, ONP, Carmen Bubar

Olympic Rain Shadow. Below you directly south lies the Dungeness delta protruding into the Strait of Juan de Fuca 12 miles away. For all the hoopla about how wet and rainy Western Washington is, the delta gets about 17 inches of rain a year, less than most places in the U.S. The Deer Park to Obstruction Point Trail is a perfect example of that lack of rainfall.

If its windy I suggest that you delay the hike across Grand Ridge until late in the day when the wind ought to subside. You could wait in the campground or hike the first 2 miles from the campground up to the ridge where you'll find shelter in the forest. Just beyond the forest, the trail starts to traverse the ridge on its south face either at or near its crest. That south face is mostly loose, small particle scree. To be out on Grand Ridge with the wind up is something close to auditioning for a sand storm scene in a movie; don't subject yourself to that misery.

From Deer Park to Obstruction Point on the eastern end of Grand Ridge is 7.9 miles with the last 3.5 miles gaining and losing a few feet at any one time as you hike across. Obstruction Point is again a place you could have driven to, but I've already spoken to that.

It's 3.7 miles southwest to Grand Lake. The first half takes you over a rolling meadow and a rock-strewn stretch of alpine trail. At the end of that distance, you'll find yourself standing at the edge of a large bowl. You can clearly see the trail descending in a slow spiral first to your left and then to your right ending at the Grand Lake, that spot of blue-green below you and at your extreme right. The trail is all grit and rock but reasonable enough. In short order you'll be at the Lake.

All of the area is in a restricted reservation designation. You found that out when you got your backcountry permit either online or at the Wilderness Information desk in the Visitor Center in Port Angeles. Check your permit to insure you set up camp in the appropriate site.

Grand Lake is well located for an otherwise hot day. It's shaded from the afternoon sun by the ridges to the southwest and the forest in that same direction. That said, the lake can be a haven for mosquitoes and deer flies. Everyone has their favorite repellent, but I'll give you this suggestion on the off chance you're interested. Most repellents rely on a variety of chemicals to do their magic. It works, but it may also be toxic over time. If you put it on your skin or your gear, you may damage both. As for your liver, you only have one as long as it works; don't beat it up unnecessarily. As for your gear, its synthetic life span can and will be eaten away by this stuff; you didn't buy your gear just to wreck it. My suggestion is lemon and eucalyptus oil, it's a much better choice. Its inexpensive, not oily, rubs in quickly, lasts for hours and is highly effective. It's also gear-safe, clothes-safe and body-safe; give it a try.

Leaving Grand Lake, the next day, you'll be climbing up to Grand Pass, dropping down to Cameron Creek and following it up-stream to Upper Cameron Basin. The climb to the pass is 2.6 miles and gains about 1,400 ft. Along the way the trail skirts around first Moose Lake and then Gladys Lake, both of which reside in alpine meadows. The closer you get to the Grand Pass the more the towering ridges on both sides of the meadows begin to close in on you. At Gladys Lake the trail swings southeast and the pass resides between two prominences on either side of it, like two posts for a gate. As you arrive at the pass take a moment to appreciate the view. Six peaks, all over 7,000 ft. are on display to your south and west. Those peaks and the ridge you're standing on are part of the two outer crescents of marine extruded basalt in the Park. Originally, they were Pacific seamounts moving northeast on the Juan de Fuca plate. When that plate ran into the Continental Plate of North America the islands were destroyed, pushed over and the end result was two Olympic Peninsula sized wrinkles of basalt. The 7,000 footers you're looking at are what's left of that pre-historic slow-motion collision.

Stepping over the pass is in this case a literal description, since the top of Grand Pass is just about one step wide. The real surprise is how steep and exposed the first quarter-mile is on its south slope. The trail slowly eases and in 1.8 miles and the loss of about 1,900 ft. of elevation you'll intersect the Cameron Creek Trail. Turn right and head up-trail following the Creek. Heading southwest in about a mile and a half the trail swings due south and enters Cameron Basin. Your camp for the night is at Upper Cameron Camp higher in the basin about a mile ahead.

Cameron Basin is a wonderous place. Its broad alpine meadow is cut through by Cameron Creek as it slowly meanders in the basin.

Cameron Pass above you to the southwest sits between two high spots on the ridge line. The gap is about a quarter mile wide and the Pass itself favors the high point to your left.

If you've built rest days into your schedule you couldn't go wrong spending one in this glorious location. Regardless of your schedule, leaving the basin and heading for the pass will be a slow and careful ascent. Cameron Pass is usually the last pass to melt out, particularly on the north side. If it's covered in snow, you'll need an ice axe and have mastered the skill of self-arrest. If the pass has melted out, you'll be climbing through the scree fields lying before you. At some point the trail quits being a trail and you'll be faced with a fairly uniform landscape of fractured grey rock. Cairns are what you'll need to find your way to the Pass. Cairns are stacked rocks intended to mark a trail. Some are small, some big, some are missing altogether. Move from cairn to cairn and don't move from one until you can identify the next. If a cairn is small, add to it; if it's missing, build one. Hikers have pointed your way today by building and improving these way markers. Help those who will follow you with the same regard as those who've gone before you.

As you reach the pass you'll be relieved by the terrain on its south face. The trail turns left and contours through a series of lush alpine meadows, brilliant with wildflowers in late July and interspersed with copse of alpine conifers. The 2 mile hike across this wonderland will deliver you to Lost Pass, a good place to take a break. The views from the pass are astounding with high ridges at every point of the compass. Directly east and about three miles distant is Gray Wolf Pass which you will cross tomorrow.

Break's over and it's time to get back on the trail. The descent from Lost Pass to the Dosewallips River is short and steep losing 1,500 feet in slightly less than a mile. Take your time and watch your step. This is not a trail where falling would be insignificant. Under foot it is rocky and there are a number of big rocks; stepping off of them is precarious.

As you meet the Dosewallips River Trail turn left. You're headed for Bear Camp 1.7 miles down-trail. The good news is the descent is only about 500 feet; the bad news is the camp is well named. Years ago, Barbara, my wife, and I were passing through Bear Camp on our way to Dose Meadows up-trail. We rounded a bend and came within spitting distance of a large male Black Bear. The bear was having a snack. He was grazing shoulder deep in a patch of lupine. Upon our arrival he raised his head, turned his head in our direction and stared at us with a "who are you and when are you going to leave" expression. All the time he was chewing a mouth full of lupine he had just ripped out of the ground. As he chewed, flowers out one side of his mouth and roots and dirt out the other, the outer extremities of the lupine inched closer and closer to his grinding jaws. He stared and chewed; we stared back. Finally, he finished off the lupine, flowers, roots, dirt and all with one last swallow; now that's "backcountry tough"! The bear went back to grazing and we moved on up the trail.

A fork of Butler Creek flows nearby through a lovely, longer than wide, meadow. A quiet place to spend the night. As you are considering where to set up camp, I would remind you that there is no camp site safe from the "night-marauders". Mice are notorious in the Olympic Mountains; Bear Camp is no exception to that rule. I've lost more gear to mice, in the dark of night, than I'd like to admit. It seems that the sweat-salt, that you have worked so hard to deposit in your pack-straps, is the mice equivalent of a pizza-delivery to your home. In spite of the opportunity, over the years I have failed to find a solution to this small but relentless malicious entity.

Tomorrow has arrived and there's one more pass to conquer. Heading down-trail 1.7 miles you'll come to the junction with the Gray Wolf Trail and more to the point the beginning of your 2,600-foot climb to Gray Wolf Pass, 5.6 miles up-trail from the junction. The ascent is an unrelenting series of long and short switchbacks all exposed due south to the day's sun. My suggestion is hit the trail at dawn and take advantage of the brief early morning shade provided by Mt. Deception. This respite won't last through the entire climb but making use of this temporal resource will make your climb a bit easier.

Reaching the Gray Wolf Pass calls for a rest. Drop your packs, rest your legs and enjoy the view. With the exception of due north, you're surrounded by 7,000-foot peaks. Take the time to savor their majesty. From here until your last day, it's all downhill, but the lower you go the less you'll see of these magnificent peaks.

Saddled up and on the trail again, you've got 4.1 miles between you and Falls Camp on the Gray Wolf River, 2,150 feet below. Most of that elevation will be eaten by the first mile and particularly the first half of the second. After that the trail contours for about a mile, then drops about 300 feet and contours again finding Falls Camp at the confluence of Cedar Creek and the Gray Wolf River.

If you're interested in another rest day, this is where I would take it. A side trip up Cedar Creek to Cedar Lake begins at the camp and climbs south up the creek about 2 miles to the lake, gaining about 1,200 feet. The lake sits in a stunning rock-walled bowl with headwalls between 1,000 and 2,000 feet on the west and south sides of the lake. It meets the definition of alpine in every respect.

The 8.2 miles of trail down the Gray Wolf to Slide Camp will be a "walk in the Park" considering what you've already been subjected to on this loop. The first 5.4 miles takes you gently down-stream to

Gray Wolf Camp, and the next 2.6 miles which aren't quite as easy, will deliver you to your last overnight at Slide Camp. The overall environment at or below Gray Wolf Camp at Three Forks, tends to be darker and colder than the alpine regions that you've traveled over the past days. Beginning at Three Forks the Gray Wolf is captured by steep and deep valley walls where the sun arrives late and leaves early every day. The forest is big and robust but it's density also adds to the overall feeling of being squeezed as you travel through it.

The last day breaks and you're almost done. Leaving Slide Camp, you'll continue down-trail to Camp Tony, cross the river and head up to Slab Camp and your trailhead, completing the last 5.4 miles of this loop hike.

You've covered 52 miles on this hike, not including side trips. A good deal of your travel was difficult climbing and descending four passes all in the 6,000-foot category. You've seen some superb alpine country and been treated to some of the best viewpoints in the Park. Pat yourself on the back. You've completed a journey that some others would have refused. You have a better sense of yourself and your skill set and can be unabashedly proud of what you've accomplished. Congratulations!

Hoh – Bogachiel Loop

SW Quadrant, Custom Correct maps, "Mount Olympus" and "Bogachiel Valley", (53 mi., difficulty 43.1, reservations, one brutal day, a ford, the Rain Forest, alpine camps, lakes, views and one primitive-trail camp)

Summary: Hoh River Trailhead, Olympus Ranger Station, Hoh Lake, Deer Lake, Twentyone Mile Camp, Flapjack, ford, South Snider-Jackson Primitive Trail, Hoh Road, Hoh River Trailhead

Day-two is a grind; but let's not get ahead of ourselves. This varied loop hike starts at the Hoh River Trailhead about 23 miles east off of U.S. 101 on the west side of the Olympic National Park, about 2.5 hours from Port Angeles. The Hoh Rain Forest is one of the major elements in the Park that helped to qualify it in 1981 as a World Heritage Site; an honor that is deserved and judiciously protected by Park staff and visitors alike.

Even though your first day is long, 9.1 miles to Olympus Ranger Station, it's relatively easy; the total elevation gain is about 300 feet. Flat trails are an anomaly in this Park and the beginning of the Hoh is the leader in that genre. Day-one is a real treat. The solitude of the Hoh Valley is hard to match. The trail parallels the river offering unlimited opportunities to shed your pack and relax on a riverside log in the shade, or shed the boots and cool your toes in this mostly glacier-fed wonder. If you're looking for advice on a rest area, I suggest Five Mile Island. It comes to mind since it's half-way to the Olympus Ranger Station, your destination for today.

In 2005 Gordon Hempton, after traveling the world, found the "One Square Inch of Silence". Can you guess where? He found it off-trail, several miles from the Hoh Trailhead. The Rain Forest is so dense and full of vegetation that it absorbs sound like a sponge. Evidently, Hempton wasn't measuring sound in the fall, when the abundant bull Elk are advertising their availability and willingness to join the effort to increase the size of the herd. Nor was he measuring sound in the dead of night, when any number of various species of owl figuratively light up the night sky with their varied "hoots". Regardless, amongst all the grandeur of the Hoh Valley, sublime quiet, soothing and solitude, can be added to the long list.

Four miles up-trail from Five Mile Island you'll arrive at Olympus Ranger Station. If for some reason these camp sites are taken, find the ranger and ask if you ought to squeeze yourselves in here or press on about 2 miles to Lewis Meadow. If it's a toss-up, squeeze in; tomorrow is going to be tough enough without adding the Lewis Meadow miles to it.

26. Hoh Lake, ONP, WC

No, you can't see Mt. Olympus from either the Olympus Ranger Station or Lewis Meadow. From the ranger station you'd have to hike 4.6 miles up-trail to Elk Lake before you could get a decent view up the Glacier Creek Valley of the Park's namesake. If you're worried about Lewis Meadows, Elk Lake is way out of your comfort zone for this hike. Maybe next time.

The sun's up early in the morning but your every thought is of the "Hoh Wall" looming to the north. Climbing the "Hoh Wall" ought to be your first concern; it's no easy feat. Heavy packs and 3,500 feet of elevation gain awaits you, spread over about 4 miles of relentless up-trail. As you climb, a front row view of Mt. Olympus slowly reveals itself. You'll feel like you can reach out and touch it. There are no easy sections of this climb but some parts are tougher than others. The worst of these starts after the first half mile and lasts well over a mile and a half as you gain 2,400 feet. Thereafter the trail continues to climb, but at a lesser rate. About a mile farther on and another 500 feet higher you'll be tested again by another short half mile climb of the last 500 feet. There's more left for tomorrow, but today's effort has come to a most thankful and astounding end.

Hoh Lake sits on a tiny bench carved out of the wall, 3,500 feet of nearly clear air that separates you from the valley below. Pat yourself on the back, few hikers dare to make this climb and now you know the reason why. Only the brave press forward toward adversity; welcome to the "Hoh Wall" club!

At Hoh Lake you've entered one of the Park's limited reservation areas. But hopefully you already know that because: you studied the Park's Wilderness Trip Planner map, contacted the Wilderness Information Center and secured the reservation permits for camping at Hoh Lake tonight as well as Deer Lake tomorrow night. If you skipped this very important step, enjoy the view and move on nearly 13 miles to the first non-limited campsite on the upper Bogachiel; a next-to-impossible trek given what you've already been through today. I can only hope you read this loop's description carefully before you started up the Hoh.

Permits and reservations are not so difficult to obtain, but if you need to reserve a sequential series of limited sites that may be more difficult. This loop hike is best made between the latter half of July to early September because of the time it takes to melt the high country snow pack and avoid an early fall snow event. You're in direct competition with other hikers wanting campsites. Reserve yours 6 months in advance.

I'll take the time here to offer a sequence of choices and alternatives if your first request cannot be accommodated. You're going to need reservations for two consecutive camp sites in two different locations within the area. In a perfect world you would secure night-one at Hoh Lake and night-two at Deer Lake. So, get the date of the Deer Lake reservation first. The reason for this is that there simply is no good alternative to Deer Lake; take a good look at the Park's Wilderness Trip Planner map. Assuming you succeed, you've got night-two anchored for the moment. Now go to work on night number one.

If Hoh Lake is available, take it and your worries are over. If Hoh Lake isn't available, find a date that it is and then check to see if on the following night Deer Lake is available. If it is, you're done. If you can't score this Hoh Lake-Deer Lake combination, keep your original Deer Lake date and search the following for night-one, in the order listed: first try C.B. Flats a short mile below Hoh Lake, then try Lunch Lake in Seven Lakes Basin, or finally try Heart Lake east of Bogechiel Peak. Alternatives 2 and 3 add several miles to a tough day-two. Hopefully one of these alternatives will be your solution to this reservation problem. If you can't solve this puzzle, pick a different hike.

If you're capable of climbing the "Hoh Wall" and then going out of your way all in the same day, you'll make this loop hike work. What absolutely doesn't work for anyone is a day that starts on the Hoh, climbs the wall and requires you to hike another 13 miles to the first camp on the Bogachiel; it can't be done. Reservations are available online at recreation.gov, 6 months prior to the start of your hike. Start solving this problem and finish it early, but also research the most likely snow-free date on the High Divide. Attempting this loop when it's not snow-free will end at least in disappointment.

Of course, you have your permit, so settle into probably one of the best view camping experiences in the Park; it's all yours until the morning sun rises. Speaking of the morning, both the climb and the view will greet you. Tomorrow you'll complete the last 1.2 miles and the last 750 feet of elevation of the "Hoh Wall". Embrace the conquest of today's challenge and get some rest; you've earned it.

You'll crest the High Divide just below Bogachiel Peak rising 200 feet above you. At just under 5,300 feet of elevation views to the south and west are yours, thanks to your efforts in climbing the wall. Head down-trail to the northwest. You are 4.2 miles from Deer Lake. About half way to the lake you'll cross a large area of open meadowland. If you're there in the last week of August or the first week of September, huckleberries carpet these meadows. Take a break and stop to pick some; they're as organic as it gets. Don't be surprised if you end up sharing these meadows with the Black Bears. Give them their space, 50 yards is the Park's rule, and as long as they're head down and grazing, life is good for all concerned. Should a bear stop grazing and stare at you, slowly get up and move a good distance away. When the bear is comfortable again, grazing will resume. Full of huckleberries or not, finish day-three setting up camp at Deer Lake. Just short of the lake you'll find the Junction of the Bogachiel ("Bogi") River Trail. Tomorrow, you'll retrace your steps to this junction and head down-trail.

You're 7.6 miles away from Twentyone Mile, the first campsite in the upper "Bogi". The trail grade is reasonable with a few switchbacks a mile above the Twentyone Mile campsite. Once you leave the higher meadows, the forest density gradually increases with the loss of elevation. If weather and snow conditions allow you to do this loop in mid-July, you may be treated to abundant wildflowers. At 3.5 miles you'll intersect, on your right, the Mink Lake Trail; continue down-trail following the "Bogi". Twentyone Mile is located at about 2,200 feet, and has one campsite nestled at the edge of the trees. It's a pleasant place to finish day-four, but not the most memorable. Neither bear wires nor toilets are available in the "Bogi", as of this writing, 2022.

The warmth of the sun, hidden to the south behind Deer Lake, won't fall on you until you're down-trail this morning. From Twentyone Mile to Flapjack, your next stop, is 10.4 miles down-trail. The trail down to Fifteen-Mile is thick with brush. Below Fifteen Mile its brushy but not as bad. With an elevation loss of about 1,600 feet, you'll most definitely be in the Rain Forest.

The environment changes quickly with elevation gain or loss. The Hoh was in the Rain Forest, the climb up the "Hoh Wall" took you to alpine, Deer Lake was at subalpine and as you approach Fifteen Mile it will again be Rain Forest, from here to the Hoh Trailhead. You can see the change in the size of the trees and their density. At today's elevations Douglas fir and western hemlock are joined with western redcedar the closer you get to Flapjack. By the time you reach the end of this day's hike alder, willow and bigleaf maple begin to populate open areas near the river. There is so little ground space and so much that wants to grow in the Rain Forest that some plants grow upon others. Licorice root ferns, four to six inches tall, jut out from the moss covering the maples. If you pull one out, wipe off the root and bite down on it, you be treated to the taste of licorice, absent the sweet.

Flapjack sits in a river bottom which lets you enjoy the sun that was missing in action early this morning. Considering the grade and condition of the trail just traveled you've arrived early in the afternoon with plenty of time to rest up for the South Snider-Jackson Primitive Trail tomorrow. This loop includes fording and you should: consult with the Wilderness Information Desk in the Olympic National Park Visitor Center in Port Angeles. I suggest you do a web search for "Stream Crossing Techniques" and read the National Park Service's web-available "Safe River Crossings" and 'Swiftwater Rescue Manual" The Rangers in the Park's Wilderness Information Center can advise you as to the advisability of your plans. In addition, you should consult the USGS website for current water conditions. Also, if you visit online the State of Washington Dept. of Ecology, River and Stream Flow Monitoring page, you can compare years of data and thereby compare it to the weather pattern in any year against the weather pattern in the current year. By doing so you'll have a better sense of what the fording conditions may be. These searches will allow you to choose your hike based on the available data.

After setting up camp, you'll need to scout out a fording point for crossing the Bogachiel tomorrow morning. There is one ford in the location of Flapjack and another two miles down-stream. Because the river is forever shifting its burden, fording locations often offer shallow and broader crossings. Expect to get more than your boots wet. The "Bogi" is always difficult to ford, and at worse uncrossable. Search for your ford and cross it early in the morning when the water is usually at its lowest.

Here's what you'll need to keep in mind if you decide to ford the "Bogi". First let me be clear. Water is a powerful force and, in this case, very cold. The cold, in short order, will adversely affect your muscle reflexes and thereby your balance. If you fall, you run the risk of drowning. Check the Resources Page, in the Appendix, for fording. Being swept down-stream, at the flow's speed, puts you at risk for colliding with rocks, an experience you don't need. Do not discount the seriousness of fording nor the threat that any river holds. More than one hiker has lost their life ignoring the rules of a safe crossing, including not crossing at all.

If you can't find a safe crossing, your only out is to hike 7.8 miles down-trail to the Bogachiel Trailhead and another 4.5 out to U.S. 101 to find a ride back to the Hoh Trailhead. What appears to be a daunting task is lessened, a bit, by the fact that the "Bogi" is a fisherman's delight. The chance of finding a friendly helper isn't guaranteed, but likely. Remember, better a daunting task than a life lost; be careful and choose wisely.

The best you can do is anticipate the strength of the flow on the "Bogi" and make an educated prediction of whether a ford may, or may not, be possible. Before you leave home, check the Washington State Department of Ecology website and navigate to Flow Monitoring. Even if the Bogachiel or any other river you're researching isn't listed, you can pick a river in the area that is active and assess its current condition. The closer the river is to the one you are researching the better the comparison. Let's assume you've done that, but now you're five days into the backcountry and your guidance will have to come from the weather that the last five days has delivered. If it has rained constantly or nearly so over the past five days, you can expect the river to be up and flowing strongly. Even a dry period followed by one or two days of downpour can quickly cause the rivers to rise. As I've said before, you are dependent on what you know and how good you are at making appropriate decisions, driven by the conditions at hand.

On a happier note, you've found and forded the "Bogi". If you did so at Flapjack follow your new found shore about a mile down-stream where it will intersect the South Snider-Jackson Primitive Trail. If you forded anywhere down-stream of Flapjack, the South Snider-Jackson Primitive Trail follows the south shore up-stream and you're probably standing on it as you dry off. If not, start moving up-stream, you'll find it shortly.

Up the Snider-Jackson you'll meet the biggest challenge on this loop. As of this writing the trail is close to nonexistent. Covered in brush and with countless downed trees, this segment demands the use of a contour map, compass and altimeter. If it becomes more than you can manage, return to the Bogachiel Trail, hike out to U.S. 101 and find your way back to the Hoh Trailhead.

You've got 10.4 miles between where you are and the Hoh Road. A little over half-way you'll reach the day's high point at about 2,900 ft, a gain of roughly 2,400 feet. The trail is primitive, not maintained, so you'll be fighting brush and down-fall all the way. The ascent starts quickly but the grade eases after the first two miles. I suggest one of two alternatives for the rest of today. You could find an off-trail hard ground campsite at about the five-mile mark, near the top of the ridge you're crossing, or push on to just short of the Hoh Road. The descending grade down the south slope into the Hoh is interrupted about 2 miles short of the Hoh Road with first a steep set of switchbacks and then a final relatively flat mile just before the road.

If you've chosen to travel most of the ten miles across the ridge, you might consider one last camp off-trail either just above or just below the switchbacks. Such a decision adds a day to the loop, but it shortens this section and gives you the opportunity to review your experience with peace and leisure. Whatever your choice, you'll need a Cross Country Wilderness Permit to camp off-trail, in a specific area and on a specific date. Remember that once you reach the Hoh Road the Hoh Trailhead is about 6 miles away. Given what you've accomplished today, I don't suggest that you also take on that 6 mile trudge up the Hoh Road to the trailhead.

Whatever you decide, eventually you'll end this loop at the Hoh Trailhead. Give yourself credit, you've completed 53 miles, some of it the toughest in the Park. You've mastered limited reservations, ascended the "Hoh Wall", hopefully forded the "Bogi" and managed the South Snider-Jackson traverse. If you're tired, you should be, but that's the price of extending your experience, meeting the challenge of the wilderness and adding to your backpacking ability

Three Passes Loop

SE Quadrant, Custom Correct map, "The Brothers-Mt. Anderson", (56 mi., difficulty 42.56, Mid-July to Mid-September only, long days, sublime high country, rivers and Marmots)

Summary: Dosewallips Trailhead, Dose Campground, Honeymoon Meadows, La Crosse Pass, Duckabush Ford, La Crosse Basin, O'Neil Pass, Bull Elk Basin, Fisher's Notch, World Record hemlock, Anderson Pass, Camp Siberia, Big Timber, Dosewallips Trailhead.

This is the first of many long days on this loop trail but it's worth the effort. Let's start by finding the trailhead. As U.S. 101 enters Brinnon on the Hood Canal, from the north, turn right onto the Dosewallips Road. Drive to the end of the road. (A special note: follow my directions, The Brothers-Mt. Anderson map is based on 1990 datum and a major slide on the Dose Road happened after its printing. As such, the map in this one instance will vary from my description.) The Dose Trailhead is 6.5 miles from the previous drive-in Dosewallips Campground. As of this writing, you'll have to hike those miles from the temporary trailhead on the Dose Road to the Dose Campground and the original Dosewallips Trailhead.

Between mile 5 and 6 is the Lake Constance "trail". You'll find the Lake Constance Trailhead on your right. This trail is little more than a scramble up Constance Creek. It's one of the steepest trails in the Park. This leg, lung, and spirit busting monster climbs 3,200 vertical feet in 1.8 miles. It's one of the few times I've ever purposely taken on a hike that rose 1,800 feet each mile. I put the Lake Constance Trail in the "once is enough" category. The lake itself is wonderous sitting on a shelf on the south flank of Mt. Constance, at 4,665 ft. nearly 3,100 feet below the summit. If you ever want to test your endurance, it's always available.

Back to today's hike, about 4 miles ahead and a half mile short of the Dose Campground you'll come upon Dose Falls. Stop opposite the falls and soak in the sheer power of water. Often the falls are littered with large trees thrown like sticks on or across the boulders that attempt to hold back the maelstrom. The Campground is just over the top of the falls. Follow the trail up-slope along the right side of the falls.

You've completed the one and only short day of this loop. Tomorrow's camp will be at Honeymoon Meadows 9.1 miles up-trail. If you're interested in shortening tomorrow and lengthening today the map offers several extensions to today's hike: Dose Forks adds 1.4 miles and Big Timber adds 4.2 miles to the length of today's hike.

27. Honeymoon Meadows, ONP, Jim Patterson

Honeymoon Meadows is 2,500 feet higher and a significant amount of the elevation gain is in the last 1.5 miles of the hike as it gently climbs away from Dose Forks 1.4 miles from the Dose Campground. At Dose Forks the main Dose Trail turns right just short of the Dose Forks Campsite and heads northwest. The West Fork Dosewallips Trail crosses the river at Dose Forks and continues to climb more steeply as it approaches the High Dose Bridge, a long half mile farther on. The bridge crosses the Dose as it runs through the narrow gorge over a hundred feet below. The steel bridge you'll cross is the third to span this gorge. The other two were beautiful log structures both of which failed under the burden of winter snow. Their remains are littered deep in the canyon, along the river. I was always a little skittish every time I crossed on the old log replacement bridge with the bones of its predecessor glowering up from the depths below. That was then and this is now, so go ahead and tramp across this modern engineering marvel, there's still a lot of today's trail that awaits you.

Big Timber camp 2 miles ahead is well named. Large Douglas firs (really Pine trees that were misnamed), western hemlock and western redcedar are sprinkled about the campsite. It's also a decent spot for fishing. Given the dense canopy Big Timber can be a cold camp even on a warm day.

As the trail heads up, leaving Big Timber, the grade gives you an idea of what lies ahead. The trail climbs about 300 feet in the first mile and then winds its way through a, fall to spring, flood plain where the underlying strata prevents absorption and forces the water to stream on the surface. Different yes, pretty no! This anomaly soon runs out and at the end of the 2.4 mile march from Big Timber you enter Diamond Meadows.

It's time for another of my side-light stories. Three of my climbing partners and I had hiked from the Dose Campground, at that time the trailhead, in the dark on a Friday night after school. We were on our way to Anderson Pass to search for climbing routes for the coming winter climbing season. As an aside, when we hiked at night, we didn't use flashlights. You'd be surprised how much your sight adapts to even the extreme low light environment of a dense forest at night.

We moved just short of a trot as we clicked off the miles. We pulled into Diamond Meadows, threw-down, crawled in and were sound asleep in a flash. We awoke early the next morning to discover that we were settled smack-dab in the middle of a troop of Girl Scouts. We broke camp in complete silence, skipped breakfast and skedaddled, saving their dignity as well as our own.

The last of today's 9.1 miles start by crossing a low marshy piece of trail consisting of a quantity of poles and half sunken foot logs that seem to be in a different arrangement each time I've crossed them. Awkward, maybe even messy, but not threatening. Shortly thereafter, the trail moves away from and above the Dose, climbing steadily and steeply just short of Honeymoon Meadows. The canyon narrows but remains deep. The sound of pounding water tumbling down unseen falls nearby should be music to your ears. Honeymoon Meadows is just around the next bend.

You'll go from canyon and cacophony to a quiet subalpine meadow, in less than a hundred yards. Rising above you, a sheer wall, the southeast buttress of Mt. Anderson. The mountain itself is out of sight from the meadow but certainly nearby.

Tomorrow our route will deny you an up-close look at Mt. Anderson from Anderson Pass. Don't despair, you'll get that opportunity a few days from now. Rest for now, tomorrow's trail will be even more demanding and more rewarding than what you completed today.

Up and at it. You'll find the junction of the West Fork of the Dose Trail with the La Crosse Pass Trail less than a half mile up-stream. Turning left and beginning an ascent of about 2,000 feet in the next 3.1 miles, the views immediately pop up. Over your shoulder to the to the north lies Mt. Anderson at 7,321 ft. What's missing is the Anderson Glacier. In place of the healthy glacier that I experienced in my youth, is a scree slope descending to a small, unbecoming water body.

While the Park retains numerous glaciers, 126 at this writing, they are disappearing rapidly in the face of climate change. The effect of this change in the Park brings pressure on the hydrology, biology and zoology throughout the Park. Water is the life blood of the Park's environment and the melting of glaciers provides a controlled ability to continuously add to stream flows in the dry months of the year. Fewer glaciers result in less stream flow, especially when it's most needed. I won't live to see the Park glacier-free, but at the rate it's going, you might. I'm saddened by the projected future of this magnificent place.

Topping out on La Crosse Pass at 5,566 ft. you're treated to views of the surrounding high country in this section of the Park. On your immediate right, west of your viewpoint is Mt. La Crosse, at 6,417, to the southwest Mt. Duckabush, at 6,250, due south Mt. Hopper, at 6,114 and in the distance Mt. Skokomish, at 6,434. To the east stand the twin peaks of The Brothers, south peak at 6,842 ft., north peak at 6650 ft. and finally northeast to the far-left Mt. Constance at 7,756 ft. and its south summit at 7,600 ft.

Time for your first descent of several on this loop. The next 3.3 miles will take you almost directly down to the Duckabush River Trail, a nice even 3,000 feet below. This is a south-facing slope and, while it is forested, tends to get quite hot on a clear summer day. Drink freely, you can fill-up again at the river where the Upper Duckabush Trail ends and, after the ford, the La Crosse Pass Trail begins.

Heading up-stream you'll come to Upper Duckabush Camp. A great place to stop. Set up camp and relax; you've had a hard day and you deserve the rest.

The trail to O'Neil Pass lies across the river, absent a foot bridge. This wasn't always the case. In my youth an old growth fir windfall fell across the river in about this location. It was bank to bank and about twelve feet in diameter. It was so big that the trail crew chopped steps up its side at either end so we could walk on its broad top to the other side. At the time I would have told you it would be a permanent bridge across the Duckabush. Oh, how young and inexperienced I was. A few years later my friends and I hiked up the Duckabush on our way to La Crosse Basin at O'Neil Pass to scout a climbing route up Mt. Steel. We stood where you're standing and to our dismay there was no sign that my "permanent bridge" had ever existed. Only one force was capable of removing that log, a raging Duckabush, most likely in response to one of our intense fall storms.

There's a reason I placed a specific time of the year for this hike. The second reason is the elevations of the three passes in this loop and in particular La Crosse Basin. You want most of the snow to be gone because streams and rivers, that need to be forded, should be running at lower levels.

Up with the sun and ready to go. If you are considering fording, you should: consult with the Wilderness Information Desk in the Olympic National Park Visitor Center in Port Angeles. I suggest you do a web search for "Stream Crossing Techniques" and read the National Park Service's web-available "Safe River Crossings" and 'Swiftwater Rescue Manual" The Rangers in the Park's Wilderness Information Center can advise you as to the advisability of your plans. In addition, you should consult the USGS website for current water conditions. Also, if you visit online the State of Washington Dept. of Ecology, River and Stream Flow Monitoring page, you can compare years of data and thereby compare it to the weather pattern in any year against the weather pattern in the current year. By doing so you'll have a better sense of what the fording conditions may be. These searches will allow you to choose your hike based on the available data.

Your first challenge is fording the Duckabush. Fording a stream or small river can be as easy as just getting your boots wet. Most of the time you might be faced with a deeper crossing. Check the Resources Page, in the Appendix, for fording. Most fording points are well identified, the trail leads you directly to the ford. Fords are often chosen because at that location the stream is shallow and wide; or those were the conditions when the trail was built. Fording is dangerous and should not be taken lightly. More than one hiker has lost their life to a failed fording attempt. Spend some time scouting your best fording option. If this isn't going to work today, it's time to reverse your direction and hike back to the trailhead; live to hike another day. Safety first!

In order for me to describe the rest of the loop I'll assume everyone had an easy crossing. With luck, you've spent less time fording the Duckabush than I have writing this section. You are now on your way to one of the prettiest places in the Park, La Crosse Basin. Marmot Lake, your introduction to the basin, is 3.5 miles beyond Upper Duckabush Camp and 2,000 feet above last night's encampment. It's a steady and reasonable grade for the first 3 miles. At that point the next half mile to the lake is rough and steep. The bear wires are down at the lake. Bear Cannisters are required.

La Crosse Basin is spectacular. With three named lakes and a number of alpine tarns scattered over an area a half mile wide and over a mile long. If you have a rest day built into your schedule, I suggest you spend it here. If you have to move on tomorrow then I suggest you spend part of tomorrow in the basin and start your hike down to Bull Elk Basin later in the day. You've reached nirvana; enjoy the experience.

The next day's hike, whatever day that is, starts at Marmot Lake and climbs1.2 miles to O'Neil Pass overseen by Mount Duckabush at 6,239 ft. nearby to the southeast. If it looks smaller now it's because you're only looking at its top 1,200 feet above where you're standing. The trail descends at a fairly even grade, giving you great views of the Enchanted Valley on the Quinault River below. For most of the descent you'll get periodic views of Mt. Anderson to the north and some good views of Chimney Peak at 6,917 ft., the high point on the Enchanted Valley's northwest wall. At the 7 mile mark below O'Neil Pass, you'll cross White Creek and enter Bull Elk Basin. It hardly compares to what you've just left but in its own way it is a peaceful and attractive setting for a campsite. If you're up for another rest day, Bull Elk Basin is your best choice as we continue on to the Dose Trailhead.

Aside from the natural beauty of the basin, I have two activities for tomorrow, if you plan to lay over. Just up-meadow to the southeast you'll find a boulder field nestled in the heather. Whenever Barbara and I stayed over in this location we never passed up a lesson in boulder-hopping, basically moving from one boulder to the next, sometimes only landing with one boot on a rock and springing off to the next, all in one sweeping movement. On the few occasions we came up short in a move, it really just amounted to jumping from a rock into the heather, not a big deal. Before I write further, there were a few occasional scraped shins, so pace yourself.

The second enticement is towering overhead. The stream that you crossed when you entered into this basin is fed by a big snowfield above you in Fisher's Notch. Backcountry rangers, in their day, used the notch as a shortcut between La Crosse and Bull Elk Basins. Yes, they descended that excessively steep gully. I'm definitely not suggesting you climb the Notch, that would be reckless for us both. What I do suggest is a scramble up to the base of the snowfield for a view of the two peaks of Mt. Anderson less than 4 miles due north. Tomorrow, as you climb over Anderson Pass, you'll be closer, but absent a scramble to the terminal moraine of the recently melted Anderson Glacier, the view from the base of the notch is as good as it gets.

The good news and the bad news, first thing in the morning. Today is another 9 mile day. You'll leave Bull Elk Basin and drop a short distance down to the Quinault River Trail. One more point of interest, if I may. Where you intersect the Quinault River Trail, I suggest you drop your packs and venture less than a mile down-trail to view the World's largest western hemlock measuring, its circumference at 273 inches, height at 237 feet and with a spread of 67 feet. You'll find it about 30 yards down a spur to your right; the only spur trail you'll encounter on this side trip.

Back to the packs and off you go only to meet a creek about a half mile up-trail. The unnamed creek isn't so much a ford as it is stepping across the boulders in its flow. Now you know why I suggested brushing up on boulder hopping yesterday.

The trail steepens significantly over the 1.7 miles from the O'Neil Trail and Quinault Trail intersection up to Anderson Pass. It's a tough stretch. You've got another 6.3 miles to go today, so take it slow and easy. Stop at Camp Siberia just over the pass and take a break. If you want to scramble up to the moraine, backtrack about a quarter mile and take the way-trail to your right a long half mile scramble to the rocky view point above what was the toe of the Anderson Glacier.

The rest of today and the rest of the loop is down-trail, that's the good news of the morning, albeit delivered at mid-day. Honeymoon Meadows is 1.4 miles ahead. Just beyond the junction with the La

Crosse Pass Trail, you may notice, close by on your right a swift flowing alpine stream. That is the beginning of The West Fork Dosewallips River. What's odd, is that it appears to be alongside the trail but slightly above it, another anomaly in the Park. Honeymoon Meadows is 2.4 miles above Diamond Meadows and Big Timber, your destination, is another 2.4 miles below Diamond Meadows. I'll skip any description here, since you've traveled this trail more recently than I.

Tomorrow is another choice, 4.2 miles to Dose Campground or 10.7miles and out to the Trailhead; your choice. By this time your packs are lighter and your legs and lungs could climb straight up a wall with little effort. Fit and trim after 57 miles, not counting side trips, on this astounding and demanding Loop, my hat's off to you. Congratulations! Your description of your trip will hopefully encourage others to prepare for the challenges and complete them successfully. The joys and difficulties delivered to you, firsthand by the Daniel J. Evans Wilderness, are now in your experience bank. I can only hope that traveling with you helped along the way.

Quinault – La Crosse Pass Loop

SW Quadrant, Custom Correct map, "Enchanted Valley-Skokomish"(56 mi., difficulty 35.43, Rain Forest, Enchanted Valley, three passes, La Crosse Basin, alpine views, fording)

Summary: Graves Creek Trailhead, Enchanted Valley, Bull Elk Basin, O'Neil Pass, La Crosse Basin, Ford the Duckabush River, La Crosse Pass, Anderson Pass, Rain Forest, Graves Creek Trailhead

This loop should be undertaken in late summer or early fall to accommodate lower flow rates on the Duckabush River. Should the Duckabush turn out to be unfordable you'll be faced with two alternatives. The first alternative would be to reverse your direction of travel and return to the Graves Creek Trailhead, making the hike an "In and Out" as opposed to a loop. The second alternative skips the ford and climbs over First Divide, down the North Fork Skokomish River, across Six Ridge to Lake Sundown and then back to the Graves Creek Trailhead. This second alternative will take three to four days. The description of the second alternative will be inserted into my narrative once you arrive at the fording site below the east side of O'Neil Pass.

Lake Quinault is an hour's drive north of Aberdeen, WA on U.S. 101. Signs at the lake will direct you to turn right on to the South Shore Road and Lake Quinault Lodge. The distance from the U.S. 101 turn-off and Graves Creek Campground and Trailhead is about 18 miles. With the exception of Aberdeen, Graves Creek is a long way from most places. You might want to add a day and stay overnight at the campground which would allow you a quick start for your first day on the trail.

Your first day will take you 6.6 miles up-trail to O'Neil Creek. You shouldn't rush this part of the hike. You'll be passing through one of only six temperate rain forests on the planet. Think of the Rain Forest as a jungle absent heat, monkeys, parrots and nasty snakes. The Quinault Rain Forest is brimming with huge conifers, maples, ferns and animals. The plants compete for every square inch of growing space, so much so that many plants grow on other plants due to the lack of available ground space. Although there are numerous record trees scattered within the Olympic Mountains, two world record holders are located in the Quinault Valley. The world's largest Sitka spruce is located at the east end of Lake Quinault and the world's largest western hemlock is a short distance beyond the Enchanted Valley Chalet. Take your time and enjoy this wonderous environment.

28. Hart Lake, La Crosse Basin, ONP, Shawn Sheltren

The trail gains very little elevation and sticks to the southern side of the Quinault River in the first 2.5 miles. At that point you'll arrive at the Pony Bridge, one of the prettiest places on the river. If it's a clear-sky day you're in for a treat. Standing on the south shore you are looking over the river as it works its way down-stream. The opposite bank is a kaleidoscopic canvas containing countless shades and textures of green. At the same time, you'll see bright splashes of yellow as the sun tracks through the forest canopy. In order for the sunshine to reach the forest floor it must travel through holes in the canopy, at various levels. As you stand there every few minutes, as the earth rotates, one splash of yellow will fade and another will take its place at a different location; this goes on all day long when the sky is clear.

Moving on, O'Neil Creek Camp is just over 4 miles up-stream. Along the way there are any number of nice places along the river to sit and absorb this grand environment. Sitting quietly in one place is a good way to see animals since they read quiet and small as non-threatening. They are not likely to approach you, however, and they won't be in a big hurry. Elk, black-tail deer, river otters, and grouse are more common sights. Black Bear, bobcats, and weasels are less commonly seen and cougars are next to never seen, although they'll see you. Adverse human-animal contacts are extremely rare. While you shouldn't worry about the animals, whenever you encounter one you should always give them the respect and space they require. If you want a better picture, use a longer lens; never approach an animal.

Morning breaks and it's time to stir. You've got a relatively easy day today. The Enchanted Valley Chalet is 6.5 miles up-trail and by the time you get there you'll begin to see the transition of lowland Rain Forest to the beginnings of the subalpine ecosystem. Enchanted Valley is broad and bears witness to the ever-meandering flow of the Quinault, shifting rock and gravel from one channel to another. The chalet was moved recently from its original placement to its present location to safeguard this historical building from the river's encroachment. Because the area has been designated as wilderness, moving the chalet was undertaken without the use of powered equipment. Regardless of that effort, the river continues to threaten and it appears that the chalet will either be moved again or removed.

The valley is often referred to as, the "Valley of 10,000 Waterfalls". The moniker arises from the hundreds of waterfalls, adorning the wall, that accompany the spring thaw. Since you are taking this loop hike in the late summer or early fall to accommodate fording the Duckabush, you're looking at the wall absent its weeping. With Chimney Peak at 6,917 ft. topping the wall to the northwest and a parallel ridge forming the southeast wall at about 6,000 ft., the valley lends itself to breezy, if not windy conditions. The reason for this is the predominant flow of weather approaching from the southwest. As such, the valley acts as a funnel. The form of the valley compresses the up-stream airflow between these two ridges and in so doing increases its velocity.

After a night's rest and the Enchanted Valley slipping away behind you, a long day awaits. As of this writing, 2022, the Park is considering quotas for camping in the Enchanted Valley. Checking with the Wilderness Information Center is advised.

About 3 miles up-trail you'll happen on a spur trail to your left and a small sign stating quite conservatively "Big Hemlock". You'll only be going a few yards out of your way but the reward, the world's largest western hemlock, is well worth your time. The fact that huge trees grow in the Rain Forest is obvious, but to have this record holder at about 3,000 feet of elevation and at the edge of the Rain Forest's upper limit is quite remarkable. Good luck at trying to get a photo that comes close to representing this hemlock's grandeur.

About a half-mile farther on you'll cross White Creek and just beyond the creek you'll intersect the O'Neil Pass Trail on your right. Following the O'Neil Pass Trail, you'll enter into Bull Elk Basin in the first half mile. Bull Elk is a great place to drop your packs and take a break. This meadowed basin rolls upward to the west until it meets the talus fields at the base of the ridge you're about to ascend. Lucky for you that the trail skirts around the western face of the ridge and has a reasonable grade that rises to the Pass. Facing south from the Basin look slightly to your right. High above you is Fisher's Notch, an incredibly steep rock chute that was often used by backcountry rangers as a short cut from La Crosse Basin above to Bull Elk Basin below. It must have saved them hours on the trail, but that said, I wouldn't recommend it as a sane alternative.

Rest time is over, gear up and up to the pass you go. You've got about 7 miles of constant elevation gain ahead of you; pace yourself. O'Neil Pass tops out at 5,000 feet, about 1,300 feet above Bull Elk Basin. Take a break at the pass. O'Neil Peak at 5,758 ft. is to the southwest at just over a mile distant. Mt. Duckabush at 6,250 ft. is to the southeast and much closer than Mt. Steel at 6,225 ft. due east. To the northeast, about 5 miles away is Mt. La Crosse at 6,417 ft. and Chimney Peak at 6917 ft. due north across the valley finishes this round-the-clock view laid out before you.

Moving down-trail 1.2 miles you arrive at the south entrance to La Crosse Basin, your destination for today. Marmot Lake is about a mile inside the Basin to the north. If you've planned a lay-over day this would be my recommendation. The basin is about a half mile wide and about three miles long. It contains four lakes and several seasonal tarns. If viewing Fisher's Notch from above is of interest follow the trail to Lake La Crosse and scramble up the 800 ft. rise north-north-east beyond the north end of the lake. The view of that 1,200 ft. plunge into Bull Elk Basin is breath-taking; I can't imagine going down it. Use extreme caution, one slip and you could be severely injured.

Whichever day you decide to head onward, you've got 4.4 miles down-trail to the intersection of the Home-Sweet-Home, First Divide Trail. This intersection is also in the vicinity of your fording of the Duckabush River. If you are considering fording, you should: consult with the Wilderness Information Desk in the Olympic National Park Visitor Center in Port Angeles. I suggest you do a web search for "Stream Crossing Techniques" and read the National Park Service's web-available "Safe River Crossings" and 'Swiftwater Rescue Manual" The Rangers in the Park's Wilderness Information Center can advise you as to the advisability of your plans. In addition, you should consult the USGS website for current water conditions. Also, if you visit online the State of Washington Dept. of Ecology, River and Stream Flow Monitoring page, you can compare years of data and thereby compare it to the weather pattern in any year against the weather pattern in the current year. By doing so you'll have a better sense of what the fording conditions may be. These searches will allow you to choose your hike based on the available data.

Drop your gear and scout the river up and down stream for a reasonable place to ford. If you can't ford the "Duck", you have two alternatives. Your first alternative is to reverse your line of travel and return to the Graves Creek Trailhead which is 27 miles and three to four days away, depending on how hard you want to push yourself. Your second alternative is to climb up and over First Divide, move down the North Fork Skokomish to Big Log Camp. There is a washout near Camp Pleasant that will require minor route-finding skills. Take the Six Ridge Trail to Lake Sundown and then move down the Graves Creek Trail to the Graves Creek Trailhead.

This second alternative is 28 miles and four days in length with day-three being a long, high and dry 10.6 mile day traversing Six Ridge. Rather than give you a brief description of this alternative, I suggest you read the following Loop Hike, Sundown Lake-O'Neil Pass Loop. Starting on the second page you can read the full description of the hike from Big Log Camp on the North Fork Skokomish to the Graves Creek Trailhead. I believe, given these details, that you will make an informed decision.

With the stress and worry of fording the "Duck" behind you, your successful fording places you at Upper Duckabush Camp, your destination for today. In my youth, a huge old growth fir fell across the "Duck" in about this location. It was so big that the trail crew cut steps at each end so that hikers could mount the log. Its diameter was so great that the top of the log was nearly flat. I considered it a bridge for all time. After all, what force could ever remove it? Several years later I returned and the log was gone. The force of a raging "Duck", produced by a winter rain storm, had won the war of nature's titans.

I hope you're well rested. Morning brings the light of a new day and what a day it's going to be. Finish breakfast, pick up any trash you find in the area, make sure you've got what you came with and head down-trail. The junction with the La Crosse Pass Trail is 1.8 miles below Upper Duckabush Camp. This is your last source of water until you cross over the Pass to the West Fork Dosewallips River.

The first quarter mile and the last half mile of this trail are the only reasonable elements of crossing La Crosse Pass. The first 3.3 miles, gains 2,700 ft. as you climb the south face of the pass. Switchbacks, long and short, are the menu for today; take your time. Needless to say, topping-out at the pass is a great place for a rest stop. There are numerous peaks for your enjoyment, not the least of which are The Brothers and Mt. Constance, key summits in the eastern range which serves as the backdrop for every west facing territorial city-scape picture of Seattle you've ever seen.

Moving down the north slope of the pass is a lot easier. The first 2 miles follow a fairly constant grade and you won't find switchbacks until you enter mile three. At 3.1 miles you'll come to the intersection with the West Fork Dosewallips River Trail; turn left and move up-trail. About a half mile later, you'll arrive at Camp Siberia, just short of Anderson Pass. Today's miles weren't long, but at least three of them were tough.

Before you settle in for the night, you might want to hike a mile up-trail and take the spur trail you'll find on your right. The spur climbs steeply up the southerly nose of a ridgeline that skirts Mt. Anderson to the east. After about a mile you'll top-out at a good view point. Directly north you'll have a clear view of Mt. Anderson's east and west peaks, both at just over 7,300 ft.

Below and between them lies what's left of the Anderson Glacier. Fifty years ago, the glacier extended down the draw, to a point due east of where you stand today. That glacier was in place for well over 2.6 million years. It stored water and fed the environment near and far with that critical resource throughout each year. Today the glacier, like many others, is gone along with its ability to feed year round the lakes and streams that are so critical to the mountains and the lowlands below.

It's another day on the trail. The first 1.7 miles descend the west side of Anderson Pass ending at the intersection with the O'Neil Pass Trail you hiked a few days ago. About a half mile before you reach that intersection, you'll cross an unnamed and boulder-strewn creek. If the creek is low, the crossing is a simple task, stepping from one boulder to the next. If the creek is running high, the task is the same but you'll need to take your time and ensure solid footing as you cross. This is no place to fall in!

From the intersection with the O'Neil Pass Trail to the Enchanted Valley Chalet it's 3.2 miles. From the chalet to the Graves Creek Trailhead is an additional 13.1 miles. You've got a number of campsites to choose from below the chalet. Your choices determine whether you now have one or two days left to finish this loop.

Reaching the Graves Creek Trailhead, regardless of the route you've traveled, you've just completed somewhere in the neighborhood of 56 miles. You've experienced some of the most beautiful basins and valleys in the Olympic Mountains, exercised your backcountry decision-making skills and perhaps expanded your physical and mental capacities. The wilderness is relentlessly teaching us who we are and what we're made of; I hope you're better as a result of this experience.

North Fork Skokomish O'Neil Pass Loop

SE Quadrant, Custom Correct maps, "Mount Skokomish-Lake Cushman" and "The Brothers-Mount Anderson", (56 mi., difficulty 48.8**, 3 passes, 2 basins, a notch, 2 fords, alpine lakes)**

Summary: Staircase Trailhead, Nine Stream, Home Sweet Home, O'Neil Pass, Bull Elk Basin, Anderson Pass, La Crosse Pass, fording the Duckabush, Home Sweet Home, Staircase Trailhead

If you are considering this loop understand that it includes two fordings. You should: consult with the Wilderness Information Desk in the Olympic National Park Visitor Center in Port Angeles. I suggest you do a web search for "Stream Crossing Techniques" and read the National Park Service's web-available "Safe River Crossings" and 'Swiftwater Rescue Manual" The Rangers in the Park's Wilderness Information Center can advise you as to the advisability of your plans. In addition, you should consult the USGS website for current water conditions. Also, if you visit online the State of Washington Dept. of Ecology, River and Stream Flow Monitoring page, you can compare years of data and thereby compare it to the weather pattern in any year against the weather pattern in the current year. By doing so you'll have a better sense of what the fording conditions may be. These searches will allow you to choose your hike based on the available data.

A lush forest in the southeast corner of the Park greets you in the first miles of this loop. You'll find the trailhead near the Staircase Ranger Station on the east side of the Skokomish River just north of Lake Cushman, in the southeast corner of Olympic National Park. Follow U.S. 101 to Hoodsport on Hood Canal and following the signs heading west. You'll follow the road as it slowly swings around to the north, follows the east shore of Lake Cushman for a couple of miles and then veers away to the junction of Forest Service Road 24. Turn left and as the road regains the shoreline it changes to gravel. At the extreme north end of the lake, you'll enter the Park and the road changes back to asphalt, ending at the Staircase Campground and Ranger Station.

There are two trails emanating close by the ranger station. The one you don't want crosses the bridge. The Skokomish River Trail follows the east side of the North Fork Skokomish River. Right out of the box you're immersed in an enchanting lowland forest replete with huge trees, mosses, ferns and a soft-afoot beautiful trail. There's a wash-out

29. First Divide, ONP

between Big log and Camp Pleasant that will require some amount of way-finding to get around it.

I took my first hike up the North Fork "Skok" in 1958, and hooked, I never looked back. Mesmerized by the magnificence of this forest dreamland and finding something new and exciting around every turn I, unlike you, was headed up-trail 3.8 miles to Nine Stream. You, on the other hand, now have a 9.1 mile day ahead. Why the difference in distance; a Boy Scout discount? Not at all. In those days the road ran all the way to Big Log 5.3 miles ahead, the difference between now and then.

At Big Log another trail leads to the east, headed for Black and White Lakes. You're not headed there and I wouldn't recommend it if you were. About 3,000 feet of elevation gain over 2.3 miles was one of my worst decisions in my Boy Scout years. Three of us, being "older scouts", by this time, got permission from Orville Schultz, the Scoutmaster, to take the trail and meet the rest of the Troop at Black and White Lakes. The troop would first climb toward Flapjacks Lakes, from Spike Camp which you passed 2 miles earlier today. Just below Flapjacks the troop would backtrack to Black and White on a linking trail. Meanwhile our climb up to the lakes from Big Timber was excruciating. A steep, thinly forested, western exposure on a hot day and we were out of water! Never again!

You're now 3.5 miles from Nine Stream, the day's end. The trail now begins to climb, but not severely. You'll soon cross Hammer Creek where I had my first wildlife encounter. I was leading the troop and we were tired enough that the banter had died away. I rounded a sharp turn in the trail and found myself eyeball to eyeball with about a dozen Roosevelt Elk. My arrival startled them and their reaction was to stamp their feet, all at once. I was frozen; what to do? Nothing, they did it for me. They quietly turned and disappeared into the forest in a matter of seconds. That was my first example of coming upon wildlife, not when I was looking for it, but when I least expected it. This pattern, of coming unexpectedly upon wildlife, has continued to this day. I go looking, they're nowhere to be found; I'm not looking, there they are.

Yes, nine streams do cross the North Fork "Skok" Trail on the way to Nine Stream and, yes, each is numbered. The old Nine Stream Shelter, long since removed, sat within a stone's throw of the river. Shelters were a vestige of a different age when the C.C.C., Civilian Conservation Corps, in the 1930's improved and/or built the trails and shelters in the Park. Some shelters have survived but where those that no longer stand, you'll find designated campsites much farther away from waterbodies to avoid fouling the waters with camping contamination.

Short rest stop. I highly recommend you not make camp and or sleep in them. Mice, mice and more mice have backpackers all figured out. They wait until it's dark and quiet, then start gnawing through your gear. Over the years I've lost more gear to mice than anything else. Don't camp in a shelter, any shelter, unless it is an absolute survival emergency!

Morning breaks and hopefully its sunny and clear. Today you'll climb 2,600 feet in the next 3.3 miles to crest First Divide at 4,688 ft. The trail is strenuous but the views grow as you climb, and this climb isn't as tough as you might think. Even if I'm wrong, today is a short day. The total mileage to the day's end point is 4 miles.

Home Sweet Home is beautifully located a short distance over First Divide on its north side. Home Sweet Home sits in a nameless headwater basin, and just up-slope of an unnamed creek which drains northwest to the upper Duckabush River 1,500 feet below. The creek may or may not have water in it depending on your timing and the past winter's snowpack. You may want to treat it as a dry camp and bring water up from Two Bear Camp, south of First Divide. From your lush alpine meadow look due west. That high ridge, some 3 miles distant is the east ridge of La Crosse Basin at O'Neil Pass, tomorrow's destination. If you think you're sitting in nirvana now, wait to see what tomorrow's revelation brings. It won't disappoint!

I mentioned marmots. I'm pretty certain that if you haven't seen them yet at Home Sweet Home you will tomorrow afternoon. Olympic Marmots, the largest member of the squirrel family, are specifically unique to the Olympic Mountains, thanks to the isolation imposed by the last ice age. These mountains were, at that time, an island in a sea of ice. Thousands of years of isolation and environmentally forced adaptive changes resulted in a type of marmot found nowhere else in the world. Because their fur falls all the way to the ground when they walk, I call them "walking rugs", they move but you can't see their feet. When curious or startled they rise on their haunches and whistle; a means of alerting the colony to intruders. Barbara, my wife, believes that they can count and therefore whistle based upon the number of intruders; I'm not convinced. You may have already seen them out in the meadow. As soon as the snow retreats, in early July, above 4,000 feet, they are on the job collecting grasses and sedges and storing them in their burrows. During the seven months of hard winter, usually October to May, marmots hibernate deep in their underground burrows. The stored foodstuffs, that you see them gathering, along with hibernation, help them survive after the snow begins to fly. As cute as they may seem, they're wild animals with a hair trigger defense response. Give them their space. You'll know what that is when they go back to comfortably grazing.

Morning breaks and you're back on the trail. It's 2 miles down-trail, a drop of 1,500 feet, several short steep grades and periodic switchbacks before you'll reach the Duckabush River. As the trail meets the river you are in the vicinity of a ford that will be yours to navigate several days from now. Take the time to assess the likelihood of fording the Duckabush when that time comes. If it doesn't appear to be fordable you'll be faced with three alternatives: 1) continue with crossing O'Neill, Anderson and La Crosse Passes and then reversing yourself, crossing the three passes again and returning to the Home Sweet Home side of the "Duck" or 2) crossing some but not all of the three Passes and then reversing your line of travel or 3) cross O'Neil Pass, follow the Quinault down-trail to Graves Creek, climb to Lake Sundown, cross Six Ridge to Big Log and finish at the Staircase Ranger Station. "Stuff happens" and in light of "stuff", you'll always be required to make informed choices as how to proceed. Choose wisely; your welfare is inseparable from the quality of your decisions.

Turn to your left following the south bank of the river as it ascends the valley headed west. The 3.4 mile climb to La Crosse Basin starts slowly. After about a mile and a quarter the trail rotates left to the southwest, crosses the Duckabush, now a smaller stream, and enters a narrow gorge with buttresses on either side of you. Passing through the gorge, the terrain opens a bit, swings north using switchbacks and then makes the final quarter mile climb to La Crosse Basin. A spur trail on your right will lead you to Marmot Lake, the headwaters of the Duckabush.

The spectacular alpine setting of the basin is inspiring to say the least. With a scattering of tarns, meadows and rock outcroppings spreading north over the length of the basin, you may want to take a rest day tomorrow just to explore this alpine wonderland. If you do, make certain that you carry a good topo map. The basin and the surrounding ridges hold a lot to explore. To the east of Lake La Crosse, through a small pass in the ridge and an up-down scramble over most of a mile lies Buck Lake. A half mile north over another ridge and just past a small tarn is Fisher's Notch. The view down the gully is, for most, terrifying. Warning, be extremely careful at Fisher's Notch, a misstep could be fatal.

From this perch you have a bird's eye view of Bull Elk Basin below, the destination of your next day on the trail. "In the day", backcountry rangers descended to Bull Elk Basin via Fisher's Notch, as a short cut, saving many miles of hiking down-trail on the O'Neil Pass Trail.

Leaving the basin, you'll climb 500 feet to O'Neil Pass, a little over a mile south. Arriving at the pass you'll get an in-your-face view of Mt. Duckabush a mile away due south and a distant view to the east of The Brothers, more than 11 miles distant. You now have about seven miles of reasonable grade down to Bull Elk Basin. You'll quickly be below treeline, so take advantage of the views down the Quinault Valley to your left and later on some peek-a-boo views straight down into the Enchanted Valley, the "Valley of 10,000 Waterfalls" on the valley's northwest side. To be precise, the wall only weeps during melt-off in the spring and early summer. If the wall is weeping, so are you, having most likely struggled in the snowpack around and over O'Neil Pass.

Slightly under 7 miles below O'Neil Pass you'll swing to the right around the nose of the north buttress holding La Crosse Basin above. Then cross a small or dry White Creek and enter Bull Elk Basin, your camp for the night. Spread out below Fisher's Notch, the north sloping basin is half heather garden and half boulder-ridden. After you've settled in, I suggest the you explore one of many areas full of boulders. Barbara and I always took the time to practice our boulder-hopping skills here. Moving from boulder to boulder without ever landing with more than one boot at a time. It's fun and the practice will be rewarded tomorrow. If for some reason you miss a boulder, at least you were practicing this day.

Up the next morning and ready to face the stiff climb over Anderson Pass. Today's hike isn't long or easy. The first half mile takes you down to the intersection with the Quinault Trail. I know you just got started, but I'd like to interrupt your progress at this point. Bear with me, you'll enjoy taking advantage of this short side trip. Drop your packs and go down-trail a short mile to a spur on your right. A few yards down the spur, you'll come upon the largest western hemlock in the world. This is one big tree and well worth a photo or two. You're already in the neighborhood, so why not drop by.

Back to your packs and up-trail you go. After about a half mile you'll come to an unnamed creek and yesterday's boulder-hopping exercise will pay off. Ordinarily I'd tell you that you'd have to ford the creek; however, a ford usually assumes some area of shallow water which doesn't describe this crossing. So, this crossing is a boulder hop more than anything else. One early summer day Barbara and I had to boulder-hop this crossing when the water was running so hard that it was washing over the tops of the rock; not our calmest crossing.

With the creek crossing behind you, it's time for some exercise. In the next mile toward Anderson Pass you'll climb just over 1,000 feet. Your legs and lungs will burn, but less so if you occasionally give them a brief rest, provided by the excuse to view the panorama to the west. Don't miss the view of the north end of the Enchanted Valley the "Valley of 10,000 Waterfalls" and Chimney Peak towering over it at 6,719 ft. This isn't a race, enjoy the hike; you'll be both rewarded and relieved when you've reached the pass. Catch your breath and continue beyond the Pass about a quarter mile to Camp Siberia. Throw down and set up camp. After a good meal and before sunset walk back up to the pass. On your way, you'll find a way-trail on your right that will take you about a mile north to a prominence above what was, in its day, a melt-water lake, trapped between the Anderson Glacier and its last moraine. Well, that was then and this is now. The glacier has completely melted and the lake is gone other than in spring with either snow-melt or in fall with rainwater. The Anderson Glacier, a tiny speck of the most recent ice age 2.6 million years ago, started its retreat between 10 and 20 thousand years before I laid eyes on it. Yet, since 1960 what was left of the glacier melted away in less than 50 years. The climate has changed! What's left of the Anderson Glacier is the "burden" that it was carrying, now strewn across the mountain side and polished rock, upon which it was working until its demise. For Barbara and I it's like viewing the resting place of a good friend; the tombstone of what was the Anderson Glacier.

Your day breaks. Time for breakfast. If you determined that the Duckabush River can be forded, based on your visit to the fording site on your way up to O'Neil Pass, then it's time to pack up and move on. If on the other hand, the "Duck" isn't fordable, then Camp Siberia will be your turnaround point as you backtrack to Bull Elk Basin and then over O'Neil Pass. If you're going to turn around, then La Crosse Pass could become a side trip before you begin your return. Either way, La Crosse Pass beckons.

Head down-trail about a mile to the junction of the La Crosse Pass Trail on your right, heading southeast. Between camp Siberia and the La Crosse Trail, you'll follow a mountain stream, the beginnings of the Dosewallips River. It flows nearby the trail and getting water shouldn't be a problem. There is next to no accessible water source on the 6.4 miles between the North Fork Dosewallips and the Duckabush Rivers.

Starting on the Dose at 3,627 feet, the trail climbs steadily giving you a front row seat for viewing Mt. Anderson over your shoulder and Mt. La Crosse to your right. After beginning with a steep climb with a series of switchbacks in the first mile and a half, the grade relents, climbing about 500 feet a mile in the last mile and a half to the pass at 5,566 feet

The view resembles a memory map of your travels. Starting at due south that rise about 2 miles out is hiding Home Sweet Home nestled just over the ridge between you and it. Rotating the view clockwise at one o'clock, deep in the Duckabush Valley, is the intersection with the O'Neil Pass Trail, and the ford you'll make tomorrow, if you are continuing on to the ford. At two o'clock is Mt. Duckabush standing guard over O'Neil Pass at four o'clock. White Mountain, the source of White Creek, is in partial view around the left side of Mt. La Crosse at five o'clock and Mt. Anderson is at six o'clock to finish the tour.

Rested up, you'll start to switchback 3.3 miles down the south slope of the Pass. After losing about 3,000 feet, with your knees complaining, you'll find yourself on the Upper Duckabush Trail slightly above the river. Turning right and up-stream, you're headed for Upper Duckabush Camp, 1.7 miles away, in the vicinity of tomorrow's ford. After you set camp take some time to assess the ford. The trail will lead you to the approximate place but remember where the trail meets the river is no true indication of where the best fording is located. Rivers are living things, raging and carrying, then slowing and depositing, shifting material in an endless cycle. In this case perhaps having moved the best fording-site.

In my youth, there used to be a giant fir windfall across this very point. It was so big the trail crew chopped steps into each end of this immovable monster bridge. Immovable? A few years later, expecting to use this bridge again, I was astonished to find it missing, obviously the victim of a fall rainstorm and the raging power of an engorged "Duck". In the end, the power of water always wins the day.

Before fording you should: consult with the Wilderness Information Desk in the Olympic National Park Visitor Center in Port Angeles. I suggest you do a web search for "Stream Crossing Techniques" and read the National Park Service's web-available "Safe River Crossings" and 'Swiftwater Rescue Manual" The Rangers in the Park's Wilderness Information Center can advise you as to the advisability of your plans. In addition, you should consult the USGS website for current water conditions. Also, if you visit online the State of Washington Dept. of Ecology, River and Stream Flow Monitoring page, you can compare years of data and thereby compare it to the weather pattern in any year against the weather pattern in the current year. By doing so you'll have a better sense of what the fording conditions may be. These searches will allow you to choose your hike based on the available data.

It's morning and time to ford the "Duck". If you're lucky, the ford results in no more than wet feet and a quick crossing. Take this fording business seriously. Hikers in the Park have lost their lives trying to ford when the water was deep. Water is heavy, a water-mass at velocity has more force-energy than you think and a rocky river bottom can be slippery. Refer to the Resources Page on fording. If the Duckabush is running too deep and fast to ford, you're faced with one really bad, and one horrendous, alternative. Either you backtrack over the three passes, 23.5 miles to get on the other side, or you hike down the Quinault, up Graves Creek, over Six Ridge and down the North Fork Skokomish to the Staircase Trailhead about 52 miles, nearly doubling the original mileage. Bad as those alternatives seem, fording when you shouldn't, could get you killed. The alternative, no matter how bad, is better. Remember that the wilderness neither loves nor hates you, it just holds you absolutely responsible for your choices.

On a happier note, I'm assuming fortune has smiled and you've forded the "Duck". Home Sweet Home lies about 1,500 feet and about 2 miles ahead. Then tomorrow it's 7.8 miles up and over First Divide and down the Skokomish to Big Log, lavishing you in the deep intensity of this ancient forest setting. Your final day is both flat, for the most part, and short. The distance from Big Log Camp to the Staircase Trailhead is 5.3 miles.

This loop trail, with all that it has to offer has been 56.3 miles in length. Regardless of how your hike finished, you'll have stories and memories for the rest of your life. You've re-tested yourself, perhaps polished up or learned a few new skills and been afforded some of the best that the Olympic Mountains has to offer. If you're a veteran hiker, this loop re-proved your abilities. If your previous experience was shy of vet status, well, you've proven you've got what it takes. Happy Hiking!

Dosewallips – Gray Wolf Loop

SE Quadrant, Custom Correct map, "Gray Wolf-Dosewallips", (61 mi., difficulty 42.94, 3 passes, deep forest, side trips, high country views in the heart of the mountains)

Summary: Dosewallips Trailhead, Dose Campground, Deception Creek, Gray Wolf Pass, Falls Camp, Cedar Lake, Gray Wolf Camp, Upper Cameron Camp, Cameron Pass, Lost Pass, Dose Meadows, Thousand Acre Meadow, Hayden Pass, Deception Creek, Dosewallips Trailhead.

To get to the trailhead take U.S. 101 to Brinnon on the Hood Canal. As you enter Brinnon, from the north, turn right onto the Dosewallips Road, Forest Service Road 2610. About 11 miles later you'll come to the trailhead. The old trailhead was at the Dosewallips Campground; however, a slide took out a portion of the road and as a result the trailhead is now about 6.5 miles from the campground. You'll be walking on the old road and at 6 miles you'll find Dose Falls to your left and a magnificent wall of pillow basalt on your right. The road continues up the right side of the falls and ends in the Dosewallips Campground, your destination for the day.

Another day begins, but no need to hurry. The trailhead is at the west end of the campground in what used to be a parking area and just beyond the Ranger Station. It's not hard to find. Your destination today is Deception Creek, an easy 6.7 miles and 2,000 feet of elevation up-trail from the Dose Campground. The trail is pleasant, the grade is easy. You'll cross two creeks, first Station Creek and then Pass Creek about a mile up-trail. Just before you get to Pass Creek keep a sharp eye out for a big conifer on your right next to the trail. It's my favorite tree on this trail. It sits patiently like a cat with its tail, its root, wrapped around its feet, its base. A half mile later you'll come to the Dose Forks junction. You'll want to take the trail to your right, the Dosewallips Trail. The trail straight ahead, is the West Fork Dosewallips River Trail that leads to Anderson Pass; not on your agenda for this loop. The Dose River Trail follows the river but seldom close enough to actually see it. Just over a mile, you'll come upon the junction with the Constance Pass Trail which passes through Sunnybrook Meadows.

Sometimes what seems like a good idea first disappoints and then becomes a plain disaster. Years back, Barbara, my wife, and I decided to take Barbara's friend on an overnight hike, the friend's first. I suggested Sunnybrook Meadows. I'd never been there and couldn't find anyone who could give me a description. Barbara and her friend trusted my experience and understanding of the backcountry. What

30. Cedar Lake, ONP

they didn't know was that I didn't have a clue as to what lay before us. We turned off the Dose Trail and started up and up and up. 4 miles and 3,000 feet later we all but crawled into Sunnybrook Meadows about two miles short of Constance Pass. The meadows amounted to a thin layer of soil over impermeable rock with almost a constant sheet of water trickling across its nearly uniform thirty-degree slope. I was dismayed and they wanted to kill me. After a fair amount of looking around I found just enough nearly flat ground for Barbara and friend. They immediately laid claim to it and I found two small trees some distance away that would block me from rolling down-meadow in the dark of night.

As long as we were in the area, I suggested a short hike up to Constance Pass and maybe Home Lake. Their mutual response, "go ahead"! By the time I got back they had turned in for the night. I wandered across the meadow, wrapped myself in a ground-cloth, snuggled up to my two guardian trees and went to sleep. Morning broke and the only words I heard were, "let's get out of here". To this day I'm still held responsible for maybe the worst first hike on record for Barbara's friend.

Moving up-trail you'll first cross Lower Twin Creek, then Upper Twin Creek and Slide Creek in that order. About a quarter mile beyond Hawk Creek, the next creek after Slide Creek, search for a break in the trees and catch a glimpse of Hatana Falls on Hidden

Creek directly across the valley. It falls near vertically on its 1,200-foot plunge running to the Dose. Its' source is snow melt off of Diamond Mountain at 6,822 ft., about 4,800 feet above you to the southwest. Although Hidden Creek isn't one of them, numerous meltwater streams run underground at some point. The water seeps into the ground at elevation, migrates downward through the soils and out of sight, until it meets and follows the slope of an impervious layer which forces the water to breach the valley wall seemingly erupting from nowhere. You can actually hear it before you can see it. It's quite a sight, a demonstration of the raw power and sublime beauty of the wilderness.

At this point you're about half way to Deception Creek. Just beyond Burdick Creek, the next creek crossing ahead, you'll enter what looks like a disaster area. The terrain flattens out and across the valley you can see the Silt Creek Canyon. Years ago, a microburst wind swept down upon this area, channeled into a turbulent and fierce windstorm created by the confluence of the Dose Valley and Silt Creek Canyon. The forest was literally blown flat, and as such, the trail twists and turns through the old growth dead-fall and up-ended stumps.

A mile farther on you'll arrive at Deception Creek. It was in 1986 that Barbara and I first met Robert Wood as he sat resting in this camp. Robert Wood is one of the few hikers I know who have hiked every mile of every trail in Olympic National Park, in both directions. For us, it was like meeting Elvis. Robert Wood wrote the book, "Olympic Mountains Trail Guide", the standard on backpacking in the Olympic Mountains. Our meeting on that day was not long but certainly memorable. Moreover, it was the beginning of a hiking-partner relationship, that lasted a few years, never to be forgotten.

The unique aura of these mountains lured and captivated the legendary like: The Iron Man of the Hoh, John Huelsdonk , the Olympic College Climbing Class, the nation's oldest mountaineering course, Minnie Peterson known as "The Packer", along with her horses, guided clients for 50 years, Jack Hughes, the quintessential ONP Ranger, Ruby Hult, the prescient author of "The Untamed Olympics", Ross Hamilton, the "Ansel Adams of the Olympic Mountains", Rowland W. Tabor author of "Guide to the Geology of Olympic National Park and Robert L. Wood who inspired us with "Olympic Mountains Trail Guide". I'm fortunate to have met most and learned from all of them.

Deception Creek is just below the 3,500-foot demarcation line in the Park wherein above this point no fires, only stoves are allowed. You won't fall below the line again until you reach Three Forks 14.4 miles up and over Gray Wolf Pass. The bear wire at Deception Creek is down.

Daybreak and back on the trail. The junction with the Gray Wolf Trail lies 1.4 miles up-trail. As you approach the junction, the valley ahead begins to broaden and swing around to the west. You won't be going that far, however. At the junction you'll head due east as you begin the 3.5 mile and 2,500 ft of elevation gain to the top of Gray Wolf Pass. Reaching the pass, it's time for a break. Even though the pass is at 6,100 ft. everything to the west, the south and the east is between 700 and 1,000 feet above you. Around the compass there are 13 peaks within that range. You truly have, a first-class perch in the heart of the Park.

Your descent into the Gray Wolf Valley begins. The first mile crosses open alpine meadows and exposed rock as it loses about 1,000 feet before the trail gets steep. In the next half mile, you'll lose over 500 feet and then it contours the east wall of the Gray Wolf Valley. It switchbacks quickly down to the Gray Wolf River and the grade eases to complete the day's 9 mile hike at Falls Camp.

If you're interested in a rest day, Falls Camp is a suitable place. The opportunity exists, if you're up for it, to hike 2.1 miles up Cedar Creek to Cedar Lake. Cedar Lake sits in a bowl with 1,000 foot walls surrounding it on three sides. I suspect that this is the end result of the glacier that carved those walls and left us Cedar Lake, as we know it today.

Rested or not, your next destination is Gray Wolf Camp 5.4 miles down-trail. The trail closely follows the river and the elevation loss is evenly spread over the mileage. Three Forks, at the confluence of the Gray Wolf River, Cameron Creek and Grand Creek, is surrounded by the noses of four major ridges. As such, it tends to be a cold camp where the sun's warmth is brief and arrives late in the morning, at best, or not at all. The good news is there's all the water you could ever want. Make sure to boil, treat or filter all of it; Giardia is everywhere.

It's morning and time to get up, clean up and get ready to move on to delightful Cameron Basin. The grade up-trail on Cameron Creek, heading southeast is as pleasant as yesterday's descent of the Gray Wolf. The grade is steady and comfortable with the first 7 miles gaining only 2,000 feet. At the 7 mile point you'll come to the junction of the Grand Pass Trail on your right, but your destination is a little over 2 miles away straight ahead to Upper Cameron Camp in Cameron Basin.

Cameron Basin is exquisite. The broad open meadow cut through by Cameron Creek is nestled between two rock ridges spreading north from Mt. Cameron at 7190 ft. directly south. To the southwest is Cameron Pass, a piece of tomorrow's objective. The Basin is a quiet place, home to deer, marmots, elk, ravens, and grey jays. A murmuring creek flowing softly as it passes by adds the gentlest of sounds, an embellishment to the hues, shapes and contrasts of a living canvas, an ambiance in which you will rest at this day's end.

As you leave the basin, the trail, such as it is, soon grows faint and then disappears into the scree that comprises the lower portion of the basin's walls. Cameron Pass is the low point between two distinct prominences about a mile west of Mt. Cameron itself. Route finding can be difficult and slow-going. The pass is a less trafficked area in Olympic National Park and as such you may have to depend on cairns, but you're likely to find the trail easy to follow. While some cairns are a foot or two tall and easy to spot, some are mere inches in height, or have disappeared entirely. The cairns that exist are the gifts of previous hikers. Ensure that you don't knock over a cairn and replace it if you do. Those who will come after you will appreciate the effort. Move from cairn to cairn stopping at each to find the next and plan a route to it. Consider the slow pace a gift as you climb 1,200 feet out of the basin and gain the last 500 feet of that in the last quarter mile.

Reaching the pass at 6,950 ft., you'll find the western slope to be broad and the grade fairly gentle. The first time Barbara and I topped Cameron Pass we were met by a browsing bull elk, who couldn't have cared less and a short distance thereafter a large boar Black Bear; happily lounging in his solitude. Always remember to give wildlife space; the Park's standard is 50 yards. The trail turns left and heads through a number of small down-slope meadows which teem with wildflowers in late July. It's 1.9 miles from Cameron Pass to Lost Pass, your next objective. The good news is that Lost Pass is about 500 feet lower than Cameron Pass.

Lost Pass is a good place to drop your gear and take a break. The view is great. To the southwest is Mt. Claywood, at 6,836 ft. and just to its left is Mt. Fromme, at 6,705 ft. Due south is Sentinel Peak, at 6,592 ft. and to the southeast is Wellesley Peak, at 6,758 ft. some three miles off. Finally, due east is Mt. Deception, at 7,788 ft. the source for Deception Creek that ran through Deception Camp several days back.

The south slope of Lost Pass is short and steep. You'll lose 1,500 feet in less than a mile. Along the way there are a few big rocks on the trail that require a knee-high step on the down-trail side. At the bottom of the slope, you'll rejoin the Dosewallips Trail. Turn right and move up-trail a bit. In short order you'll come to Dose Meadows, your camp for the night.

Tomorrow you'll start on your way down the Dose and back to the trailhead. In my estimation it would be an excruciating day if you hiked all the way out. Barbara and I have done the 14 miles to the Dose Campground and it wasn't fun; 17 miles in one day is beyond most everyone. I suggest one of two alternatives: you could hike the first day 10.4 miles to Dose Forks and on the second day hike the remaining 7.9 miles back to the trailhead, or take three days to hike out. If you elect the latter, I suggest that the morning of the first day you hike the 2.3 miles up-trail to Hayden Pass going by Thousand Acre Meadow, enjoying the peaks surrounding the pass and getting a peek into the Upper Elwha Valley to the west. After that short hike back to Dose Meadows, pack-up and head down the Dose to Deception Camp about 4.8 miles away. On day-two hike the 8 miles down to the Dosewallips Campground and then finish the loop on day-three with the remaining 6.5 miles out to the trailhead. Your choice!

However, you finished the loop, the important point is that you did it. Just over 61 miles, not counting your side trips. That's a lot of hiking. I truly hope you enjoyed the experience. Some days were longer or tougher than others, but you managed, met all the challenges topographic or otherwise, and got a taste for the more remote areas in the Olympic Mountains. This is not a land for the faint-of-heart but it is a place to test and grow your stamina, your appreciation of the wonders that await and the breathtaking raw beauty the Olympic Mountains have to offer.

Sundown Lake – O'Neil Pass Loop

SE Quadrant, Custom Correct maps, "Mount Skokomish-Lake Cushman", "Enchanted Valley-Skokomish" and "The Brothers-Mt. Anderson" (68 miles, difficulty Anderson 76.79 or O'Neil 53.58, lush valleys, high ridges, alpine lakes, perhaps a ford or two)

Summary: Staircase Trailhead, Six Ridge, Lake Sundown, Graves Creek, Enchanted Valley, O'Neil Pass, (Anderson Pass, La Crosse Pass, ford the Duckabush), First Divide, Skokomish Valley, Staircase Trailhead.

If you are considering this loop that includes fording, you should: consult with the Wilderness Information Desk in the Olympic National Park Visitor Center in Port Angeles. I suggest you do a web search for "Stream Crossing Techniques" and read the National Park Service's web-available "Safe River Crossings" and 'Swiftwater Rescue Manual" The Rangers in the Park's Wilderness Information Center can advise you as to the advisability of your plans. In addition, you should consult the USGS website for current water conditions. Also, if you visit online the State of Washington Dept. of Ecology, River and Stream Flow Monitoring page, you can compare years of data and thereby compare it to the weather pattern in any year against the weather pattern in the current year. By doing so you'll have a better sense of what the fording conditions may be. These searches will allow you to choose your hike based on the available data.

Loop hikes in the Olympic Mountains come in all sizes and some with alternatives; this loop has both. The Sundown Lake-O'Neil Pass Loop starts at the North Fork Skokomish River Trailhead less than an hour's drive from Hoodsport on U.S. 101. There's a big brown sign in Hoodsport that points you to Lake Cushman. Take the Lake Cushman Road to the lake. After following the lake for a while, it will veer away. Stay on the road until you come to a "T" intersection. At that intersection turn left on Forest Service Road 24. The FS Road 24 turns to gravel before it returns to asphalt as it enters Olympic National Park and ends at the Staircase Ranger Station adjacent to the campground. The trailhead is at the ranger station, in fact there are two trails that start there. Do not cross the bridge! Take the trail straight ahead on the east side of the North Fork Skokomish River.

If you haven't noticed already, you're about to spend the next few days in a verdant old-growth forest composed primarily of western redcedar, Douglas fir (really a pine species) and western hemlock. These giants of the forest are joined by rhododendrons, sword ferns, lichens, moss and abundant wildlife. The wildlife, except the deer flies and mosquitoes, are for the most part shy and skittish. Even though

31. La Crosse Basin, ONP

the Park has had very few adverse animal-human encounters, please remember to give any animal you come across its space. Want a better picture, bring a longer lens. Wildlife is hardwired into fight or flight. Crowd them into a space from which they can't retreat and you're in for a nasty surprise, not to mention possibly prematurely ending this wonderous loop hike. You'll have a better than average chance at seeing any or maybe all of the following: Roosevelt Elk, Black Bear, Olympic Marmot, river otter, bobcat, eagles, ravens, and most likely hear but not see multitudes of song birds. One bird I know you'll come across but not see is the Pacific wren. Barbara, my wife, and I hiked for years in the low forests entertained by, but never seeing, what we called "Happy-Bird" sharing the longest song in the forest. It's a true audio treat!

This Loop Hike has two alternative routes. The "Passes and Fords" alternative comprises Staircase to Graves Creek to Anderson Pass to La Crosse Pass to the Duckabush ford to First Divide and back to Staircase; 68 miles in total. I'll take time to describe the "non-ford" alternative which crosses O'Neil Pass, when this narrative has you just beyond the Enchanted Valley Chalet, on the Quinault River. The alternative omits a fording of the Duckabush River, then travels over the First Divide and back to Staircase. Again, about 68 miles total.

Moving up-trail 5.3 miles to Big Log Camp, you'll notice, with the exception of the first mile, one of the lushest forests in the Olympic Mountains. A thousand shades of green, accented by the unending textures of various plants all bathed in the murmur of the North Fork

Skokomish River, flowing placidly on its eternal journey from the mountains to the sea. Today's hike ends at Big Log Camp. The purpose of this short first day was to get you settled in and give you a chance to get comfortable with your gear. Tomorrow will be a long day.

Tomorrow's here and she's ready for the day; are you? Leaving Big Log and moving up-trail a short half mile, you'll cross the river and intersect with the Six Ridge Trail on your left. The Six Ridge Trail is difficult primarily because it gets little use and less maintenance. The Six Ridge Trail works its way down-stream at first and then takes you from the bottom of the Skokomish Valley up a difficult and switchback-laden climb to 3,500 feet in under two miles. The good news, the rest of the trail sticks to the top of Six Ridge staying at just about the 4,000-foot level. Climbing out of the valley, at the end of the switchbacks, you'll crest the ridge traveling through subalpine forest until the trail nearly reaches treeline about a half mile short of Belview. This trail is difficult between Six Ridge Pass and the Lake Success junction. The confusion of game trails requires good navigation skills. Arriving at Belview you'll be treated to a lush alpine meadow; it's time for a break.

The broken ridge about 2 miles to the south, the far side of the Six Stream Valley, is approximately the division between Olympic National Park and the Olympic National Forest. Just south of the division, in the Olympic National Forest lies the Wonder Mountain Wilderness, a trail-less, primitive place of deep solitude. Behind the ridge directly to the north is Lake Success. Way-finding over a 5,000-foot pass and across the 2.4miles between the Six Ridge Trail and Lake Success is a challenge better saved for another day.

Resisting the urge to linger in the beautiful setting of Belview's meadow, reality strikes and it's time to move on. Lake Sundown, today's camp is 5 miles southwest toward the western end of Six Ridge. The trail stays just at treeline treating you to views south. At the 3 mile mark you'll pass by McGravey Lakes, another chance to rest and your first water source since you left the North Fork Skokomish River at Big Log Camp. Lake Sundown is just 2 miles down-trail slightly, below your current elevation, but low enough to put you back in the forest until you arrive at the lake.

You've put in a 10.6-mile day and you deserve to rest and enjoy the view, hopefully including a great sunset to finish the day. Lake Sundown sits in a glacial-carved bench at the southwest end of Six Ridge and the northwest end of an unnamed broken ridge running southeast to the Park boundary. If you've got the energy, after dinner take a short trek to the Wynoochee Pass-Graves Creek Trail intersection. Turning left you'll find Sundown Pass a half mile farther on. From Sundown Pass you have an unobstructed view of the South Fork of the Skokomish running to the southeast. Capitol Peak at 5,054 ft. is about 3 miles due south and Mount Tebo at 4,654 ft. is six miles to the southeast. Back to camp and a good night's rest. Tomorrow you'll lose most of today's hard-won elevation as you descend to the Quinault River Trail.

Tomorrow arrives and off you go. As the trail leaves Lake Sundown, it switchbacks steeply down to the junction of the Wynoochee Pass-Graves Creek Trail 1.6 miles and 1,200 feet below the lake. Heading down-trail to the north, the Graves Creek Trail loses elevation slowly for 2 miles, drops 500 feet in a flurry of switchbacks and then returns to following the creek down-stream. The remaining 3 miles lose another 900 feet and join the Quinault Trail a stone's throw east of the Graves Creek Campground and the Graves Creek Trailhead. Turn right up-trail through the Quinault Rain Forest a little over 2 miles to Pony Bridge, your refuge for the night.

Pony Bridge moves the trail from the south to the north bank of the river. That's important, but what's spectacular is the setting. On a blue-sky day far below the Rain Forest canopy, the crossing is in deep shade and engulfed in a thousand shades of green, common in the Rain Forest. With persistence, the sun pierces the canopy when a combination of holes at different levels fall into alignment. The result? Splashes of golden sunlight spread across small patches of green and as the earth rotates, they close and open, extinguishing the light here and initiating it anew there. This light show continues for most of a cloudless day.

The Rain Forest holds a tremendous biomass. There is so much that wants to grow in this region of the Park that a plant's desire, its need to take root, outstrips the supply of raw earth in which to do so. Plants like the Licorice Root Fern, (Polypodium glycyrrhiza) an epiphyte, take root on other plants. For the Licorice Fern, it's the moss on the big leaf maple trees (Acer Macrophyllum). You'll find these ferns sticking out of the moss. They're about five inches tall and if you pull one out and chew its root it tastes just like licorice but without the sugar. There are an abundance of plants and animals in the Olympic Rain Forest. Why not; it's a virgin and protected ecosystem. The soils are deep, having avoided continental glaciation, the temperatures are temperate, thanks to its neighbor the Pacific Ocean, and the rainfall is abundant, over 135 inches a year, every year. As such, the Rain Forest environment does prompt you to have wet weather gear handy. Such a small price for the reward of visiting one of only six temperate rain forests on earth.

It's tomorrow already and you're back on the trail. This day's goal is the Enchanted Valley 10.5 miles up the river. Water's no problem, even without the Quinault, there are over a dozen streams and streamlets along the way, a few with names and some patiently waiting for one. The grade couldn't be more accommodating rising slightly over

1,000 feet across the miles between Pony Bridge and the Enchanted Valley. For the most part, the trail wanders up the river bottom. Because of the amount of exposure, on a sunny day it can get hot. Just above Pyrites Creek the valley narrows and the trail contours along the bottom of the valley's north wall. About a mile farther on the trail crosses a bridge to the south side of the river and enters Enchanted Valley.

The Enchanted Valley lies at about 2,000 feet of elevation. Its broad bottom is a maze of present and past channels that the Quinault has carved over the ages. It meanders back and forth never staying in one channel for very long. On your right about half way up the valley you'll see the Enchanted Valley Chalet, a summer-only ranger station from 1954-2013; it is now closed. More importantly, the chalet was placed on the National Historic Register in 2007. It was built in the early 1930's as a destination lodge for commercial tourism, a booming business in the early 1900's. As of this writing, 2022, the Park is considering quotas for camping in the valley. You may want to contact the Wilderness Information Center regarding quotas.

The river, moving around as it does, started to progressively encroach on the chalet in the early 2000's threatening its stability and very existence. After many discussions and ideas about how to save this national treasure, in 2017 the Park decided to move it about a hundred feet to the southern edge of the valley. They were granted permission but the question was how to move it. Enchanted Valley is within the area protected by a wilderness designation. As such, mechanized equipment, other than emergency rescue equipment, is prohibited only hand tools and human power is allowed.

Facing this monumental task with its withering requirements, the Park's Rangers set themselves to a task that must have looked to them as an exponential challenge. With the help of a contractor, they raised the chalet off its foundation and placed beams beneath the structure. Using chains, "come-alongs", a form of ratcheted cables and pulleys, and hydraulic jacks, they winched the chalet inch-by-inch to the base of the south wall of the valley floor. Finally, their repositioning work done, the chalet was, for the time being, out of the path of the Quinault. Everyone associated with or following this human miracle breathed a sigh of relief.

The river has continued its advance! Although it once again came too close for comfort, as of this writing, it has been meandering away, towards the north, on its endless journey. Will it return? Absolutely. The National Park Service is evaluating alternatives, the most likely of which may be the chalet's removal. As of this writing no final determination has been made

Looking north, you face a steep glacier carved wall, the southern buttress of Chimney Peak at 6,917 ft. This 3,000-4,000 foot wall is a spring melt-off treat, lending the Enchanted Valley the moniker "Valley of 10,000 Waterfalls". In late spring and early summer, the snowpack high above melts into hundreds of falls and rivulets, cascading off the wall to the valley floor in a gravity-fueled extravaganza, as the high-country sheds its winter's cloak.

The murmur of water flowing is everywhere in the valley, round the clock. It acts as a backdrop to the peacefulness. Sleep well in this Enchanted Valley, tomorrow is just hours away and a decision will be at hand; shorter or longer, one pass or two and how do you feel about fording the Duckabush River? I've used shorter and longer as a means to differentiate between the choices; in truth, they are about the same length but have distinctly different challenges.

The "O'Neil Pass" alternative. Inevitably morning breaks and it's time to get organized for the day's hike. You've decided to take the "O'Neil Pass" version of this loop. Today's order of march is first to Bull Elk Basin about 3 miles away and then up and on to La Crosse Basin 7.6 miles farther on. This will be one of the longer and harder day's travels on this shorter loop.

As you move up-valley it narrows and swings east as it starts to gain elevation. Near the next stream crossing you'll come upon a spur trail to your left. Will you spend a few minutes to take this short side trip and see the largest western hemlock in the world? I hope you do. It's a living monument and remarkably so, considering that it's at the eastern and elevation edge of the Rain Forest environment. Above this point first subalpine and then true alpine environs take hold.

Back on the trail and a short distance ahead, it's time to execute your short loop decision. You've arrived at the junction of the O'Neil Pass Trail on your right; turn right and press on. Turning right, you'll climb a short way into Bull Elk Basin, a beautiful subalpine basin crowded with heather and spotted with clumps of trees. Look southeast high on the ridgeline and you'll see a notch at the top of an extremely steep ravine. You're looking at Fisher's Notch. Believe it or not, rangers used this as a shortcut between La Crosse Basin, your destination for today, and the Quinault Valley. I'm not at all that daring and I'd advise you to look, but not attempt, this outlandish route.

The trail crosses the basin, then crosses White Creek. The first mile beyond White Creek gains 700 feet of elevation before the trail settles down to a less heart-pounding climb, as you rise above Enchanted Valley and up to O'Neil Pass 6.5 miles father on. Reaching the pass, proceed another long mile to Marmot Lake and the glory of La Crosse Basin, one of the most idyllic places in the Park. The basin is worthy of a layover day, including a better look from O'Neil Pass and the 270° view it affords. Take your map and compass; you'll need it for peak-finding. There are a number of lakes and tarns in La Crosse

Basin. As you explore, keep track of your position relative to Marmot Lake. Otherwise, you might end up roaming around; oh, so much more than you might have planned. The bear wires are down at Marmot Lake and Bear Cannisters are required.

It's a hiking day again and today you'll first lose all this hard-won elevation just for the chance to regain it again headed for Home Sweet Home. On the trail down to the Duckabush River the high-country view gives way to a healthy subalpine forest. 3.4 miles down-trail you'll come to the junction with the Home Sweet Home trail on your right. You are now standing opposite the Upper Duckabush Camp on the far bank and facing the ford you chose not to chance.

The "Anderson Pass" alternative. You've elected the "Anderson Pass" alternative route. Your decision requires two fordings and the "you-won't-know-till-you-get-there" possibility of how difficult an experience that may be. As you move out of the Valley about a mile and a quarter, you'll come to a spur trail on your left. If you follow it, in short order you'll be face to face with the largest western hemlock in the world. Back on the trail to Anderson Pass and about a mile farther on you'll find the intersection of the O'Neil Pass Trail on your right. Move straight ahead toward Anderson Pass 1.7 miles farther on and 1,500 ft above where you stand.

Regardless of your predetermined decision; I'll point out the rough parts now and save the beautiful parts for later. As you start up Anderson Pass, within the first mile you'll arrive at an unnamed creek, your first fording. The difficulty of fording this creek is directly tied to the time of year, last winter's snow pack and your definition of difficult. If the snow pack was substantial and it's earlier than later in the summer, the creek can run like a raging bull at the ford, making it very difficult if not impossible to ford. Bush-whacking either up or down stream is both futile and seriously dissatisfying. There is no better place to ford this creek than where you now stand. Consider the challenge and danger associated with the decision you're about to make. If the creek is running like a raging bull, remember that at this point you're only a mile up-trail from an alternative that doesn't pose such a risk. Finally, if this creek is running high and strong, I'd bet that the Duckabush River isn't going to treat you any better. Hopefully conditions are more favorable upon your arrival.

The rise to the pass from here is a leg-burner; take breaks and drink plenty of water. Gaining the pass, your stop for the night is Camp Siberia about a mile and a half ahead. Camp Siberia and this short day is the alternative to hiking over La Crosse Pass to Upper Duckabush Camp some 8.2 miles ahead. If you stay at Siberia, you'll have time to go back up to Anderson Pass and hike the spur trail on the right to a prominence overlooking what used to be the Anderson Glacier years ago. Climate change, you bet! This Glacier had been in place for over 2.6 million years but within a few decades it's gone and has been replaced with the stark scene that lies before you.

Back on the trail next morning. Today you'll climb 2,000 feet over La Crosse Pass, 3.1 miles up and 3.3 miles down the other side to the Duckabush River. From there you'll head up-stream 1.8 miles to Upper Duckabush Camp. This is another long hard day, so take a break at the pass; get out your map and identify the eight named peaks awaiting your curious gaze. Remember La Crosse Pass is at 5,566 ft., so all the peaks you're looking for are at higher elevations.

Before fording, you should: consult with the Wilderness Information Desk in the Olympic National Park Visitor Center in Port Angeles. I suggest you do a web search for "Stream Crossing Techniques" and read the National Park Service's web-available "Safe River Crossings" and 'Swiftwater Rescue Manual" The Rangers in the Park's Wilderness Information Center can advise you as to the advisability of your plans. In addition, you should consult the USGS website for current water conditions. Also, if you visit online the State of Washington Dept. of Ecology, River and Stream Flow Monitoring page, you can compare years of data and thereby compare it to the weather pattern in any year against the weather pattern in the current year. By doing so you'll have a better sense of what the fording conditions may be. These searches will allow you to choose your hike based on the available data.

After you arrive at Upper Duckabush Camp, spend some time, after you've set up camp, finding your fording location for tomorrow. Just like the previous fording of the unnamed creek, the Upper Duckabush, based on conditions, can pose some level of difficulty. The same reasoning applies: snowpack, recent rains and the time of year. If the Duckabush is not fordable, you have two tough choices. You can either hike down the Duckabush and find a way back to Staircase or retrace your steps and traverse O'Neil Pass, ending up on the opposite bank. Remember this, the Park has lost more than one fording hiker in its history. Your mortality is always on the line in the wilderness. Refer to the Resource Page on fording.

It's tomorrow and assuming you've forded the Duckabush River, the rest of your day is a pleasant climb to Home Sweet Home just short of First Divide. Good, bad or otherwise you've got 1,500 feet and 2.1 miles beyond the Duckabush ford before you reach Home Sweet Home. You climb out of the uppermost limits of lowland forest and enter the subalpine zone where life for flora and fauna is a seasonal fight for survival in which some win, some lose and none are unaffected.

Home Sweet Home sits at the head of an alpine meadow; a place, fit for Heidi and Grandfather, right out of Johanna Spyri's storybook, "Heidi". The view due west is back up to O'Neil Pass. You're nearing the end of this loop and hopefully this evening's sunset will be cloaking the mountains and valleys in spectacular light. Surrounded by beauty and friendship you may be inspired to share some of your previous backpacking experiences; don't be shy, go ahead and embellish a bit.

Yesterday's gone and today breaks. Your trail today goes over First Divide a short mile up-trail and then drops into the North Fork Skokomish drainage 6.8 miles back to Big Log Camp. As you proceed down the "Skok" you'll pass Two Bear Camp and then Nine Stream Camp. Go ahead and ask; are the streams really numbered? The answer is, yes, the streams are numbered. There are nine of them on the way back to Staircase; imagine that! There is a wash-out near Camp Pleasant that will require minor route-finding skills.

Have you heard or seen a grouse yet? In my view grouse are one of the oddest birds in the Park. They'd rather walk than fly. They have an affinity for viewing their surroundings from downed trees, far enough off the ground to not get surprised, but close enough to forage. Surprise, they don't sing or chirp, they grunt. Listen carefully, that noise may not be your partner's growling stomach.

Leaving Big Log, this last morning on the trail, you've got an easy 5.3 miles between camp and the trailhead. You most likely were aware, but if you didn't know then you do now, there's a big difference between tough and easy, high and low and wet or dry. Welcome to the Daniel J. Evans Wilderness. I hope you liked it enough to return some day.

You've just completed a minimum of 68 miles. If you extended the loop via Anderson Pass, La Crosse Pass and then got turned back by the raging Duckabush you've covered at least 86 miles, if not more, depending on your route. Either way you deserve the "Silver Boot" award for self-exposure to long trail backpacking and all the beautiful and a bit of the ugly that came with it. You've now joined a very special group of Olympic Mountain hikers. By the way you can drop your pack while I sing more of your praises. My hat's off to you!

Loop Hikes Done in Over 10 Days

High Country – Elwha Loop

NW & SW Quadrants, Custom Correct Maps, "Elwha Valley" and "Quinault – Colonel Bob", (98 mi., difficulty 92.72**, long days, a difficult route, way-finding, dry camps, great alpine views, a fording, steep climbs and descents, up and down 11,000 ft.)**

Summary: Whiskey Bend Trailhead, Humes Ranch, Dodger Point, Elwha ford, Remann's Cabin, Camp Wilder, Low Divide, Lake Beauty, Kimta Peak, Three Prune, Kurtz Lake, Elip Creek, Sixteen Mile Camp, Chicago Camp, Hayes River, Mary's Falls Camp, Whiskey Bend Trailhead

The trailhead for this loop is Whiskey Bend. That said, as of this writing, 2022, a washout out on the Olympic Hot Springs Road has caused the Olympic National Park to establish a temporary trailhead on the Olympic Hot Springs Road at Madison Falls about 1.5 miles off of U.S. 101 and 8 miles distant from Whiskey Bend. Either way, turn left off of U.S. 101, 15 minutes west of Port Angeles, where U.S. 101 slows to 25mph and turns abruptly right to cross the Elwha Bridge. Don't cross the Bridge!

Depending on whether or not the road has been repaired, your first day may be a hike up the Olympic Hot Springs Road. Just beyond the Elwha Ranger Station the Whiskey Bend, a gravel road, spurs to your left. At the end of the Whiskey Bend Road is a turnaround parking area and the Whiskey Bend Trailhead proper. Your first of many choices on this hike occurs 1.2 miles up-trail where you could move straight ahead or turn right and drop down to Rica Canyon and Goblin Gates. After visiting Goblin Gates you'll be following the river up-stream to Humes Ranch. If your choice was to move straight ahead, you'll press on to Michael's Cabin. Turn right and after another short mile, you'll turn right again and drop down to Humes Ranch. Either way, from the trailhead to Humes Ranch is a distance of about 3.5 miles. The campsite is in a relative flat area below the cabin and nearer the Elwha which was the Humes' Garden in the day.

Morning puts you back on the trail climbing the Long Ridge Trail to Dodger Point. Several items of importance, Dodger Point is at times a dry camp; alpine tarns exist but only until the summer's heat dries them to dirt. Make sure to carry enough water for today and tomorrow. Long Ridge is long and exposed; today is going to be tough. You've got 11 miles and 4,850 feet of elevation ahead of you, primarily steep and rocky.

From Humes Ranch to the Long Ridge Trail Bridge, across the Elwha, is a half mile. A short stretch of this part of the trail crosses above a landslide that periodically reoccurs. As the old trail slides

32. Mt. Olympus from Dodger Point, ONP

away a new section is built above the slide and with each rebuild the grade down to the bridge has gotten steeper over time. As you cross the bridge to your left is the bottom end of Convolution Canyon a part of the Grand Canyon of the Elwha, a deadly serious class VI and V run demanding expert kayaking skills and experience. To your right is Geyser Valley. There are no geysers, but as you can see, the breadth and power of the river is on display as it sorts the smallest to the biggest rocks with great efficiency.

Leaving the bridge headed west the Long Ridge Trail is at first deceptive, climbing only a few hundred feet over the course of its initial mile. Don't think that the rest of the trail will be as kind. The next five miles will strain your legs as well as your lungs before the grade lessens a bit above 3,500 feet. The last 4.5 miles tracks through the last of the low elevation forest as progressively an alpine environment begins to show itself.

At 10.5 miles you'll come to a junction. Dodger Point is half a mile to your left and 500 feet above you. The trail to the right leads to a tarn and a small creek, if they haven't gone bone dry.

The views from Dodger Point are exquisite. Robert Wood, the author of "Olympic Mountains Trail Guide", an information masterpiece born out of his keen eye and a dedication to detail, said, "...Dodger Point is one of the superlative viewpoints in the Olympics and the 360-degree panorama is outstanding." Near and far all around the compass, peaks are visible from Mt. Angeles to the north then circling to your right, Elk Mountain, Windfall Peak, McCartney Peak, Mts. Cameron, Claywood, Norton, Dana, Wilder, Scott, Ludden Peak, Stephen Peak and Mt. Olympus.

If you are considering fording the Elwha, you should: consult with the Wilderness Information Desk in the Olympic National Park Visitor Center in Port Angeles. I suggest you do a web search for "Stream Crossing Techniques" and read the National Park Service's web-available "Safe River Crossings" and 'Swiftwater Rescue Manual" The Rangers in the Park's Wilderness Information Center can advise you as to the advisability of your plans. In addition, you should consult the USGS website for current water conditions. Also, if you visit online the State of Washington Dept. of Ecology, River and Stream Flow Monitoring page, you can compare years of data and thereby compare it to the weather pattern in any year against the weather pattern in the current year. By doing so you'll have a better sense of what the fording conditions may be. These searches will allow you to choose your hike based on the available data.

The sun's up and it's time to depart and head down-trail to a fording of the Elwha at Remman's Cabin, losing nearly all of the 4,500 feet of elevation you gained yesterday. Starting down-trail to the Elwha you'll find the tarn. The trail swings hard left and the day's challenges begin. The descending route is identified as a way-trail. It is seldom used due to the combined difficulties of way-finding and the fording of the Elwha. Early on in the history of this area blazes in trees and colored flags helped mark the way. Very few of the blazes remain, the reason being evident by the amount of dead fall in the forest. Flags have been banned for decades; I doubt you'll see any. That leaves cairns as the only on-the-ground assistance which may be available to you.

If you are not comfortable with your ability to meet this challenge, you should not attempt this loop. On the other hand, if you intend to move forward, you'll need to spend a good deal of time studying, in great detail, a quality topographic map and know how to read a compass. You'll come to a point down-trail where being able to orient your physical position relative to compass bearings will mean the difference between success and failure.

Let me just put this in your face! If you're good at reading maps, know your compass skills and have a keen eye for the surrounding topography you'll manage this route with some difficulty. Anything less in your skill department will result in you throwing in the towel semi-lost in the woods with only one remaining clue still working for you; Dodger Point is uphill to the northwest! Return there and hike out the way you came in.

If you're moving forward down to the Elwha, as you leave the tarn the trail initially heads east then swings to the southeast and skirts below a scree field just below Dodger Point. You'll lose about 800 feet by the end of the first mile, marked by crossing over the bottom quarter of a narrow treeless overgrown avalanche chute.

The next mile drops at about the same rate. At the end of about two miles, you'll find yourself starting to steeply descend the south-facing nose of Long Ridge. Stop! Before you descend you need to read the lay of the land before you. Facing you across the valley is the north-facing nose of a buttress on Mt. Dana to your south. On either side of the buttress there is a valley. The correct start point for the descent is when the Elwha River, which is to your left in the direction of south-southeast, and the river to your right, the Goldie River, is aligned in the direction of south-southwest; a spread of 50 degrees. Move right or left until these two rivers appear in the orientation described.

The descent is steep. It swings first to the east, then back to the west and then it drops straight down toward the Goldie, losing about 400 feet of elevation. At that point it abruptly turns east losing elevation more gradually and contours around the nose of Long Ridge for the last time. The trail then begins to swing north as it crosses the Semple Plateau, loses less than 500 feet in the last mile and delivers you to the west bank of the Elwha, in the vicinity of Remann's Cabin on the opposite bank.

Up and down stream a short distance from Remann's Cabin you'll find gravel bars and hopefully fordable places in the late summer and early fall when flow rates on the Elwha are at their lowest. Fording is serious business. Refer to the Resource Page in the Appendix for fording. Hikers have lost their lives attempting fords. Choose wisely; your well-being depends on your choices. Good news, you're across the Elwha and Remann's Cabin is your destination today.

On the trail again in the morning, your hike will be long, 9.8 miles but with little net elevation gain. Camp Wilder is half of a two-day break from steep trails. In the second day you'll cover another 8.1 miles, the last 2 of which climb 1,400 feet to your destination, Low Divide. Camping is not allowed at the lakes but is allowed at Low Divide.

As it was on Dodger Point, anything above 3,500 feet is stoves only, no open fires are permitted. This will be true for the next several days. As you leave Lake Margaret headed west, you'll begin the roughest part of this loop. A half mile below the lake you'll cross the North Fork Quinault River, albeit a small creek at the crossing point. A few hundred yards later you'll find the northern end of the Skyline Trail on your right. Bear cannisters are required on the Skyline Trail. Turn right. Lake Beauty is your destination 7.6 miles and a steep climb up, down, up, down and up again all to gain a little over 1,500 feet. This is your introduction to one of the toughest way-trails in the Olympic Mountains. Depending on how late in the season and the amount of snow delivered to the Sky Line Ridge last winter, Lake Beauty may be the last water available to you for the following two days. Lake Beauty marks the end of anything like a trail on the Sky Line. From Lake Beauty to Three Prune is way-finding territory. Kimta Peak is in the middle of this stretch and definitely qualifies as dry; Three Prune can be so as well.

Heading for Kimta Peak will test your way-finding skills and your strength. The trail is poorly marked by cairns in some places and very old blazes in trees. Take your time and refer constantly to your map, compass and altimeter. There are numerous game trails in the area. They are confusing and are not likely to lead you to Kimta Peak.

From Lake Beauty the trail heads southwest, a short mile then turns south and drops through Hee Haw Pass a notch in the ridge that you've been following on your left. The trail drops down and then runs southwest again bobbing up and down across the rocky east face of the Sky Line Ridge to the nose of a buttress. At the buttress the trail is very near the crest of the down-sloping nose and high above the head of Promise Creek. At that point it drops very steeply losing about 500 feet over a quarter mile.

At the bottom of the steep drop the trail heads southwest and switchbacks down a second steep pitch. It then swings to a mostly westerly heading and contours what is now the south face of the Sky Line Ridge. The trail swings around to the south just below Kimta Peak at 5,399 feet and just above the ravine carrying Kimta Creek down to the North Fork Quinault. Start looking for a suitable campsite, flat clear ground is at a premium around Kimta Peak. I'd suggest looking on your right in the first quarter mile after the trail turns south above the ravine in which the creek begins.

You've just completed the most challenging 5.6 miles of the Sky Line. I hope that you enjoyed some of the best high-country views since you left Dodger Point. The trail will progressively improve as you head south 5.2 miles to the day's end at Three Prune Camp at 3,600 feet.

Three Prune itself does not have a water source, but a short trek to the north over the ridge is a bowl that holds Three Prune Lake. If the Lake is dry, your next option is Kurtz Lake down-trail. Leaving Three Prune you'll find the junction of the Elip Creek Trail 1.5 miles ahead. Turn left at the junction and follow the trail about half a mile. Drop your packs and scramble up slope about 200 feet and search for Kurtz Lake which sits on a small shelf on the north side, your side, of the ridge you've been following since the junction. You may find water, but if you're looking for a campsite your choices are Three Prune or

Elip Creek campsite on the North Fork Quinault, 4 miles and 3,000 feet below. There is no bear wire at Elip Creek campsite and the privy is across the creek from the campsite.

Whatever you do, the next destination is Sixteen Mile Camp on the North Fork Quinault, an easy 5.7 miles up-trail. Sixteen Mile is at the upper reaches of the Quinault Rain Forest. The growth of everything green is robust to say the least. It's also in a fairly deep valley and as such can be a cold camp.

The trail now follows the north bank of the river to Low Divide. The trail passes over the divide and loses elevation down to Chicago Camp on the Elwha 6.6 miles away. The next days of hiking are a bit long, but otherwise not strenuous. Its 9.2 miles down to Hayes River. Sections of the trail are overgrown between Lake Margaret and Camp Wilder and a small section of trail a half mile above Hayes River has been undercut by a landslide. The gentle loss of elevation continues the next day 6.8 miles to Mary's Falls Camp. The next day's 8.7 miles will put you at Whiskey Bend. Given the explanation that I started this loop with, either Whiskey Bend or Madison Falls is your trailhead. If it's Madison Falls you've got one last 8 mile day to get back to Madison Falls, the temporary trailhead.

Whichever trailhead is yours; you've hiked at least 98 miles on this long loop in the Park. Way-finding was a challenge you met head-on and succeeded at following the route no matter the difficulty. Maybe you've done this before or maybe it was your first experience; either way you've grown in confidence and honed your skill set. It wasn't easy; testing yourself never is. My congratulations for facing and meeting the challenges as each presented themselves. Good Job!

Four Rivers Loop

SW and SE Quadrants, Custom Correct maps, "Quinault-Colonel Bob", "Elwha Valley", "Gray Wolf-Dosewallips", "The Brothers-Mt Anderson", "Enchanted Valley-Skokomish", (111 mi., difficulty 101.17**, lush Rain Forest subalpine lakes and forests, 3 passes, alpine basins, four river drainages, 1-day of road-hiking)**

Summary: North Fork Quinault Trailhead, Wolf Bar, Sixteen Mile, Low Divide Hayes River, Hayden Pass, Dose Meadows, Dose Forks, Honeymoon Meadows, Anderson Pass, O'Neil Pass, La Crosse Basin, Home-Sweet-Home, First Divide, Big Log Camp, Lake Sundown, Graves Creek Campground, North Fork Quinault River Trailhead

(Quinault-Colonel Bob map) I've described this loop starting from the North Fork Quinault River Trailhead, but you could do the same loop starting at the Dosewallips Trailhead. If you start on the Dose, you'll add 11 miles to the length of this loop. The summary identifies significant points along the loop. Regardless of trailhead or rotation, the summary remains true. Starting at the Dose Trailhead, which is 6.9 miles east of Dose Forks, will require at least one more day to the hike than starting at the North Fork Quinault River Trailhead.

The North Fork Quinault Trailhead is about 17 miles east of U.S. 101 on the North Shore Road of Lake Quinault. Lake Quinault is one hour north of Aberdeen, if you are arriving from the south, or three hours west and then south of Port Angeles. In either case you'll be approaching Lake Quinault on U.S. 101.

North Fork Campground is a mile short of the trailhead. If you decide to camp in the campground, you could hike the 11 miles to Sixteen Mile Camp on your first day. On the other hand, if you've spent most of the day getting to the trailhead you might want to hike the 2.5 miles to Wolf Bar or the 5.1 miles to Halfway House. Either choice will reduce the remainder of the hike to Sixteen Mile Camp the following day. Regardless of your decision, the trail gradient from the trailhead to Halfway House is minimal and from there to Sixteen Mile is at the low end of moderate.

The North Fork Quinault Valley is a lowland Rain Forest with a dense forest, huge trees, ferns, moss and plenty of animals. Your chances of seeing animals is usually in an inverse proportion to how much noise you make. Years ago, in my youth, I was hiking up the North Fork Skokomish on the opposite side or these mountains. My friends and I had been on the trail long enough that day that we'd run out of idle chit-chat. Quietly I led our small group around a blind curve in the trail and instantly found myself less than twenty feet from about a dozen elk. They were as startled as I was

33. Mt. Duckabush from O'Neil Pass, ONP

and their reaction was to stamp their feet in unison. I stopped and I thought my heart had done the same. The elk on the other hand, simply turned away and walked into the forest. By the time you could count to ten they had completely disappeared without making a sound. Needless to say, "stuff happens"; this time for the good of all concerned.

The trail underfoot up the North Fork Quinault reflects the deep forest that it penetrates. From the trailhead to Low Divide it's mostly cushioned by duff, has a few rocky sections restricted to multiple stream crossings and the inevitable downed trees that you'll need to navigate, unless the trail crew found them first. The later in the hiking season you hike this loop the fewer trees you'll have to navigate. Thank the National Park Service trail crews and the volunteers of the Washington Trails Association.

The trail crosses from the west bank to the east bank of the river just before you arrive at Sixteen Mile Camp. You should expect a shallow fording of the river which at this elevation could be considered a stream. Only once did I ever find a convenient cluster of small logs and brush at the crossing point that allowed a nearly dry crossing. Sixteen Mile at about 1,700 feet of elevation is still well within the Rain Forest. As such, the dense canopy lends itself to a camp that is relatively dark and cold. It's a one-night stay and there is plenty of near level space available; things could be worse.

Another day on the trail. Throughout this loop it should be incumbent upon you to pack out your trash and even trash that isn't yours. So, before you move on up-trail please take the time to police the area. Leave each camp as you found it, or more to the point better than you found it. From Sixteen Mile to Lake Margaret and Lake Mary is 4.2 miles. The grade is steeper today but not abusively so; you'll gain about 500 feet per mile. The lakes are a great place for a midday rest, but you can't camp there. Camping is allowed just west of the lakes on Low Divide.

You're over half-way to today's destination; so, relax and take in the beauty of Low Divide. For the eager beavers there is the opportunity to take a five mile roundtrip day hike to Martin's Lakes. The Martin's Park Primitive Trail starts at the southern end of Lake Margaret and initially heads due south. You'll gain about 1,000 feet of elevation on a trail that doesn't get all the use that the North Fork Trail does; it can suffer from a lack of maintenance.

(Elwha Valley map) With the rest break over, you've got 2.4 miles down-trail to Chicago Camp on the Elwha River. You'll lose about 1,000 feet in the first 2 miles as you descend, at times steeply, to the end of today's hike. If you're a fisherman, as of this writing, the Park does not allow fishing on any part of the Elwha River. Make sure that you've read and understand the current fishing regulations and restrictions within the Park, they are well enforced. The best news is no one needs a fishing license in the Park or Olympic National Forest.

Leaving Chicago Camp, you've got about 9 miles of trail and very little elevation loss down-stream to Hayes River. I hope the day is clear and warm. If so, this stretch of trail will be an idyllic experience on the Elwha. It's fresh, green and easy traveling as the route follows the river in a slow bend from northeast to due north on its way to Hayes River. In my youth there was an actual telephone at the Hayes River Ranger Station. I don't know if it worked because, thankfully, I didn't have a problem that would have warranted it's use.

Up in the morning and ready for the next trail. Today will be a bit longer than yesterday's jaunt down the Elwha and also more strenuous. This trail can be dry in the summer; the first water source you can count on will be at, or slightly before Dose Meadows 10.6 miles away. The Hayden Pass Trail leaves the Elwha and the Hayes River Ranger Station behind as it begins its 8.3 mile climb to the pass. Starting in a slow climb to the northeast the trail swings around to the southeast to cover the majority of the mileage. The first mile climbs about 700 feet as does the second. At the 2 mile point the trail turns to the southeast and the grade settles to about

500 feet a mile over the next 5.5 miles. With most of the elevation gained, the last mile is an easy approach to Hayden Pass at 5,847 ft.

The views from the pass are outstanding on a clear day. Immediately to the south is Sentinel Peak and Sentinel's Sister within a mile of the pass. To the southwest is Mount Norton 3.5 miles distant. Much farther west you can see Mount Wilder, and Mount Dana. To the northwest and farther out still is Mount Scott and Dodger Point both sitting just east of the famed Bailey Range, fronting the east slope of Mt. Olympus. Immediately to your northwest is Mount Fromme at 6,705 ft. which, because of its location, is blocking your view of the higher Mount Claywood at 6,836 ft. You truly are in the heart of the Olympic Mountains.

There's 2.3 miles left on today's menu as you drop down to Dose Meadows. Along the way, a long mile down-trail, you'll pass Thousand Acre Meadow; a way-trail leads off to your right. From late July to early August, depending on the spring weather, this large alpine expanse can be a most glorious display of wildflowers, similar to a lot of the Olympic Mountain's open high country. Dose Meadows finishes this tough day, up and over Hayden Pass. Tomorrow will be a long stroll down the Dosewallips River.

(Gray Wolf-Dosewallips map) Leaving Dose Meadows you'll arrive at Bear Camp just short of two miles down-trail. Just beyond Bear Camp is Butler Creek, perhaps more notable to me than you. Barbara, my wife, and I were packing in from the Dosewallips Campground to Dose Meadows. Just as we approached Butler Creek, we came across a large Black Bear munching lupine. We stopped and watched while the bear continued to uproot the lupine. With each chew, the flowers at one side of his or her mouth and the roots at the other came closer and closer to a well-deserved swallow. Finally, blooms, roots, rocks and all were swallowed without so much as a grimace. We always knew bears were tough, but this exhibition raised our appreciation for that trait to a new level.

With one exception, I'll leave the many stories that any number of camps, trails and creeks could prompt, on your trip down the Dose to Dose Forks 9.5 miles beyond Butler Creek. Six miles ahead and directly across the valley, if you look closely, you'll see Hatana Falls, the lower end of Hidden Creek as it plunges nearly 1,200 ft. to the valley floor in its dash to join the Dose.

If you have planned or considered a resupply point, the Dosewallips Campground is your only opportunity on this loop. If you've already arranged the resupply, you and your resupply-helpers know that getting to the Dose Campground requires a 6.5 mile trek up a closed road from the Dose Trailhead. The Dose Campground is 1.4 miles east of Dose Forks.

(The Brothers-Mt Anderson map) From wherever you spent last night, the distance between Dose Forks and Camp Siberia, up the West Fork of the Dosewallips River, is 8.7 miles. Along the way you'll gain 2,300 ft. of elevation. For the most part, the West Fork Dosewallips River Trail is well maintained and is certainly doable. That said, it's best to be informed about several points along your route today. A half mile above Dose Forks you'll cross the High Dose Bridge; be thankful that it's made of steel. The previous two wooden renditions were put to their rest, in the chasm below, by winter snow storms. The next 2.3 miles to Big Timber Camp are easy. Between Big Timber and Diamond Meadows there is a quarter-mile stretch of the trail that crosses over a wash caused by an impervious sub-stratum. This piece of the trail is more like hiking up a shallow creek bed than a trail; it's short but bothersome.

Just above Diamond Meadows the trail crosses the West Fork, unfortunately not in a pretty manner. Over the years the crossing has been made by stepping over brush and small logs, wading through a knee-high flow, or a combination of both. Needless to say, any trail report on this leg of the hike will include a less than flattering description of this particular crossing. Finally, the elevation gain between Diamond Meadows and Honeymoon Meadows is about 1,000 feet. It is not distributed evenly across the 2.5 miles that separate the two. The first half gains about 200 feet and the last half picks up the rest. With your legs and lungs feeling the grade on the upper half the trail, you will slowly approach a roaring West Fork Dose, that you can't see. When you get to what you would think was spitting distance of the river you can hear it but not see it. The trail will take one last turn to your left and almost immediately top out just above the unseen waterfall you've been approaching. You've arrived at Honeymoon Meadows and your destination is a mile farther on at Camp Siberia.

After you're settled, and if you have the energy, you might want to hike the half mile up to Anderson Pass. When you get near the pass, you'll find a spur trail on your right. It will lead you up to an overlook that will give you a front row seat for viewing Mt. Anderson's two peaks both at just over 7,000 feet. Mt. Anderson, like all the peaks in the outer eastern and northern basaltic arc of the Olympic Mountains, are composed primarily of marine extruded basalt, a volcanic rock formation. Along with the peaks in the inner eastern and northern basaltic arc, combined, they contain the vast majority of the tallest peaks in the Olympic Mountains, with the exception of Mount Olympus, the tallest. Oddity that it is, Mt. Olympus is the product of the orogenic uplift of the seafloor, a primarily sedimentary rock formation; a byproduct of plate tectonics. The entirety of the Olympic Mountains is affected by this ongoing process but nowhere in the world is the rate of orogenic uplift greater than that of the Clearwater Valley just south of the Hoh River.

Day breaks and you'll be leaving Anderson Pass behind. You'll descend at a rate of about 800 feet a mile across the next 1.7 miles where you'll meet the O'Neil Pass Trail on your left. A half mile before you reach the O'Neil Pass Trail, you'll cross an unnamed creek. The crossing is usually simple; a matter of stepping from one large boulder to the next. If the flow rate is high, however, the creek can be sloshing over the tops of those boulders. There is little to do about the crossing but be safe and take care; wet or dry it's not a place where you'd want to fall.

Meeting the trail to O'Neil Pass, turn left and a half mile later you'll be crossing the lower end of Bull Elk Basin. The basin, basically a large sub-alpine meadow, is a great place to take a break before you start the over 7 mile climb to O'Neil Pass. White Creek runs through the basin and you should fill-up on water before you leave; water on the climb is scarce at best and most often entirely absent.

With the exception of a few steeper sections, the trail gains 1,400 ft. across the next 7 miles. Your exertion will be seriously eased by the ever-widening views on your trek to the pass. When you arrive at the pass, Mt. Duckabush at 6,250 ft. will be standing watch over you, about a half mile to your southeast. All around the compass you're treated to "peeks at peaks" ranging between 5,000 and nearly 7,000 ft in height. I hope it's a clear day.

(Enchanted Valley-Skokomish map) Leaving O'Neil Pass you'll move down-trail 1.2 miles to a spur trail on your left leading you another mile to Marmot Lake in the gorgeous La Crosse Basin. The Basin is an alpine wonderland that changes its mood with the day's shifting light. Some of the most beautiful pictures in these mountains have been taken here. In particular, you might recall an astounding photo of La Crosse Lake hanging on the wall at the wilderness desk in the Olympic National Park Visitor Center, in Port Angeles. La Crosse Lake is a mile north of Hart Lake in the north end of the basin; go grab a photo for your own collection. The strong implication here is that you may want to spend a lay-over day in this locale.

Regardless of your decision, leaving La Crosse Basin is an inevitable reality that must be faced. The next two days are relatively easy and I believe enjoyable. Today you'll lose about 2,300 feet of elevation following the trail 3.4 miles down into the upper Duckabush Valley. You'll arrive at the intersection trail on your left that leads to the Duckabush River just yards away; an opportunity to fill your water bottles.

The trail to Home-Sweet-Home, today's destination, turns to your right. The trail climbs 1,500 feet steadily rising out of the dense forest of the Duckabush and transitioning into a sup-alpine meadow at the end of the second mile. Home-Sweet-Home sits in the meadow with grand views to the northwest. Surrounded on most of three sides by a mix of Alpine and sup-alpine forest, the place gives you the feeling of a bird sitting on a perch. Regardless of today's weather, Home Sweet Home can be a very windy camp.

Your second of these two easy days begins with you crossing First Divide, less than a mile up-trail. Once across you'll drop down into the North Fork Skokomish River drainage. Today's hike slowly loses elevation once you've passed through Two Bear Camp, 3.3 miles away, and have arrived at Nine Stream. From Nine Stream to Big Log Camp, today's destination, is another 3.8 miles and only 600 feet lower in the valley. There is a wash-out near Camp Pleasant that will require minor route-finding skills. Technically the North Fork of the Skokomish is not part of the Rain Forest but it's hard to tell the difference. Much like the Quinault Valley, it is cloaked with huge trees and more vegetation than a herd of vegans could consume.

Big Log Camp in my youth was the end of the road and the beginning of the North Fork Trail. Today, the road ends and the trail begins 5.5 miles south at the Staircase Ranger Station. Hopefully, you're not looking for an exit which makes that last bit a piece of trivia.

Morning brings the dawn and a tough day on the trail. Backtrack up-trail a short half mile to the intersection with the Six Ridge Trail on your left. As you take the turn, the trail immediately crosses the North Fork Skokomish and puts an end to easy hiking. The trail climbs 2,000 feet up the northeastern nose of Six Ridge in a seemingly endless chain of switchbacks. Less than a mile and a half later the trail eases heading west-southwest. Between Six Ridge Pass and the junction of the Success Lake Trail, you'll find it difficult to find the trail due to all the game trails and very little use. Take your time and navigate carefully. The trail gradient over the better part of the next six miles rarely exceeds 200 feet a mile. At about the 9 mile mark the trail passes by McGravey Lakes. This is the first water source since you crossed the North Fork this morning. The good news, in the next 1.5 miles you'll drop down to Lake Sundown, your refuge for the night. The Six Ridge Trail is not frequently used, intermittently maintained and generally falls into the hiking category of a "rough-go".

Having survived yesterday you'll enjoy today, so much better. It's 8.5 miles down-trail to the Graves Creek Campground, your last camp on this loop. Leaving Lake Sundown and reaching the Sundown Pass Trail, turn right and proceed 1.3 miles to intersect the Wynoochee Pass Trail, a drop of 1,200 feet from Lake Sundown. Turn right again and you're on your way following Graves Creek 6.2 miles down to the Quinault. Interrupted by a short set of switchbacks at about its mid-point, the trail maintains a fairly constant drop of about 300 feet a-mile. When you arrive at the Quinault River Trail turn left and the Campground is a short mile farther on.

(Colonel Bob-Quinault map) Tomorrow won't be a hard day but it may turn out to be the worst day of this loop. You'll wake up at the campground situated at the end of the Graves Creek Road but the trailhead you left from is at the end of the North Fork Road. These two places are just shy of 9 miles apart. Throughout the day you'll have access to all the water you might need, plenty of river views, a few guard-rails to sit on and a nearly level road to follow. The truth, every mile looks almost identical to the last. The alternative of doing the loop in a counter clock wise rotation wouldn't have taken this miserable road hike out of the equation. You would have just hiked the road in the opposite direction.

Road-hiking aside, you can be proud of your accomplishment. You hiked 111 miles following four rivers and climbed a number of passes and divides. Your reward is the joy of accomplishment and a host of photos and memories that so many others have experienced or others will experience. You've proven your endurance on the trail and your determination in the face of some tough parts of these mountains. Above all, you dug deeply and found the inner strength to demonstrate your willingness, capacity and sheer grit to overcome the challenges of the wilderness. My congratulations for your dedication and skills, as evidenced by this long hard loop. Well done!

Very Long Loop Hikes

The following two loop hikes are the longest in the Olympic Mountains and each will require a good deal of planning, including reprovisioning along their routes. The "Six Passes-Two Divides Loop" is 162 miles in length, and "The Grand Loop of the Olympic Mountains" is even longer at 309 miles.

Backpackers with less than exceptional skills, endurance, and experience should refrain from taking on the challenges and risks associated with either of these serious endeavors. Even if you have the skills and experience to undertake either of these loops, you should think long and hard about the difficulties involved.

If you are serious about attempting either of these loops, there are several pieces of important information that you need to understand:

In spite of the Book's narrative nature in which the static details of any of these hikes can be enumerated: distances, altitudes, compass directions etc., dynamic elements: trail conditions, weather, re-routing of trails, Park restrictions and the behavior of any animal at any time cannot be guaranteed. You are headed into a wilderness where you are your first and best resource. The Book cannot and does not identify nor assume responsibility for every problem, difficulty or hazard that you may encounter. You truly are on your own. If that reality concerns you then I suggest you reconsider. Even when your estimate of your self is, in your mind, a match for a chosen quest, the unexpected, the unbelievable and the unplanned can fall upon you at any time. When it does, you are the only resource for a resolution of the event.

These loops are an aggregation of other shorter loops described in this book. You should reference those loop segments and make use of the index to thoroughly inform yourself. To be as informed as possible, you should re-read each segment as it appears in each of the descriptions of each loop. For example, a description of Gray Wolf Pass appears in a number of different loops. While each description is factual, not every fact is included in any individual loop's description. Therefore, use the index and read all the descriptions of Gray Wolf Pass. In doing so, you will acquire a more thorough understanding of that segment.

Weather can pose challenges on these hikes. The longer you are exposed on these loops, the greater the chance that weather will become, at least temporarily, a major challenge. Rarely, extremely rarely, will the Olympic Mountains go 20 to 40 days without adverse, if not, travel-stopping weather. Summer weather usually arrives from the west and the worst of it from the southwest. After several days of good weather, you should keep an eye to the sky. The presence of lenticular clouds is an indicator that the weather is going to change; usually it will get worse.

Getting your permit to do either of these loops will be a challenge in itself. Don't expect to simply walk up to the Wilderness Information Center desk and get a permit as easily as you might if your trip were 3 or 4 days in length. Even though the W.I.C. issues over a hundred thousand permits a year, the smallest fraction of those barely reflect the length of what you're planning. Start working out the details with the W.I.C. well in advance of your start date.

On Day-6, Day-14 and again on Day-41 of "The Grand Loop of the Olympic Mountains", you'll need a Cross Country Permit for camping off-trail in a non-designated camping space. This permit can only be obtained at the Park's Wilderness Information Center in The Olympic National Park Visitor Center in Port Angeles. The rangers in the W.I.C. will help you with the permit.

Reprovisioning is an absolute requirement for these longest of loops. You are not allowed to cache provisions within Olympic National Park. You'll need to organize someone to meet you, relieve you of your trash and provide you with replacement provisions for the next leg of the loop. No one can carry 20 to 40 days of food, fuel, and trash.

Do Not Solo Hike either of these loops. If you are your only resource and something critical happens, your resource bin may go from adequate to abysmal in a flash. These loops will take you into some of the most remote areas of the Olympic Mountains. Summoning help may not be possible, or even if it is, it could take days for it to arrive. Every person who will hike with you on either of these loops must be thoroughly vetted as to their experience, mental and physical stamina, and their understanding of the risks involved. Either of these loops will push hikers to the limits of their abilities. There are enough things that could go wrong, could not have been foreseen or just happen in an undertaking such as this.

Safety is everyone's first responsibility. Every member of the party should be thoroughly versed in the route, terrain and challenges of each segment of the loop. More than one member of your group should have training in wilderness first aid at a level that can manage an injury where evacuation could take days. More than one member of your group should be familiar with and experienced in fording rivers.

If you are considering a loop that includes fording you should: consult with the Wilderness Information Desk in the Olympic National Park Visitor Center in Port Angeles. I suggest you do a web search for "Stream Crossing Techniques" and read the National Park Service's web-available "Safe River Crossings" and 'Swiftwater Rescue Manual" The Rangers in the Park's Wilderness Information Center can advise you as to the advisability of your plans. In addition, you should consult the USGS website for current water conditions. Also, if you visit online the State of Washington Dept. of Ecology, River and Stream Flow Monitoring page, you can compare years of data and thereby compare it to the weather pattern in any year against the weather pattern in the current year. By doing so you'll have a better sense of what the fording conditions may be. These searches will allow you to choose your hike based on the available data.

Six Passes – Two Divides Loop

SE, NE and SW Quadrants, Custom Correct maps, "Mount Skokomish-Lake Cushman", "The Brothers–Mt. Anderson", "Gray Wolf-Dosewallips", "Elwha Valley", "Quinault-Colonel Bob", "Enchanted Valley-Skokomish", (162 mi., difficulty 118.11, seven rivers, forests, alpine meadows, a ford, viewpoints, dramatic changes in elevation, reprovisioning)

Summary: North Fork Skokomish River Trailhead, First Divide, fording the Duckabush, La Crosse Pass, Dose Forks, Gray Wolf Pass, Three Forks, Cameron Creek, Cameron Pass, Lost Pass, Thousand Acre Meadow, Hayden Pass, Low Divide, North Fork Quinault, Graves Creek, Enchanted Valley, O'Neil Pass, Home Sweet Home, North Fork Skokomish River Trailhead

(Mount Skokomish-Lake Cushman map) The trailhead for this hike is near the Staircase Ranger Station in the SE corner of Olympic National Park. To get to the ranger station: follow U.S. 101 to Hoodsport, WA on Hood Canal, turn west on the Lake Cushman Road, turn left at the "T" intersection of Forest Service Road 24. The road turns to gravel and then back to asphalt as you enter the Park. The Staircase Ranger Station will be on your right just before the road crosses the North Fork Skokomish River. The trailhead is next to the overnight parking area at the end of the road just east of the ranger station. I would suggest that you check-in with the ranger, if one's available. This is more of a good idea than a requirement.

Before we get started, let's review the difficulty and magnitude of this endeavor. At 162 miles this is the second longest loop hike in the Olympic Mountains. It's unlikely, if not impossible, for you to carry all the supplies that you'll need without reprovisioning. There will be a number of trail segments that gain or lose over 1,000 feet a mile. You will be exceptionally lucky if you avoid some degree of adverse weather over the course of time required to complete this loop. If you find the Duckabush unfordable, your alternative course will add 15 miles and a hike over Anderson Pass to your itinerary. If you are strong, skilled, accustomed to being on the trail, and experienced in finding backcountry solutions to problems that will arise, then those resources and your determination will go a long way toward achieving your goal.

I'll describe the loop on a day-by-day basis. The description that follows is a balance of time, calories and effort with a bias toward enjoying the ambiance of being in the wilderness. The description is based on my approach to wilderness hiking; you may see it differently. While the trail segments remain the same, where and when you camp

34. West Side of Hayden Pass, ONP, Pablo McLoud

is at your discretion. Remember, however, that your permit should be the last word regarding where you'll be at any given point in time. In an emergency, your life could depend on it.

If you've spent part of today picking up your wilderness permit at the Park's visitor center in Port Angeles or maybe shopping for some last-minute supplies, given the time it takes to get to the trailhead, you might consider spending a night at the Staircase Campground and start off early and fresh in the morning.

Regardless of how you've arrived, let's get on the trail. Your first day's destination is Nine Stream 9.1 miles up-trail from Staircase. Yes, the streams that flow into the North Fork Skokomish, "Skok", are numbered. Well sort of! From Four Stream to Nine Stream the statement is true; not so much for the three creeks below Four Stream.

The first 5.3 miles will take you from the trailhead to Big Log Camp. Along the way you'll pass through Spike Camp which in my Boy Scout days, was the trailhead for both Flapjack Lakes and the North Fork Skok Trail. The trail to Spike Camp follows the original and now abandoned road. While this entire valley, below about 3,000 feet of elevation, is near, but technically not, a Rain Forest; it has that lush and intensively vibrant feel of the Bogechiel, Hoh, Queets and Quinault valleys on the Pacific side of these mountains. Ancient conifers, mostly western redcedar, western hemlock and Douglas fir stand silent amidst a flourish of undergrowth so dense and green it presents itself as an impenetrable guardian holding back time and keeping hikers on the trail.

As you take a break at Big Log Camp, you may notice another trailhead for Black and White Lakes; heading directly up the east valley wall and gaining 3,000 ft. in 2.3 miles. I made this climb once and that was enough. When I arrived at the lakes, I found them situated in a cirque on the northwest flank of Mt. Gladys. The cirque and the lakes leave little to write home about, however, the views from the ridge just above the lakes are spectacular. At some time in the future, you may want to explore this area as a side trip from Flapjack Lakes; it's a much easier approach.

Enough about side trips, your break is over and you have another 3.8 miles to cover to get to Nine Stream. The remaining trail gains about 500 ft., is relatively gentle, pleasant and for the most part easy on your feet. The forest is dense and the river is near, creating a cooling effect on a hot summer day, or a likeness to a refrigerator if it's cold and cloudy. Time to set up camp and get some food and rest.

Breakfast is over and you're packed up, ready for a new day. Beyond Nine Stream the trail abruptly begins a 2,500 ft. climb to First Divide, 3.3 miles ahead. The trail follows a northeasterly course slowly shifting around to the north after passing Two Bear Camp along the way. About a quarter mile below the Divide two surprises await you. The trail turns quickly from north to east and serves up progressively better and better views of Mt. Duckabush at 6,250 ft. 2 miles west and Mt. Hopper at 6,114 ft. less than a mile off to the southeast.

Crossing First Divide you'll leave the Skokomish River behind and enter into the Duckabush drainage. The first thing that you'll encounter is the idyllic setting of Home Sweet Home situated in a lovely alpine meadow with an extraordinary view of the upper Duckabush region including O'Neil Pass, which you'll cross in one of your last days on this loop. It's time to drop your packs and enjoy this delightful setting.

Well, time waits for no one; pack-up and get down to the "Duck". You've got the last 2 miles of today's 6.3 mile trek from Nine Stream to Upper Duckabush Camp. The trail averages a loss of about 600 feet a mile, has its fair share of switch backs and rapidly swallows the alpine views as it descends into a vibrant subalpine forest.

As you approach the Duckabush River, you'll find a spur trail on your right that takes you directly to the river's bank. This may be a fording spot, however, remember that trails are more or less static and rivers are most definitely dynamic. They forever shift their rock and sand burden from one point to another. There is no rule that says that the trail will deliver you to the best fording location!

If you are considering this loop, that includes fording, you should: consult with the Wilderness Information Desk in the Olympic National Park Visitor Center in Port Angeles. I suggest you do a web search for "Stream Crossing Techniques" and read the National Park Service's web-available "Safe River Crossings" and 'Swiftwater Rescue Manual" The Rangers in the Park's Wilderness Information Center can advise you as to the advisability of your plans. In addition, you should consult the USGS website for current water conditions. Also, if you visit online the State of Washington Dept. of Ecology, River and Stream Flow Monitoring page, you can compare years of data and thereby compare it to the weather pattern in any year against the weather pattern in the current year. By doing so you'll have a better sense of what the fording conditions may be. These searches will allow you to choose your hike based on the available data.

Drop your gear and spend some time evaluating where your best opportunity lies. This is a situation where you'll be investing in your safety. The end products of fording tend to be at the extremes of either success or failure; seldom is there any middle ground. Over the years hikers have lost their lives in an attempt to ford a river that wasn't fordable. Apply yourself to making informed decisions regarding this next commitment. Refer to the Resources page for fording.

(The Brothers-Mt. Anderson map) If for any reason you believe that fording is not a safe option, you do have a viable alternative. You can skip the fording and proceed to La Crosse Basin, just below O'Neil Pass 3.4 miles farther up the Duckabush. In order to regain your original itinerary, you'll have to descend the west side of O'Neil Pass to the North Fork Quinault and cross over Anderson Pass to Honeymoon Meadows. Such a decision adds about 15 miles to your total mileage, adds at least one extra day to your trip but rescues your opportunity to complete the rest of this loop.

On the other hand, you've successfully forded the Duckabush River and are settling in at Upper Duckabush Camp. You'll need the rest. Tomorrow you'll climb over La Crosse Pass, no easy feat from the Duckabush.

Having packed-up all your gear and policed the campsite for trash, yours or others, you're on the trail again. The first 1.8 miles of down-trail to the intersection with the La Crosse Pass Trail is the only easy part of today; enjoy it. The La Crosse Pass Trail switchbacks 2,894 feet up the south wall of the Duckabush Valley. If you anticipate that the day will be hot, I suggest you hit this climb as early in the day as possible; anyone for breakfast in the dark? There is no water source on this trail until you reach the West Fork Dosewallips River 6.4 miles north of where you stand. Take the opportunity to replenish your water supply while you can.

As you climb the valley wall the regional scenery will begin to present itself and by the time you arrive at the crest the view is spectacular. Looking due south, you'll see Mt. Hopper and rotating to your right you'll see, in order, Mt. Steel, Mt. Duckabush, O'Neil Pass, White Mountain, Mt. La Crosse, all three peaks of Mt. Anderson, Mt. Elk Lick to the east and then The Brothers, Mt. Lena and Mt. Bretherton. I hope it's a clear day.

On the trail again there's a lot more to see in the days ahead. In the first mile and a half the trail descends at a rate of about 500 feet per mile. In the last mile and a half, the trail switchbacks through a steeper descent and joins the West Fork of the Dosewallips near Honeymoon Meadows, your camp for tonight.

Honeymoon Meadows lies east of and in the shadow of Mt. Anderson. If you're up for it, a side trip up to Anderson Pass will give you a glimpse of your future and the past. It's 1.4 miles up to the pass where you'll find a spur trail on your right. Follow the spur as it climbs a prominence overlooking what's left of the Anderson Glacier. For 2.6 million years the Anderson Glacier has held forth in the rock-strewn basin and what now is a rock chute to the north. I first visited this spot in 1960 and what you now see as rock was, at that time and for eons before, solid glacial ice. Without debating the cause, what you're looking at is evidence of climate change. Sad but true. Mt. Anderson's East Peak is hidden behind the rock outcropping to the north. But it's Middle and West Peak are clearly visible.

As for your future, gaze southeast into the Enchanted Valley 3,000 ft. below. Days from now you'll be passing through this most intriguing section of the Quinault Rain Forest. Forming the northwest wall of the upper valley is the "Valley of 10,000 Waterfalls", so called due to the numerous waterfalls that plunge to the valley floor during spring melt-off. The wall is capped by Chimney Peak standing at 6,917 ft. Climbing the southeast wall of the valley will take you to O'Neil Pass and La Crosse Basin. You'll be doing this in some of the latter days of this loop.

Morning breaks and the day begins. Today's destination is Dose Forks, down-trail just short of 8 miles. As you descend 1,800 ft. from Honeymoon Meadows, you'll pass through Diamond Meadows and Big Timber before you cross over the High Dose Bridge and shortly thereafter arrive at Dose Forks. The distance between each of these locations is near equal to one another, each separated by about 2.5 miles. The trail's first mile drops more steeply than the rest of today's hike. All in all, this is not a difficult hike with the exception of crossing the Dose about a half mile above Diamond Meadows. The crossing is always wet, but consistently fordable. I've crossed it when it's been choked with enough small logs and branches to be almost dry and on other occasions calf-deep. It's more of an inconvenience than any manner of threat. After Diamond Meadows the next crossing will be the High Dose Bridge that spans a significantly deep and narrow chasm. After the high bridge you'll cross the Dose once more immediately before you arrive at Dose Forks.

The Dosewallips Campground, 1.4 miles east of Dose Forks, is the first reprovisioning point on this long loop. More specifically, the campground is over 6.5 miles from the current Dosewallips Trailhead at the end of the Dosewallips Road. The road used to run all the way to the campground until a washout turned it into a trail, adding the 6.5 miles from the campground to the new trailhead. I'll leave the details of reprovisioning at the Dose to you and your helpful friends.

(Gray Wolf-Dosewallips map) Leaving Dose Forks you'll be headed to Deception Creek Camp 5.3 miles up the Dosewallips River. Except for the added weight of reprovisioning, today is short and relatively easy. You'll gain about 1,500 feet on your trek to Deception Creek Camp with an average gradient of slightly less than 300 feet a mile. The bear wire is down at Deception Creek so you'll need a Bear Cannister.

At 1.1 miles you'll find the Constance Pass Trail on your right. This trail climbs to Constance Pass gaining over 4,000 feet in 5 miles. Obviously, this trail is not for the faint-of-heart but the reward is astounding. This is a through-hike, not a loop, that traverses the west face, of the center section, of the east range of the Olympic Mountains. If you ever get around to doing this hike, make sure you camp at Home Lake, just north of Constance Pass; you won't be disappointed.

You've got another 4.2 miles ahead of you today. Along the way take a break to view Hatana Falls. About a quarter mile north of Hawk Creek, the fourth creek you'll cross after the Sunnybrook Meadows junction, put down your load and search for a clear view across the valley. Hidden Creek, true to its name, will be out of sight until it becomes Hatana Falls dropping hundreds of feet to join the Dose. It's buffered by dense forest on either side which creates a narrow window in which to view its majesty.

Just beyond Burdick Creek, the next creek you'll cross is another act of nature, a testament to her raw power. The trail will abruptly enter what appears to be a war zone. For less than a quarter mile, the trail winds its way through an area that was the location of a microburst in the late 1970's. Microbursts are the result of strong downdrafts of wind created by storm fronts resulting from large and compressed differences in air pressure. In this case, the effect was enhanced by the terrain. Look across the valley and you'll see the Silt Creek valley. It was the Silt Creek valley wedged between Mt. Anderson and Mt. Diamond to the south and the Sentinel's Sister, Sentinel Peak and Wellesley Peak to the North that helped to enhance the microburst. The downward slope and the compressive shape of the lower end of the Silt Creek valley brought a sledge hammer force to the exact spot upon which you're standing. The destruction that you bear witness to was most likely produced in under 5 minutes; never underestimate the potential energy and sometimes lethal force of nature!

Deception Creek Camp is 1.5 miles ahead. Arriving early in the day will give you time to rest in anticipation of tomorrow's climb over Gray Wolf Pass. The bear wire at Deception Creek is down; a Bear Cannister is required.

Barbara, my wife, and I met Robert Wood, the author of "Olympic Mountains Trail Guide", the definitive work on backpacking in these mountains, in this exact spot on a bright summer's day in the mid 1980's. He and a couple of his friends were on their way up to Thousand Acre Meadow; we were headed down-trail to the Dosewallips Trailhead. It was shortly thereafter that our trails merged into a fondly remembered hiking relationship.

Rising early this morning will allow you to climb part of the Pass in the shadow of Mt. Deception. You'll find the Gray Wolf Pass Trail just over a mile up-trail from Deception Creek. Turning east at the trail junction you're facing a 3,000 ft. climb to the Pass, 3.5 miles from the junction. There is no easy part of this climb and it gets harder and hotter once you've lost the early morning shadow of Mt. Deception.

Reaching the Gray Wolf Pass you deserve a break. Put down your burden and enjoy the view. To the west is Mt. Cameron at 7,190 ft. You'll cross Cameron Pass on the opposite side of the mountain a few days from now. To the south is Wellesley Peak at 6,758 ft. and at a greater distance Diamond Mountain at 6,822 ft. Due east however, is the most spectacular sight. Less than two miles distant are The Needles, a significantly unique formation within the Olympic Mountains. Anchored by Mt. Walkinshaw on the north and Mt. Deception on the south, The Needles formation contains eleven peaks and spires all at or in excess of 7,000 ft.; an aggregation found nowhere else in the Olympic Mountains.

The rest of today is down-trail 4.1 miles to Falls Camp on the Gray Wolf River. The first three-quarters of a mile is a rock-strewn alpine traverse after which the trail descends rapidly through the next mile and a half and crosses the Gray Wolf River. A half mile later the trail again crosses the river and thereupon delivers you to the confluence of the Gray Wolf with Cedar Creek at Falls Camp. If anyone hasn't had enough exercise for the day, a side trip, 4.2 miles roundtrip, up Cedar Creek to Cedar Lake, would be rewarded by this alpine lake set in a rocky cirque.

Breaking camp, your destination is Three Forks, an easy 5.4 miles down-trail. Before you arrive at Three Forks, across the river, you'll come across Gray Wolf Camp. I suggest setting up camp and crossing the river in the morning. Either way, you'll discover that the Three Forks locale is well named. It exists at the confluence of the Gray Wolf, Cameron Creek and Grand Creek. Look up in any direction and all you'll see are the buttresses and valleys that these three watercourses have carved over time. If it's hot, you'll enjoy the cool air and shade; if it's cool already, it'll be a cold morning that awaits you.

Up and at it, your first challenge is to cross both the Gray Wolf and Grand Creek. Having accomplished that feat, you'll head up-trail along Cameron Creek about 9 plus miles to Upper Cameron Camp in beautiful Cameron Basin. The first 7 miles follows a moderate grade climbing 1,900 ft. along the way. The last 2 miles, or so, take you from 4,000 ft. to 5,400 ft., the general elevation of Cameron Basin.

The basin is a veritable wonderland, an open meadow has replaced the glacier that initially formed it. The meadow is often sprinkled with wildflowers and heavily grassed while Cameron Creek slowly meanders throughout its length. All of this beauty is contrasted against a background of shear-walled Mt. Cameron to the southeast and Cameron Pass to the south west. Overall, you'll spend tonight in the embrace of the high country.

The sun's up and you have a relatively short but tough day ahead of you. First, you'll climb over Cameron Pass, a way-finding exercise that's doable. You'll cross a series of alpine meadows chocked with flowers, from mid-July to early August, and cross over Lost Pass descending to Dose Meadows, your destination. The distance is 4.3 miles, however, there are elevation gains and losses that will make it a challenge.

The first mile climbing to Cameron Pass gains 1,000 feet. The trail, to the extent that you'd consider it a trail, follows a series of cairns up and across a bowl littered with rock scree with a high degree of uniformity in both coloration and size. Some cairns are big, some small, some nonexistent for whatever reason. The going is slow. Move to the cairn, stop and search for the next, repeat often. In making this climb I've found cairns three feet tall and some three inches tall, not to mention nonexistent. If you find a missing cairn or one that was so small you struggled to find it, do the next hiker a favor and add a rock or four or ten, whatever it takes to improve the journey. Thank you!

Cresting Cameron Pass you'll be surprised at how different the terrain is on its western slope; it's downright gentle by comparison. Heading south you'll cross through a succession of alpine meadows each with their own astounding array of wildflower grandeur and color. At the end of a short two miles, you'll arrive at Lost Pass. The good news is that you're on top of the pass this time; or is it? The trail down from Lost Pass loses 1,500 feet in less than a mile. If that wasn't enough, the top portion of this trail has you stepping down off rocks that are knee high; your legs and joints are barking already!

The best news is you're down, survived in one piece and on the doorstep of Dose Meadows, a very short distance up the Dose Trail to the east. As I said, today was short but not easy. Tomorrow will be over 10 miles in length but not nearly as challenging as today has been.

(Elwha Valley map) Get up, eat up, clean up and pack up; today will be long, less difficult, scenic and you'll finish, out of the sun's heat, in the cool dense conifer Rain Forest of the Elwha Valley. You've got 2.3 miles up-trail to Hayden Pass, gaining about 1,400 ft. along the way. About halfway to the pass, you'll cross over the Dosewallips River; more a mountain stream than a river. Shortly thereafter you'll climb steeply to the southeast and then abruptly turn due south. You'll be circling past the western end of Thousand Acre Meadow to your left. It's a short off-trail jaunt to visit the edge of this very large and glorious alpine wonderland. Thousand Acre Meadow is one of the largest meadows in the Olympic Mountains, at a half mile wide and over a mile long.

Arriving at Hayden Pass, as usual, you'll be treated to alpine wilderness views. Sentinal Peak appears to be but a stone's throw away southeast of the Pass and Sentinal's Sister resides just to your right and a bit farther out. Behind you is Mt. Fromme, hiding Mt. Claywood, directly behind it from where you stand. Hayden Pass is the crossover trail from the Dose drainage to that of the Elwha.

The Hayden Pass Trail down to Hayes River on the Elwha loses about 1,500 feet in the first 4 miles before the trail gradient increases and then eases up considerably in the last mile. You'll find Hayes River a pleasant finish for this long day. Tomorrow you'll start to move up the Elwha headed for Anderson Pass. A half mile up-trail from Hays River a 20 foot section of the trail is being undercut by a landslide. Move carefully through this section.

As you leave Hayes River in the morning, you'll be hiking 8.8 miles up-stream to Chicago Camp, just below Low Divide. There are numerous ups and downs along the way, but the total elevation gain for today is about 500 feet. The forest is dense and provides a fair amount of shade if the sun's out, or adds to the gloom of a cloudy day, if that's the case. About a half mile up-trail from Hayes River there is a small undercut caused by a landslide. The trail doesn't closely follow the river bank and it swings far away in the vicinity of Godkin Creek. If you're planning a rest break, I'd suggest Camp Wilder on Leitha Creek about a half mile below Godkin Creek. Sections of the trail are overgrown between Camp Wilder and Lake Margaret; map and compass skills will be needed.

Arriving at Chicago Camp, you're at today's destination. This is the end of easy hiking up the Elwha. As of this writing all fishing on the Elwha is closed; check with the wilderness desk. If you plan on fishing anywhere else make sure you've checked the fishing regulations. They vary quite differently from one location to the other and are rigorously enforced. The best news is, you won't need a state fishing license inside the Olympic National Park or the Olympic National Forest.

Up the canyon northwest of Chicago Camp lies the head of the Elwha. The Happy Hollow Trail, which is difficult, will take you 3.8 miles up to the Elwha Basin where it ends and the Elwha Basin Trail begins. The Elwha Basin Trail is a short 1.8 miles but the 1.8 miles becomes very difficult teetering on non-existent the rest of the way to Dodwell-Rixon Pass. From Dodwell-Rixon Pass to Chicago Camp is one of the most challenging parts of the famed Bailey Traverse. The Traverse, in spite of its difficulty, is one of the most frequented off-trail adventures in Olympic National Park. The stories that are told are nearly endless and the element of getting nearly lost on the traverse is a common feature of the telling.

The day begins and you have a 10 mile hike over Low Divide and down the North Fork Quinault to Trapper. The trail climbs rapidly after the first half mile, gaining 1,400 feet by the time you've completed the 2.4 miles to Lake Margaret and Lake Mary, on Low Divide. The steepest stretch is in the last quarter mile of the climb. Low Divide is a pleasant spot where you can enjoy the lakes, meadows and views of Mt. Seattle to the northwest and Mt. Christie to the south.

(Quinault-Colonel Bob map) Cresting the Divide you'll enter the North Fork Quinault drainage. As you make your way down-trail, at 0.7 miles you come to the intersection with the northeast end of the Skyline Trail, one of the most scenic and toughest trails in Olympic National Park. If you are interested in doing the Skyline at some future date, I would highly suggest that you do your homework and read some of the trail reports before you commit to being tested by the Skyline. Your ability of way-finding will determine your level of success.

You've got 7.6 miles of down-trail with the loss of 2,400 feet of elevation before you reach Trapper. Along the way you'll slowly transition from a subalpine to a Rain Forest environment. But first, you'll have to ford the North Fork Quinault at Sixteen Mile Camp. Most any current trail report about the North Fork will include the fording conditions. On one very lucky occasion I crossed the river on a jam of brush and small logs without getting my feet wet. More often, however, it's an ankle-deep and bitterly cold fording. Needless to say, bridges and foot logs are not on the menu at Sixteen Mile.

Just beyond Sixteen Mile is Twelve Mile Camp and Geoduck Creek entering the North Fork Quinault from the east. The trail moves away from and above the river, crossing two small unnamed creeks in the next mile and a half and remains so as you arrive at Trapper. You may want to refresh your water supply at the creeks. If not, Kimta Creek is about a half mile down-trail of Trapper. Whatever your choice, water is available.

Your last day on the North Fork Quinault probably begins with the greeting of a cold morning. The river follows a deep valley route through an intensely dense forest. Sunshine and warmth, particularly in the morning, is hard to come by. Just over 8 miles lies before you as you finish this section of the loop. As the trail leaves Trapper, it swings to a southeasterly course. At the 5 mile mark it bends around to the southwest and arrives at Wolf Bar Camp. The North Fork Trailhead is 2.5 miles away and about a half mile farther is the North Fork Campground, your destination for today.

Today will be easy in some respects and difficult in others. Between the North Fork Campground and the Graves Creek Campground, your destination today, is a 9 mile slog. Slog because this is a hike down the North Fork Road to the bridge spanning the Quinault River and then a longer hike up the Graves Creek Road to the campground. Either the campground at the North Fork or the one at Graves Creek is your reprovisioning point; the last one on this loop.

(Enchanted Valley-Skokomish map) Hiking through the Rain Forest is truly a walk through Mother Nature's backyard. Huge trees: Douglas firs, western redcedars, western hemlock, big leaf and vine maples, are accompanied by wildflowers, ferns and mosses of an astounding variety. Temperate weather and rich soils allow the west side of the Olympic Mountains to rest its lowland feet in one of only six temperate Rain Forests on earth. This national treasure exists because of the foresight and joint protection of the U.S. National Parks Service and the U.S. Forest Service.

You've got two short days ahead of you. The first takes you 6.6 miles up the Quinault River to O'Neil Creek Camp. Along the way, you'll pass over the Pony Bridge, a delight on a clear sky day. The entirety of the Quinault River Trail will closely follow the river until you pass beyond Enchanted Valley.

Leaving Graves Creek Trailhead, you'll have a delightful day hiking beside the Quinault River. You'll cross several unnamed creeks, the fourth of which will be at O'Neil Creek Camp. Oddly enough O'Neil Creek is not the creek you crossed; it's on the opposite side of the river. Given that today is a short hike day, take the time to relax and enjoy the peace and serenity of your surroundings.

Your second day on the Quinault River will not be difficult, but it offers an alternative which makes today longer but tomorrow shorter; your choice. From O'Neil Creek Camp to Enchanted Valley is 6.5 miles. The upper end of Enchanted Valley is a transition zone between Rain Forest and subalpine terrain. The valley runs to the northeast bordered by 6,000 ft. cliffs to the northwest and a ridge to the southeast shared by White Mountain, Mt. Claywood and Mt. Fromme. The northeast ridge is crowned by Chimney Peak and due to the spring melt-off each year that creates innumerable cascades, Enchanted Valley is often called the "Valley of 10,000 Waterfalls".

If you choose to camp in the Enchanted Valley, your next day to Marmot Lake, over O'Neil Pass in La Crosse Basin, will be the longest day on this loop, 12.8 miles. On the other hand, if you hike through Enchanted Valley and camp in Bull Elk Basin, sometimes called White Basin, your hike to the pass and then Marmot Lake will be about 7 miles long. Either way, the climb from Bull Elk Basin to Marmot Lake does not give you access to a water source. In addition, most of the climb is at or above treeline. As such, this can be a long, hot, and dry day.

On the bright side of things, the views up to and on O'Neil Pass are beautiful and La Crosse Basin is so wonderful that you may decide to spend an extra day in the basin. If you intend to lay-over and explore the basin, make sure you do so with a map and a compass. There are several lakes and a number of viewpoints that I'm sure you'll enjoy. The bear wires are down at Marmot Lake, bring a bear canister.

You have two days left on this loop. The first day will have you descend O'Neil Pass to the Duckabush and then ascend past Home Sweet Home and over the First Divide to Nine Stream camp; a total distance of 9.4 miles. Take your time. The views and serenity on the bank of the Duckabush, the meadow that holds Home Sweet Home, the views from the First Divide and the hushed quiet at Two Bear Camp along the way, provide a wonderful alternative to just putting your head down and pushing through to Nine Stream.

Your last day will bring you all the way down the North Fork Skokomish to the Staircase Trailhead, a distance of 9.1 miles. Be aware that there is a washout near Camp Pleasant. Route-finding will be required. Huge trees and a verdant understory lend an alure to the finishing of this very long loop hike. With the exception of hiking the North Fork and the Graves Creek Roads, every day brought you a different version of spectacular and a host of tales to be told and retold across time. 162 miles, accentuated by large changes in elevation and several long days of hiking, was no small undertaking. Congratulations for the strength and dedication that you brought to this challenge. I daresay, you've joined the ranks of the few who have embraced the difficulty and lent their resolve to this long and arduous loop. Take pride in what you've conquered and be humbled by what you've experienced. Well Done!

The Grand Loop of the Olympic Mountains

NE., SE., NW., & SW. Quadrants, Custom Correct maps, "Lake Crescent–Happy Lake", "Seven Lakes Basin–Hoh", "Hurricane Ridge", "Elwha Valley", "Gray Wolf-Dosewallips", "Quinault–Colonel Bob", "Mount Skokomish-Lake Cushman", (309mi., difficulty 302.91, 42 days, roughly 64,500 ft. of elevation gain and loss, peaks, passes, valleys, streams, rivers, creeks and lakes, Rain Forest, alpine meadows, way-finding, fording, dry camps, off-trail camping, this is the toughest loop of them all)

Summary: This Loop includes punishing segments. The Grand Loop will require support. I can't imagine anyone capable of carrying all the food, supplies and gear required by the longest of these loops, without reprovisioning. You and I have both seen some big loads hauled by some very strong hikers, but I don't believe there's anyone that can carry all of what this challenge requires, in one load. You will have to coordinate and establish resupply points at reasonable and critical locations along your route. Caching is not allowed in the Park. As such, you'll need someone to bring you fresh supplies and take away your refuse. I'll identify these resupply points as the description of the loop unfolds. They are spaced between ten to fourteen days apart. My reference to support isn't restricted to food and gear. It also includes someone, at the resupply point that is capable of discussing your condition and helping you determine your potential for the remainder of the hike.

This loop is the longest of them all. It's the loop hike of all loop hikes and it will test you every way possible. The following sentence reflects the length and complexity of what lies ahead. If you're fit, skilled, determined, have the stamina of a mule, well equipped and organized, your adrenalin's pumping and you've a smile on your face, then gather your partners, devise a plan, identify and acquire your necessary resources, get your permits and give it your very best shot. You and yours may well be the first to accomplish what others view as impossible. Let me emphasize again that your planning is directly correlated to the product of your applied efforts and skills. I encourage you to truly study the topo maps especially regarding the descent from Dodger Point and The Skyline Trail, most particularly between Three Prune and Lake Beauty. Reprovisioning is absolutely necessary so organize your support team; this hike is a 41-day venture.

Where I've given greater attention to describing elements of the previous hikes, I've reduced each day's hike to a few sentences. "The

35. Panorama of the Olympic Mountains, ONP

Grand Loop of the Olympic Mountains" contains segments of most of the hikes in this book. The index can direct you to descriptions of the specific places and trails that constitute the "Grand Loop".

If you are considering this loop, that includes fording, you should: consult with the Wilderness Information Desk in the Olympic National Park Visitor Center in Port Angeles. I suggest you do a web search for "Stream Crossing Techniques" and read the National Park Service's web-available "Safe River Crossings" and 'Swiftwater Rescue Manual" The Rangers in the Park's Wilderness Information Center can advise you as to the advisability of your plans. In addition, you should consult the USGS website for current water conditions. Also, if you visit online the State of Washington Dept. of Ecology, River and Stream Flow Monitoring page, you can compare years of data and thereby compare it to the weather pattern in any year against the weather pattern in the current year. By doing so you'll have a better sense of what the fording conditions may be. These searches will allow you to choose your hike based on the available data.

Day-1 and your off! (Hurricane Ridge, Lake Crescent-Happy Lake Ridge maps,) The trailhead, as of this writing 2022, would be Madison Falls just inside the Park boundary on the Olympic Hot Springs Road. If the current washout on the road has been repaired and even if it hasn't, you'll start this loop at the Elwha Ranger Station, roughly 4 miles up the road from Madison Falls. Contacting rangers where and when you can along this loop is a good idea. Letting other hikers and rangers know where you've been and where you're headed next, on your long and challenging journey, informs people of your general location across a given time span. From the Elwha Ranger Station to the Olympic Hot Springs Campground is 10.2 miles (+1,710 ft.), your destination for today. No open fires are allowed at the Olympic Hot Springs Campground, stoves only.

Day-2 begins at the Olympic Hot Springs Campground and will end 5.3 miles later at Appleton Pass. (Seven Lakes-Basin-Hoh map,) This pass could be a dry camp. Although there is a tarn, Oyster Lake, I'd suggest getting water at the bottom of the switchbacks. They start just after you've crossed the South Fork of Boulder Creek about a half mile below the pass proper (+3,050 ft.).

Day-3 You'll be descending Appleton Pass. After 2.5 miles you'll come to the junction with the Sol Duc Trail, turn left. Your destination is Heart Lake 3 miles and 1,720 ft. ahead (-2,070 ft. +1,720ft.).

Day-4 Today will be a difficult descent from the High Divide to the Hoh Valley, to the south. Above the Heart Lake you'll head west 2.2 miles to the junction with the Hoh Lake Trail on your left. The views from the High Divide are some of the best in the Park, however by the time you've finished this loop you will have visited every great viewpoint in the Park. The first part of the descent takes you to Hoh Lake and then down to the Hoh River. This descent is long and brutal, losing 4,280 ft. across 6.2 miles, containing at least three exceedingly steep drops. Take your time and keep a keen eye on the trail. At the bottom of the descent, you'll intersect the Hoh Trail. Turn right and you'll come upon the Olympus Ranger Station, your destination (+540ft., -4,280 ft.).

Day-5 Today will be long but not hard. You'll be hiking from Olympus Ranger Station to the Hoh Campground 9.1 miles downstream. You'll follow the Hoh River and lose only 480 ft (-578ft.). The Hoh Campground is your first reprovisioning opportunity and your first opportunity to check-in with the Park's rangers, if they're around.

Day-6 Today is another "walk-the-road" day. From the campground you'll hike 6 miles down the Hoh Road to just past the entrance station, (Bogachiel Valley map) where you'll find the South Snider-Jackson Primitive Trail on your right. Up the Snider-Jackson you'll meet the biggest challenge on this loop. As of this writing the trail is close to nonexistent. Covered in brush and with countless downed trees, this segment demands the use of a contour map, compass and altimeter. Most of the first mile is flat brushy terrain and thereafter the trail climbs to a crest at about 4 miles and 3,302 ft. of elevation. The trail climbs moderately in the first three miles and then shifts to an easy grade in the last mile to the crest. This trail runs through dense rain forest, but as you cover that last mile before or just after the crest you should find a doable, not great but doable, site to camp for the night. This will be a dry camp. If you choose to camp off-trail you are required to get a Cross Country Permit from the Wilderness Information Center at the visitor center in Port Angeles. (+2,902 ft., -178 ft.)

Day-7 You'll start somewhere on the Snider-Jackson Primitive Trail, near its crest between the Hoh and the Bogachiel Rivers. The complete traverse from the Hoh to the Bogachiel Valley is a total distance of 10.2 miles. Reduced by your efforts of the previous day, the Bogachiel River ought to be about 6 miles distant. As the trail meets the Bogachiel River you'll need to find a place to ford. There are two usual fordings: one, 1.5 miles down-stream, found by following the trail to your left, or two, a mile up-stream, the trail on your right. If you are fording, you should: consult with the Wilderness Information Desk in the Olympic National Park Visitor Center in Port Angeles. I suggest you do a web search for "Stream Crossing Techniques" and read the National Park Service's web-available "Safe River Crossings" and 'Swiftwater Rescue Manual" The Rangers in the Park's Wilderness Information Center can advise you as to the advisability of your plans. In addition, you should consult the USGS website for current water conditions. Also, if you visit online the State of Washington Dept. of Ecology, River and Stream Flow Monitoring page, you can compare years of data and thereby compare it to the weather pattern in any year against the weather pattern in the current year. By doing so you'll have a better sense of what the fording conditions may be. These searches will allow you to choose your hike based on the available data. After fording the "Bogi" your destination is Flapjack Camp on the opposite bank. (-2,722).

Day-8 You're headed up-trail 10.4 miles to Twentyone Mile Camp. The trail is an easy grade, for the most part, as you ascend the Bogachiel Valley. The last 4 miles above Fifteen Mile Camp can be pretty overgrown, but passable. (+1,634 ft.).

Day-9 (Seven Lakes Basin-Hoh map) Today will be a relatively short hike but one that quickly gains elevation. The trail climbs about 2,000 feet in the next 4.1 miles where it intersects the Mink Lake Trail, on your left. It continues to rise up, but much more slowly over the next 3 miles before it crests the ridge and drops half a mile down to Deer Lake, the end of today's hike, (+1,986 ft., -680 ft.).

Day-10 The first part of today's hike takes you 3 miles down Canyon Creek to Sol Duc Falls. Just beyond the falls, at the shelter you'll begin to climb as you follow the southeast and up-stream to 7 Mile Camp. This day's travel adds up to 7.9 miles, (+1,400 ft., -1,560 ft.).

Day-11 Another day starts with you backtracking down-trail a short mile to the junction with the Appleton Pass Trail on your right. The climb to Appleton Pass, your destination and a dry camp, is 2.5 miles but it gains a lot of elevation along the way, (+2,070 ft., -250 ft.)

Day-12 On the trail again, today you'll drop down to Boulder Creek and move down-trail 4.6 miles to the junction with the Boulder Lake Trail. Turning left onto the Boulder Lake Trail you'll ascend 2.7 miles to Boulder Lake, your stay for the night, (+1,940 ft., -2,750 ft.).

Day-13 As you leave Boulder Lake behind, the trail climbs steeply at first as you gain the crest of the Happy Lake Ridge. (Lake Crescent-Happy Lake Ridge map) The trail follows the ridge crest 5 miles to a spur on your left that will take you a half mile to Happy Lake and day's end (+960 ft., 160 ft.).

Day-14 Packed up and having left Happy Lake, today's hike headed east will end 11 miles later at the Elwha Ranger Station. The trail at first contours the Happy Lake Ridge for about 2 miles and then descends sharply in the last 2.5 miles arriving at the Olympic Hot Springs Road. Follow the road down to and across the Elwha Bridge then down-stream a short half-mile to the ranger station. If you choose to camp off-trail you are required to get a Cross Country Permit from the Wilderness Information Center at the visitor center in Port Angeles. The Elwha Ranger Station is a reprovisioning opportunity. (+300 ft., -4,910 ft.).

Day-15 This day begins with a 6 mile hike up the Whiskey Bend Road which you'll find on your left a short distance up the Olympic Hot Springs Road (Elwha Valley map). Whiskey Bend is the end of the road and the beginning of the Elwha River Trail. Proceed up-trail 1.9 miles to Michael's Cabin and leave the main trail as you swing right. You'll travel 0.3 miles from Michael's Cabin to a second turn to the right. In another 0.3 miles you'll come to Humes Ranch. Below and to the left of the Humes Cabin there is a clearing near the Elwha, your camp for today. (+808 ft., -198 ft.).

Day-16 A tough day begins by hiking up-stream from Humes Ranch and crossing the bridge over the Elwha, the beginning of the Long Ridge Trail. This is going to be an 11 mile climb to the Dodger Point lookout, a dry camp, at 5,763 ft. The steepest grade happens in the second mile, but none of this hike is easy. The views from Dodger Point are some of the best in the Park, (+4,863 ft., -100 ft.).

Day-17 Today may not be the most demanding physically, but it will certainly be a challenge for your way-finding skills. The 5.3 mile drop from Dodger Point to the Elwha is a seldom used way-trail obvious in some places and easily confused with animal trails in others. If you haven't truly studied your topo map at this point, I'd stop and do so now. Don't proceed with this segment until you are comfortable with the challenge it presents. Early on in the history of this area blazes in trees and colored flags helped mark the way. Very few of the blazes remain; the reason being evident by the amount of dead fall in the forest. Flags have been banned for decades; I doubt you'll see any. That leaves cairns as the only on-the-ground assistance which may be available to you.

If you are not comfortable with your ability to meet this challenge, you should not attempt this segment. Return to overnight at Humes Ranch or Lillian Camp and then head up-trail to Remann's Cabin on the Elwha. On the other hand, if you intend to move forward, you'll need to spend a good deal of time studying, in great detail, a quality topographic map and know how to read a compass. You'll come to a point down-trail where being able to orient your physical position relative to compass bearings will mean the difference between success and failure.

Let me be blunt! If you're good at reading maps, know your compass skills and have a keen eye for the surrounding topography you'll manage this route with some difficulty. Anything less in your skill set will result in you throwing in the towel, semi-lost in the woods, with only one remaining clue still working for you; Dodger Point is uphill to the northwest! Return there and hike out the way you came in and then proceed up the Elwha.

About a mile southwest and below your campsite you'll find a tarn. At the tarn the trail splits one track continuing to run southwest and one that veers east on your left. The trail heading left and down to the Elwha initially heads east then swings to the southeast and skirts below a scree field below Dodger Point. You'll lose about 800 feet by the end of first mile, marked by crossing over the bottom quarter of a narrow treeless overgrown avalanche chute.

The next mile drops at about the same rate. At the end of the two mile mark, you'll find yourself starting to steeply descend the south facing nose of Long Ridge. Stop! Before you descend you need to read the lay of the land before you. Facing across the valley is the north facing nose of the buttress of Mt. Dana to your south. On either side of the buttress there is a valley. The correct start point for the next descent is when the Elwha River which is to your left in the direction of south-southeast and the river to your right, the Goldie River, is aligned in the direction of south-southwest. Move right or left until these two rivers appear to be close to 50 degrees of angle between the two rivers.

The descent is steep. It swings first to the east, then back to the west and then it drops straight down toward the "Goldie", losing about 400 feet of elevation. At that point it abruptly turns east losing elevation more gradually and contours around the nose of Long Ridge for the last time. At 1,900 ft. the trail begins to swing north and levels out as it crosses the Semple Plateau. It loses less than 500 feet in the last mile and delivers you, after a total of 5.8 miles, to the west bank of the Elwha in the vicinity of Remann's Cabin, on the opposite bank. If you are considering fording, you should: consult with the Wilderness Information Desk in the Olympic National Park Visitor Center in Port Angeles. I suggest you do a web search for "Stream Crossing Techniques" and read the National Park Service's web-available "Safe River Crossings" and 'Swiftwater Rescue Manual" The Rangers in the Park's Wilderness Information Center can advise you as to the advisability of your plans. In addition, you should consult the USGS website for current water conditions. Also, if you visit online the State of Washington Dept. of Ecology, River and Stream Flow Monitoring page, you can compare years of data and thereby compare it to the weather pattern in any year against the weather pattern in the current year. By doing so you'll have a better sense of what the fording conditions may be. These searches will allow you to choose your hike based on the available data.

Having met the challenge of the descent you now must ford the river. You ought to find a ford up or down-stream a short distance from Remann's Cabin. If you can't find a passable ford, abandon the attempt and head back up to Dodger Point and exit the area by descending Long Ridge then proceed up the Elwha. ""stuff happens""! Hikers have lost their lives fording, when and where they should not have made the attempt (-4,312 ft.).

Day-18 will be a short and easy day. You'll hike 4 miles up-trail to the Hayes River Ranger Station. Sixty years ago, there was an actual telephone at the Ranger Station for emergencies, (+149 ft.).

Day-19 sends you up to Hayden Pass and then on to Dose Meadows a distance of 10.9 miles. Climbing to the pass, the trail gains about 2,700 ft. of its elevation in the first 4.5 miles and spreads the rest of the 3,100 feet over the last 3.8 miles topping out on Hayden Pass at 5,847 ft. The descent to Dose Meadows, your destination, drops 1,400 ft. in the next 2.3 miles to finish your day (+4,247 ft., -1,397 ft.).

Day-20 (Gray Wolf-Dosewllips map) Today's 9.5 mile hike will take you up and over Lost Pass and Cameron Pass. The Lost Pass Trail is just down-trail from Dose Meadows on your left. This will be one of the steepest climbs you'll do on this loop, 1,500 feet in 0.9 miles. The alpine meadows between Lost and Cameron Passes are a wildflower paradise in late July as the trail rambles easily across them. Descending from Cameron Pass is another exercise in way-finding. From the pass the trail spirals down through a mass of indistinguishable and nearly unicolored scree. The trail is marked by small cairns, large cairns and at times, no cairns. Any hint of a path is dependent on the number of hikers who have passed through this season. You can help those who will follow you by enlarging or replacing cairns as you descend. At the bottom of the scree field, you'll regain a decent trail winding through Cameron Basin down to Lower Cameron Camp 5.6 miles from Cameron Pass, (+1,910 ft., -2,800 ft.).

Day-21 Today is an easier day as you hike down-trail 4.9 miles to Three Forks. Three Forks is a cold camp, the result of its location at the bottom of three converging valleys: Grand Creek, the Gray Wolf River and Cameron Creek (-1,350 ft.).

Day-22 Today the trail heads up-stream on the Gray Wolf River Trail 5.4 miles to today's destination, Falls Camp. If you're interested, you can hike up Cedar Creek near camp to Cedar Lake 2.1 miles and 1,500 feet above Falls Camp, (+2,150 ft.).

Day-23 First, climbing over Gray Wolf Pass, you'll drop down into the Dosewallips drainage and spend the night at Deception Creek. The bear wire is down at Deception Creek so bring a Bear Cannister. This 7.5 mile hike over the pass starts gaining significant elevation in the second mile and tops out on the pass at 6,150 feet, 4.1 miles later. The descent isn't any easier losing 2,900 ft. in even less mileage, 3.5miles. Where the Gray Wolf Pass Trail intersects with the Dosewallips Trail turn down-trail 1.4 miles to Deception Creek, your destination (+2,350 ft., -3,000 ft.).

Day-24 Heading south, down the Dosewallips River, you'll arrive 6.4 miles later at the Dose Forks junction. (The Brothers-Mt. Anderson map) The trail to your left will take you to the Dosewallips Campground, your mid-day destination. The Dose Campground will be the most inconvenient resupply point on the entire loop. Your helpers will have to pack in your supplies from the Dosewallips Trailhead 6.5 miles east of the campground. Resupplied and on the trail again, return 1.4 miles up-trail to Dose Forks, cross the West Fork Dosewallips River and hike 5.2 miles up-stream to Diamond Meadows. Neither leg of today's hike will be strenuous, but the necessity of resupplying will make it long. (+956 ft., -1,414 ft.).

Day-25 Today's destination is Bull Elk Meadows on the Quinault side of Anderson Pass. While the hike is shorter, 6.1 miles, the elevation gain and loss will be tiring. Once over and on the descent from Anderson Pass, you'll come to a junction with the O'Neil Pass Trail on your left. Turn left and a half mile farther on you'll enter Bull Elk Basin, your camp for the night, (+2,372 ft., -664 ft.).

Day-26 The hike today will take you 7 miles up-trail to O'Neil Pass and another 2.2 miles will deliver you to your camp at Marmot Lake in La Crosse Basin. The climb has some steeper sections in it, but for the most part the trail rises steadily. The bear wires are down at Marmot Lake, Bear Cannisters are required. La Crosse Basin is one of the most picturesque places in the Park, and is often the subject of published photographs, (+1,200 ft., -200 ft.).

Day-27 Leaving La Crosse Basin, you'll follow a tributary of the Duckabush River 3.4 miles down to the confluence of a second tributary and the Duckabush proper. The trail then climbs 2.1 miles and 1,500 feet heading southeast to Home Sweet Home, just below the First Divide, and your home for the night, (+1,703 ft., -2,195 ft.).

Day-28 (Mount Skokomish-Lake Cushman map) The First Divide is 0.7 miles up-trail and the rest of the day is 7.1 miles down-trail to Big Log Camp on the North Fork of the Skokomish River. Before you get to Big Log you'll have to deal with a wash-out near Camp Pleasant. You'll be moving out of a subalpine environment into a denser mature lowland forest as you follow the North Fork of the Skok south to your day's end at Big Log Camp, (+490 ft., -3,188 ft.).

Day-29 (Enchanted Valley-Skokomish map) Nearly 11 miles and a lot of elevation are on today's menu before you reach Lake Sundown. From Big Log you'll move a short distance up-trail to the junction with the Six Ridge Trail. You'll climb steeply in the first 3 miles. The trail is hard to find due to little use and game trails. Navigation skills are required between Six-Ridge pass and the Success Lake junction. This section of trail is difficult but climbs at a lesser rate through the next 5 miles. The last 3 miles loses elevation as you drop down to Lake Sundown, today's destination (+3,000 ft., -700 ft.).

Day-30 Beginning the day's 8.3 miles, you'll head down-trail and at 0.3 miles you'll intersect with the Sundown Pass Trail on your left. Moving straight ahead, first to the southwest and then west, swinging round to the north. After a series of switchbacks, you'll intersect the Wynoochee Pass Trail, 1.6 miles below Lake Sundown. Turning right and headed down-trail again you'll follow the Graves Creek Trail to the Graves Creek Campground 6.3 miles ahead. This can be another resupply point (-3,154 ft.).

Day-31 (Quinault-Colonel Bob map) This may be the worst day on this loop. You'll hike down the Graves Creek Road to the Bridge and cross the Quinault. After crossing you'll hike up the North Fork Road. This road-trek is 10.5 miles long and ends in the North Fork Campground. If you didn't resupply yesterday, do it today. (+300 ft., -400 ft.)

Day-32 The next four days will be as challenging as anything you've faced so far on this loop. Elevations vary severely every day. Given the need to hike this segment later in the hiking season, when water is in short supply on this route, two consecutive days of dry camping should be anticipated. If that isn't enough, this route is infrequently traveled and way-finding will come into play. That said, hike back down the North Fork Road a long half mile to the Irely Lake Trailhead on your right. The first mile gains a hundred feet but then the trail climbs steadily through the remaining 6.3 miles. First it follows Big Creek on your left. Big Creek turns and rises to the west but the trail continues north. It crosses the outlet creek draining from Three Lakes and starts to climb, swinging off to the west. There is no bridge for crossing Big Creek. Crossing at 1,200 ft., the trail climbs steeply at first and then settles down for the last of the 2.5 miles to Three Lakes, (+2,680 ft.).

Day-33 Leaving Three Lakes the trail contours the east face of Tshletshy Ridge heading north 4.4 miles to Three Prune. Bear Cannisters are required on the Skyline Trail.

At the 2.9 mile mark the trail passes the Elip Creek Trail on your right. Kurtz Lake is about .75 miles down the Elip Creek Trail and about 200 feet above the trail. If Three Lakes was in a dry state, you may want to explore Kurtz Lake as a water source. Three Prune is 1.5 miles farther on along the Tshletshy Ridge. At Three Prune, which is your destination, you may want to make the scramble off-trail over the low ridge just north of your camp. Three Prune Lakes on the northside of the ridge may be a water source, (+420 ft.).

Day-34 The trail from Three Prune to Lake Beauty will test your way-finding skills. With your topographic map in hand, pay close attention to direction, distance and elevation. This segment takes you 5.2 miles from Three Prune to just below Kimta Peak. This will be a dry camp. As you approach Kimta Peak the ridgeline you've been following turns abruptly from northerly to easterly. Your best chance to find a reasonable campsite is in the last quarter mile before the trail turns east. If you intend on scrambling up to the Peak, start your scramble just before the trail turns east to Lake Beauty. This side excursion will take you 139 feet above the trail and about a quarter mile west of the summit of Kimta Peak, (+1,160 ft.).

Day-35 You've already had to do some amount of way-finding to get to Kimta Peak and you'll do a lot more today on your way to Lake Beauty. In the first 2.6 miles of this segment the trail jogs up and down as it heads east. Given this trail's infrequent use and the abundance of animal trails, way-finding will be based on direction, distance and elevation,

Your starting elevation is 5,260 ft. where the trail turns from north to east, just below Kimta Peak, set your altimeter. In the first half mile you'll drop to 4,800 ft. then drop abruptly down another 160 ft. and then contour to the southeast a short quarter mile at that elevation. Drop to 4,400 ft. and contour east at that level for a half mile. Leaving 4,400 ft. drop down 50 ft. and contour southeast around one buttress, into and back out of a creek drainage, regaining 4,400 ft. as you round to the east side of the second buttress. Changing direction to the south, travel a short 200 yards and gaining about 75 ft., you'll arrive at a ridge climbing steeply to the northeast. Follow the ridge to an elevation of 5060 ft. Looking upward to the north, you'll see a rock promontory. Ascend at first to the north then slightly to the northeast, as you near the crest you'll attain Promise Creek Divide at 5,300 ft. You're looking down into a small cirque. Contour the north wall until you are due northwest of the low point in the cirque, a dry tarn in the summer. Start a slow descent northeast from 5,300 ft. to 4,800 ft. over the next half mile and then contour at or slightly above that level for another quarter mile to the northeast. You've arrived at the crest of, or just beyond, a buttress running down to the southeast. Heading east, follow the northeast face of the buttress as you descend to 4,300 ft. over the next quarter mile, to the crest of a second buttress to the north. Look upward to the north, you'll see a gap in the ridge line above, that's Hee Haw Pass, a short half mile distant. Once through the pass head northeast a half mile, skirting below a peak on your right, to the junction of the Lake Beauty spur trail at 5060 ft. Turn left and you'll find Lake Beauty a short half mile away; your destination for today at 4,681 ft. Congratulations, you've just completed 5.9 difficult miles; one of the toughest sections of one of the toughest hikes in the Olympic Mountains (+2,289 ft.-1660 ft.).

Day-36 This is the last day on the Skyline trail and it will be easier than the last two. It's 3.5 miles, descending the ridge face northeast, to Seattle Creek. The trail then ascends the south buttress of Mount Seattle heading southeast, swings around the nose and descends to the northeast to Low Divide, todays camp, (+1,079 ft., -2,140 ft.).

Day-37 (Elwha Valley map) Today is long but not difficult as you hike down-trail to Hayes River 11.2 miles away. A half mile south of Hayes River a small section of trail has been undercut; be careful and the trail between Lake Margaret and Camp Wilder is overgrown in places; a test of your navigation skills. The trail drops from Low Divide to Chicago Camp and then loses very little elevation thereafter, (-1,860 ft.).

Day-38 You did this segment on day-19. Once again, the hike sends you up to Hayden Pass and then down to Dose Meadows a distance of 10.9 miles. Climbing to the pass, the trail gains about 2,700 ft. of its elevation in the first 4.5 miles and spreads the rest of the 3,100 feet over the last 3.8 miles, topping out on Hayden Pass at 5,847 ft. The descent to Dose Meadows, your destination, drops 1,400 ft. in the last 2.3 miles to finish your day (+4,247 ft., -1,397 ft.).

Day-39 This hike at 4.4 miles is shorter than yesterday, but not easy. Leaving Dose Meadows down-trail you'll intersect the Lost Pass Trail on your left. Climbing to Lost Pass is difficult. It climbs just over 1,500 feet in slightly less than a mile. The trail meanders through alpine meadows on its way to Cameron Pass. Descending Cameron Pass will be easier since you ascended it on day-20 and hopefully enlarged or rebuilt cairns your first time through this scree field. Below is Upper Cameron Camp your stop for the day, (+2,000 ft., -1,200 ft.).

Day-40 Today you'll descend Cameron Creek to the Grand Pass Trail, go over the Pass and drop down to Grand Lake. The climb over Grand Pass is as steep but longer than Lost Pass. Climbing the Pass, you'll gain 2,400 feet, in 1.8 miles. The remaining 2.6 miles down to Grand Lake is relatively easy, (+2,400 ft., -2,900 ft.).

The distance between Grand Lake and Madison Falls, the end of the loop, is 24.3 miles. There are no designated campsites along the way which will require either camping off-trail or off-road or a very long and hard day of hiking. If you choose to camp off-trail or off-road, you are required to get a Cross Country Permit from the Wilderness

Information Center at the visitor center in Port Angeles. The Rangers at the W.I.C. will advise you.

Day-41 Climbing 3.7 miles above Grand Lake you'll arrive at Obstruction Point. You'll hike 7.8 miles down the Obstruction Point Road to Hurricane Ridge. (Hurricane Ridge map) Follow the Hurricane Hill Road 1.4 miles to the Hurricane Hill Trailhead and another 1.4 miles up-trail from the trailhead you'll come to a junction on your left, with the Elwha to Hurricane Hill Trail. The trail to the Elwha Ranger Station, 6 miles and 5,200 ft. below. Turn left and begin the descent. If you choose to camp off-trail you are required to get a Cross Country Permit from the Wilderness Information Center at the visitor center in Port Angeles.

Day-42 This is your last day on this loop. You'll complete the long miles of the segment from Grand Lake to the Elwha Ranger Station and then hike out the Olympic Hot Springs Road to Madison Falls the current trailhead, as of this writing. The elevation gain and loss for the Grand Lake to Madison Falls is, (+850 ft., -4,968 ft.).

Congratulations! You have successfully finished not only the longest loop hike in the park, given the distance and the terrain, it's the most difficult. Few hikers, if any, have preceded you in this achievement. In total you've covered 309 miles, gained and lost over 61,000 feet of elevation, and been on the trail 42 days, a triumphant feat!

36 .Hart Lake, ONP

Though beautiful,
breathtaking and often brutal,
the Olympic Mountains are
truly memorable. Forever a
part of you and who you are.

Appendix

Acknowledgements

"Loop Hikes in the Olympic Mountains" is an outcome of my continuous development across the years. My parents, Harold and Kathryn Paschal, introduced me to the Boy Scouts and therein my initial experience of the wilderness.

I owe a debt of gratitude to Orville Schultz and Ken Peterson the adult Scout Leaders for BSA Troop 505, Bremerton, WA. Without their dedication and a willingness to sacrifice their personal time, numerous energetic young boys might not have acquired a pervasive appetite for the outdoors.

I'm grateful for my teenage hiking and climbing partners Dan Baker, Denny Pruitt, Craig Anderson and others. Together we grew to understand the importance of teamwork. As partners, we helped each other accept the discomfort, stress, danger and physical effort that confronts everyone in the wilderness.

I feel an exceptional thankfulness to George Martin, Glen Kelsey and Chuck Maiden who initiated and led the Olympic College Basic Mountaineering Course; the first and oldest of its kind in the U.S. Along with Kent Heathershaw, they instilled in me the value of patience, a belief in incremental self-development, the skill of self-assessment, and a measured respect for the inherent dangers of the wilderness.

Immense credit is due to four critically important people in the writing of this book. Florence Justin guided me through Sophomore English and taught me how to reach out to others with my thoughts. My wife Barbara, through countless edits and wise counsel, helped me polish the manuscript. A special thank you to Bryan Bell the former Supervising Ranger at Olympic National Park's Wilderness Information Center. He is one of the very few people sufficiently qualified to review the book and who contributed greatly to the accuracy and specificity of its details. Finally, I owe Tom Schindler a debt of gratitude. Tom's Custom Correct Maps led me to the mountains and brought me safely home through a lifelong pursuit of the Olympic Wilderness.

Above all, I'll be rewarded in my final years with the memories and moments of exquisite surroundings and the companionship of friends and family; so much joy in so many precious places.

Resources

Information

Olympic National Park Wilderness Information Center (backcountry questions)
https://www.nps.gov/olym/planyourvisit/W.I.C..htm

Olympic National Forest
https://www.fs.usda.gov/activity/olympic/recreation/hiking

Hood Canal Ranger District, Quilcene, 360-765-2000

Pacific Ranger District, Quinault, 360-288-0203

Pacific Ranger District, Forks, 360-374-6522

Fording

The National Park Service article, "Safe River Crossings"

The National Forest Service, "River Crossing Safety on Glacial Streams"

Pacific Crest Trail Association's, "Stream Crossing Safety while Hiking and Backpacking"

River flow

Washington State Department of Ecology: Homepage
https://ecology.wa.gov then navigate to Flow Monitoring

Weather Characteristics

https://www.accuweather.com/en/us/olympic-national-park/98381/september-weather/29517_poi

Climbing

"Olympic Mountains, A Climbing Guide"

Hiking

"Olympic Mountain Trail Guide"
olympicnationalparkvisitor.info

Water Pathogens

National Parks Service, purify water
https://www.cdc.gov/healthywater/drinking/travel/backcountry_water_treatment.html

First Aid

First Aid Kit Checklist, REI

"Mountaineering First Aid" 5th edition, Mountaineers Books

"Wilderness Basics" 4th edition, Mountaineers Books

Nutrition

"Lipsmackin' Backpackin': Lightweight, Trail-Tested Recipes for Extended Backcountry Trips"

Backpacker and Outside magazines, nutrition

The Basal Metabolic Rate (BMR) Calculator estimates your basal metabolic rate https://www.calculator.net/bmr-calculator

Gear

Browns Outdoor, Port Angeles, WA, USA 1-360-457-4150
REI, USA, NEMO, Britain, MEC, Canada, Bergfreunde EU, EXPED, Swiss

Ten Essentials

National Park Service, Ten Essentials

Navigation

"Wilderness Navigation" 3rd edition, Mountaineers Books

Custom Correct maps at

Brown's Outdoor, Port Angeles, 1-360-457-4150
Discover Your Northwest, Seattle, 1-877-874-6775
Metskers Maps, Seattle, 1-206-623-8747

Wilderness Trip Planner

Contact:
Olympic National Park
Wilderness Information Center at:
olym_W.I.C.@nps.gov or 1-360-565-3100

Trail Conditions

Annual Trail Conditions, reported in November 2021

This book, like all trail books, are only as accurate as they were when they were published but the Olympic Wilderness is constantly changing. Always check on trail conditions before you go hiking. Go to my website, loophikes.com where there's an archive of trail conditions and revisions to Custom Correct Maps. Trail conditions for each year reflect Olympic National Park's updates on trail conditions usually posted in the late fall of the previous year.

Fitness, Stretching and Nutrition

Your preparedness will define you

You may be someone who is in great shape and has a good deal of experience. If so, you may not find anything in this section that is new. If you're not well experienced, I encourage you to take a few minutes and read the information and ideas that my wife and I have successfully used for decades of backpacking. I'll describe elements that have survived our trips and skip the ideas that didn't survive the true test of the trail. We're no different than anyone who backpacks or wants to backpack. Carrying loads over rough terrain and steep trails teaches backpackers to travel as light as you can while at the same time carrying your essentials, attending to the needs of your body and balancing your effort with enjoyment.

Your eagerness and interest in the challenges that the Olympic Mountains hold are a critical first step in furthering your backcountry development. Your mental state can only sustain your efforts in direct proportion to your physical condition. I've written this book to entice you; but enticed or not, your degree of success is truly based on your physical state and stamina. What I'll present is intended to add to your current level of development and preparedness. I'll address three basic elements of physical success on the Olympic Mountain trails.

I've borrowed this advice from Ed Vestures' book, "No Shortcuts to the Top". "Getting to the top is optional. Getting down is mandatory." The first requirement of hiking or backpacking is returning to your trailhead. Fulfilling that requirement hinges on your fitness, stamina and the choices you make. I've broken your preparedness into three segments: Fitness, Stretching and Nutrition.

Fitness

Building the Stamina You'll Need

Let's start with walking; you'll be doing a lot of it and it will be demanding. The first parameter is a sustained pace of two miles an hour. Let's assume a day-hike of 8 miles round trip as a starting metric. That will require you to walk for about 4 hours. Rest breaks are allowed but they can't be counted against this 4 hour test.

Start this exercise with a simple walk. If that attempt is a success, move on to a new incremental goal, adding length and uphill, downhill challenges steadily. Make sure you find actual stairs for practice. Especially challenging are at school sports fields with multiple levels of stairs in the bleacher seating area. Ascending and descending for miles on nearly all trails will require you to build significant muscle strength to protect your knees and other joints. My experience has been that at least 3-5 days are essential for your body to get used to each increment of distance and the degree of ascending and descending before you move on to the next level. You may have your own standard, but I knew I was ready for an incremental upgrade when my current level wasn't exhausting me. Do not interrupt your schedule because of inclement weather. Backcountry weather is a condition that you must accept and become accustomed to especially in the Olympic Mountains.

Level trails, with the exception of the first ten miles of the Hoh River Trail are rare. Let's be clear. The Olympic Mountains frequently have extremely long and steep grades. There is no shortage of rough trails with a lot of stepping up and down. Your hips, knees and calves bear the brunt of gravity both going up and coming down. Regardless of up or down, you use the same muscles but you use them in different ways. Your muscles will tire in a direct correlation to you level of fitness. As they tire, they underperform at controlling your downward movement. As they weaken, their effect is an increase in jarring which increases the wear on your joints. Weak muscles and extended jarring can cause joint injuries, where rehabilitation can be lengthy.

Barbara, my wife, and I prepared each year by daily walking, jogging, bicycling and swimming all year long. Each year we started hiking on trails as soon as portions of them became snow-free. We began with day hikes of increasing length with day packs and progressed to long day hikes with fuller loads. As spring turned to summer, we started with a single overnight then two and sometimes three overnights. As the backpacking season got into full swing we hiked farther and farther into the backcountry building our stamina and our ability to hike day after day. By late July into August, we usually had a 10-14 day backcountry experience planned.

Only once, in all our years, were we kept from attaining our backpacking goals. After years of trail hiking, we had decided to go up the Sol Duc Trail to Appleton Pass and then hike off-trail in Cat Basin. An extended stretch of very bad weather pinned us down at Appleton Pass for four days. We knew our limits and doing a first off-trail hike in dense fog was not in our skill-set. We hiked out on day five of ten, but we're hopeful that another opportunity would be part of our fortune.

Stretching

Your Body is a Work Horse; Treat it Well

Part of preparing yourself physically includes a regimen of stretching, at least morning and night but often during the day as well. What follows are a set of stretches that don't require gym equipment but do require your dedication and commitment.

Packing heavy loads for hours on end as you seek the grandeur of the Olympic Mountains strains and tightens your muscles and joints. If you don't practice a regime of stretching, your body will lose its ability to perform at an optimum level. Stretching is to the body what maintenance is to your car. In either case, attending to these critical needs will result in a greater degree of success and help you achieve your goals.

The complete set of stretches should be done:

- After a long drive to the trailhead
- After your lunch break before you continue on the hike
- At the end of the day's hike before you set up camp
- Before you go to bed and just before you get back on the trail the next morning.

Repeat this pattern each day and you'll be rewarded with improved balance and agility as you face the challenging terrain. Below are some suggestions of stretching exercises that have helped me a great deal. However, everyone is different and has different abilities and potential disabilities; so, no one list of stretches is good for everyone. The real idea here is to do gentle stretches every day before your Loop Hike and during the actual hike and afterwards to help your joints and muscles be as healthy as possible for your travels.

A) Hip flexors and Quads

Stand in good Core Alignment

1. Step back with one leg about a foot or more and come to a low squatting position
2. Keep your torso in Good Core Alignment
3. Your front leg will be bent at 90 degrees at your knee and your foot is planted solidly on the ground
4. Hold the position for a count of 30-60 seconds
5. Repeat with other leg
6. 3 repetitions with each leg

B) Hamstrings:

1. In Good Core Alignment stand with feet about 2 feet apart with arms straight and hands together.
2. Keeping the back straight, bend at your hip joints, not bending at your waist or low back.
3. Slowly rotate and slowly reach with your hands toward one foot.
4. Hold position for a count of 30-60 seconds
5. Slowly straighten up and repeat rotating and reaching toward your other foot and hold for a count of 30-60 seconds.
6. No Bouncing, no yanking and move slowly
7. Do 3 repetitions for each leg

C) Calves:

1. Spread your feet shoulder width apart as you lean on a tree trunk/rock
2. Right foot behind you, knee straight with heel on the ground
3. Keeping left leg straight bend right knee keeping most of your weight on your left leg
4. Keep left foot, leg, torso in a straight line
5. Bend your arms to increase angle of lean
6. Hold for a count of 30-60 seconds.
7. Stand up and repeat with opposite leg
8. 3 repetitions for each leg

D) Back Arches:

1. Feet spread about 2 feet apart
2. Place hands on waist
3. Slowly arch your back allowing your head to gently drop backward
4. Hold for a count of 5-10 seconds and return to Core Alignment
5. Repeat 3 times

E) Pectorals:

1. Stand in Good Core Alignment, feet, torso, head aligned looking straight forward
2. Step alongside a tree and reach out to it with your right hand and touch the tree with your arm at 90 degrees connecting your torso, arm and tree in the same plane
3. Without moving your hand on the tree, step forward about 6 inches to create a gentle stretch in your shoulder

4. Hold for a count of 30-60 seconds
5. Repeat with your left arm
6. Repeat 3 times

Doing these stretches throughout each day will bring relief to your whole body. The load of your pack acts as an unnatural force; a force that your body must accommodate over hours on the trail. The trail itself: long, rough and steep, adds to the burden on your body; give it the relief that it requires. Good maintenance reaps better performance.

Nutrition

Put the Best Fuel in Your Body

A) Metabolism

Everyone's metabolism differs and individually your metabolism changes depending on your level of activity. This book focuses on backpacking in the Olympic Wilderness where your activity will come close to extreme and nutrition is the key to fueling a metabolism matched to that activity. Metabolism, like the engine in your car, takes raw fuel, food/nutrition and converts it to energy that allows and sustains movement, strength and endurance. There is a science to nutrition in support of extreme efforts. I suggest researching nutrition and performance training for strenuous sports. REI, Backpacker Magazine, Outside Magazine, Runner's World and Triathlete websites will be useful.

Backpacking in the Olympic Mountains, particularly on extended routes, places a mammoth demand on your body. Heavy loads, steep trails, constant balance demands, and weather, day after day, can take a toll, but your choices can make a difference. One of the critical tools to help you avoid exhaustion is the fuel that you feed your body. The informed use of calories, water, carbohydrates, fats, fiber and proteins will make a critical difference in your performance over time.

B) Calories

Your caloric burn rate while backpacking is at least two to three times the rate of a normal day at work, depending on your job. Long before you venture on a multi-day backpacking trip research all the calories, protein, carbohydrates, fiber, and healthy fats of each and every meal you are planning. Study the BMR Calculator on-line to understand what calories you might need with the activity level adjustment the site offers.

C) Water

Finding water in the Olympic Mountains is highly dependent now on recent weather and climate change. Read this book carefully for details on when you will need to gather extra water for "dry days" and where and when you can gather water to filter. Giardia is everywhere in the Olympic Mountains, even in fast running streams and waterfalls. All water should be filtered, boiled or treated. Some people think iodine tablets are a good substitute for filtering but most people object to the taste or find acute abdominal distress with those tablets.

Water is as critical in the long run as oxygen is in the short run. Insufficient amounts of either will kill you. Water is the key to metabolism. Without water your body cannot convert food into fuel for your body. Everyone needs at least half a gallon of water each day. Backpacking requires much more water distributed throughout the day's hike. Drink often. Strenuous activity, like climbing from Cameron Creek to Grand Pass, involving hours of a non-stop 20 per cent grade, will cause you to sweat profusely and demand you rehydrate. At such intensity through perspiration and respiration you can lose up to two liters of water an hour.

Get ahead of the hydration curve by drinking a good amount of water before you get on the trail in the morning. Taking a break on the trail, even if you don't shed your pack, is another good time for a snack and more importantly water. Don't wait until you're thirsty. Being thirsty is the body telling you it needs water. Do your best to stay ahead of the hydration curve; your body will reward you.

D) Carbohydrates:

Study information on simple and complex carbohydrates to understand why the latter will give you more lasting energy. Eating simple carbos can give you a "sugar high" and a quick drop in glucose and subsequent energy drop. Also study healthy fats like nuts and nut butters as well as much-needed protein and fiber. Different foods are easier to digest while you are strenuously exercising and again research is important. Lastly, weigh what you plan for each meal in order to correctly calculate room in your pack, your ability to carry the food and to ensure that you have enough energy from it.

A Peronal Tip:

Barbara, my wife, and I have logged hundreds of miles with a stove, a pot, two cups and two spoons. We've eaten meals without firing up the stove. We would eat everything in our cups and our pot until they are nearly clean. We'd boil water in the pot along with our cups and spoons, after five minutes pull everything out and let it air dry, and finally use the hot water for tea, and at times a spit bath. Denser, more efficient, less weight, less fuss and wonderful years on the trails.

Books Worth Reading

Hiking, biking, Climbing and Fishing Olympic National Park

Best Easy Day Hikes Eric Molvar
Hiking Olympic National Park Eric Molvar
Your Guide to Olympic National Park Michael Joseph Oswald
Olympic Mountains Trail Guide Robert L. Wood
Day Hiking, Olympic Peninsula Craig Romano
Bicycling America's National Parks: Oregon & Washington David Story & Denise Coello
Olympic Mountains Fishing Guide David Shorett
Olympic Mountains, A Climbing Guide The Mountaineers Books

General Guides of Olympic National Park

Olympic National Park Tim McNulty
Olympic National Park Impressions James Randklev
Visitor's Companion to Olympic George Wuerthner & Douglas W. Moore
Olympic National Park a Timeless Refuge Nicky Leach & Jeff Nicholas
Olympic National Park Mike Graf
Olympic National Park Adventure, Explore, Discover Susan Jancowski
The Olympic Rain Forest Ruth Kirk & Jerry Franklin
Gods and Goblins Smitty Parratt
Council of Bears Pete Merill
Olympic Peninsula Jeff Burlingame
Spotlight on the Olympic Peninsula Erica Chickowski
Campfire Songs Irene Maddox & Rosalyn Blankenship
The Olympics A Wilderness Trilogy Ross Hamilton & Janet Scharf
Where the Mountain Meets the Sea Tim McNulty & Pat O'Hara
Olympic Peninsula from the Air Nicky Leach

History of Olympic National Park

High Divide: Olympic Mountain Adventures Gary L. Peterson & Glynda Peterson Schaad
Island of Rivers Nancy Beres
The Land that Slept Late Robert L. Wood
Olympic Battleground Carsten Lien
The Last Wilderness Murry Morgan
The Water Link Daniel Jack Chasan
Images of America Series: Forks Larry Burtness & Chris Cook
Early Settlers on the Upper Elwha Alice Bretches Alexander
Untamed Olympics Ruby El Hult
The Elwha Bridge Project Clallam County Public Works

History of Olympic National Park Continued

Footprints in the Wilderness Chris Morgenroth
Women to Reckon With Gary Peterson & Glynda Schaad
Postmistress Mora, Wash. 1914-1915 Jacilee Wray & Doreen Taylor
Lake Crescent-Gem of the Olympics Alice Alexander
Great Shipwrecks of the Pacific Coast Robert C. Belvk
The Graveyard of the Pacific Anthony Dalton
The Final Forest William Dietrich
Juan de Fuca's Strait Barry Gough
Across the Olympic Mountains Robert L. Wood
Men, Mules and Mountains Robert L. Wood
Strait Press Bill Lindstrom

Science of Olympic National Park

Northwest Mountain Weather Jeff Renner
Mountain Flowers Harvey Manning & Ira Spring
Lipsmackin' Vegetarian Backpackin' Christine & Tom Conners
Mountains Without Handrails Joseph L. Sax
Exploring the Olympic Mountains Carsten Lien
The Restless Northwest Hill Williams
The Weather of the Pacific Northwest Cliff Mass

Level of Difficulty

Each loop hike in this book is given a difficulty rating. The aggregate rating is derived from the application of the following ten criteria:

1. **Length:** every 5 miles is a 0.5
2. **Elevation gained and lost:** every 100 ft. is a 0.1
3. **Water availability:** every dry day is a 5
4. **Fording:** is a 4
5. **Way-finding:** every mile is 1
6. **Rocky trail:** 0.3
7. **Overgrown trail:** every mile is a 0.5
8. **Dead-fall:** contained within a mile is a 1
9. **Washout:** contained within a mile is a 1.25
10. **Exposure to heat or wind:** every mile is a 0.75

Index

Index

Index

Photo Index

Cover

View toward Grand pass from Elk Mountain, William D. Bacchus, Physical Scientist, Olympic National Park.

Title Page

Waterfall in the Enchanted Valley during spring snow-melt, ONP

Notes

Notes

Notes

Notes

Printed in the USA
CPSIA information can be obtained
at www.ICGtesting.com
JSHW042119210923
48551JS00001B/1

* 9 7 9 8 2 1 8 2 2 4 9 1 2 *